… it gets you away from the madness

… it was life or death for me. Definitely… *Emma*

It took a really long time but the rhythm and flow here just began to settle and whatever else I had going on in my head, that became a part of me. *Alex*

I feel safe here. *Simon*

… people would come at any time of day or night and we were able to put together a meal of some sort, even if it was 11 o'clock at night. So, that welcome, I think, was really important. *Anne*

I love the work I do there… I never thought in a million years I would milk a cow. And I think it's excellent. I love it. *Emma*

I think care for the environment was … something which I learnt at Pilsdon. *Sarah*

Pilsdon doesn't hold anything against you if you just say, 'Look, I just need a break,' …This is a unique opportunity to look after myself and I've learnt to love myself… I try to care for myself in a better way. *Daniel*

But what Pilsdon done for me… it gave me hope and chances that I never thought I'd ever get. *Michael*

I think it is amazing that a handful of idealists, you know, people with a dream, and a bunch of other people with really significant difficulties in their lives have been able to make this thing happen for the last 60 years. *Sarah*

WHAT SOME WHO KNOW PILSDON HAVE SAID ABOUT THE COMMUNITY:

Pilsdon is about people and this oral history opens up the community's sixty years wonderfully. What a lot of stories there are to tell and what a difference has been made for the better. It was founded and keeps going because of a vision about who we are as people and how we can live with each other. It depends on good people working hard not just for themselves but for others with a commitment to live in the here and now by the values of the kingdom of God. Pilsdon gives hope to large numbers of individuals and the sorts of stories it tells are the hope of the world.

The Rt Revd Nicholas Holtam, Bishop of Salisbury

In any diocese, the bishop is grateful to have something that helps lift people's horizons beyond the limits of church on Sundays and fundraising to keep the building intact, so to have a real community that actually practises what it preaches is a huge blessing. I was always grateful for the community at Pilsdon with its rich life, grounded in the practice of hospitality and ready to say yes. Yes to the stranger and the traveller; yes to the unhurried seasons of the year; yes to the essentials of the Christian faith as it is actually lived out in practice. Life in community is demanding, as we all know and I marvelled at the succession of wardens with their differing charismas and complementary gifts who served Pilsdon during my time in Salisbury. I learnt from each one, and never doubted that the Trustees would appoint the right successor when the time came. So the community has never grown stale, and has been able to respond to ever-changing demands, and I bless the moment when Percy and Gaynor were led to this place to offer a place of security and serenity to those who so badly needed it.

The Rt Revd David Stancliffe, Former Bishop of Salisbury

I recently revisited *Pilsdon Morning*, written by Gaynor Smith in 1982. Gaynor was married to Percy Smith, the founder of the Pilsdon Community in 1958, and she outlined how the community was conceived, run, and the ethos behind it. Having the opportunity to read *Living Life in Common* confirmed to me what an inspirational place the community is, and though we are sixty years on from its inception, and the world with its health and safety requirements and legislation is very different, the wardens, members and guests are still people who give and receive that support and love through community life.

Amanda Streatfield, Chair of the Pilsdon Community Board of Trustees

LIVING LIFE IN COMMON

Stories from the Pilsdon Community

Marian Barnes,
Mary Davies and
David Prior

Matador
Unit E2 Airfield Business Park,
Harrison Road, Market Harborough,
Leicestershire. LE16 7UL
Tel: 0116 2792299
Email: books@troubador.co.uk
Web: www.troubador.co.uk/matador
Twitter: @matadorbooks

ISBN 978 1803130 507

British Library Cataloguing in Publication Data.
A catalogue record for this book is available from the British Library.

Printed and bound in the UK by TJ Books Ltd, Padstow, Cornwall
Typeset in 11pt Sabon by Troubador Publishing Ltd, Leicester, UK

Matador is an imprint of Troubador Publishing Ltd

Contents

About the Authors

Marian Barnes was a Professor at the Universities of Birmingham and Brighton. She is the author, co-author or editor of 16 books, numerous book chapters, journal articles and other publications on mental health, ageing, care, user and citizen involvement. She is currently a volunteer at the Pilsdon Community.

Mary Davies is a historian, specialising in oral history, and worked at Goldsmiths University, London and the University of Leiden. For the past 5 years she has been a member of the Pilsdon Community and led the research project in 2018 on which this book is based.

David Prior had a career in local government and as a Senior Research Fellow at the University of Birmingham. He is the co-author of 3 books on aspects of social and public policy, plus numerous chapters in edited collections and articles in academic journals. He is currently a volunteer at the Pilsdon Community.

Foreword

This absorbing discussion of the growth of the Pilsdon community in West Dorset is based on oral histories, participant observation and some penetrating analysis of how this community works today. Of the three authors, Mary Davies is a Christian, a current member of the community and an historian who led the project on which this book is based. Marian Barnes and David Prior, responsible for most of the writing, have long-standing interests in the experiences of those with mental health problems and in public policy; as both non-Christians and volunteers their outsider/insider status is what makes this book so accessible. Ultimately it is the stories of those seeking refuge in Pilsdon that are so moving. As the authors note '…the intersection between the physical space, the routine of everyday life and the spiritual life of the community creates for many people a distinctive context in which they undergo different kinds of transformation.' (Ch4.)

I am fascinated and impressed firstly by the way in which Pilsdon has offered people a chance to 'live their faith in a way that they had not been able to find in the established church '(ch2.); secondly, at the openness and fluidity of the community that has enabled 'guests' with a wide range of mental health issues to come and go according to their needs; thirdly at the resilience of the trustees, members and other volunteers, particularly during the pandemic with its attendant lockdown and social isolation. As a Christian myself, all of this has provoked reflection on the life and structure of our more conventional church communities today. How best to move forward is a question all are now asking.

As a sociologist I have also been reminded of the important interface between religion and secular concerns. There has been a steady flow in Pilsdon between the community and surrounding people and agencies, with it seems little hostility and much tolerance, understanding and trust. A fine balance has been sustained between the substantial administrative needs of the community, the guidelines for acceptable behaviour (e.g. non-compulsory church services but compulsory attendance at communal meals) and individual freedom of choice. The social structures of Pilsdon have allowed for all of this and the renewal of the community as people come and go.

Pilsdon is a far cry from the way in which 'community care', following the closure of long stay institutions, is managed nationally. In rural communities, such as the one in which I live, collaboration between members of the church, the parish council and others during the pandemic has initiated a new type of highly appreciated neighbourhood support for those who are socially isolated, physically or mentally unwell or in economic difficulties.

None of these different community responses, however, can meet all social need and we continue the long wait for a coherent and properly funded community care system.

Sue Balloch, Emeritus Professor of Health and Social Care, University of Brighton; Parochial Church Council Secretary, St. Mary's Parish Church, Newick, East Sussex.

CHAPTER 1

Introduction: The Pilsdon Community and its story

The Pilsdon Community is located in a remote, marshy vale in rural west Dorset, in the south west of England. It has been there for over 60 years and has had a significant impact on the lives of those who have been part of the community during this period. We describe more fully what the community does and how it operates in subsequent chapters, but, briefly, its primary purpose is to offer a place of welcome and refuge to people of all backgrounds and circumstances whose lives are in crisis, which may be the result of mental illness, alcohol or drug addiction, relationship breakdown or homelessness.

This purpose is grounded in the Christian faith of the founders and members of the community for whom living in community according to the values of friendship, acceptance and hospitality is a core expression of their faith. The community is a registered charity. The small group of members, headed by a warden, live there full-time and invite people in crisis or experiencing longer term troubles to live and work alongside them as guests, looking after the small farm which provides much of the community's food. Guests may profess any religious faith or none and there is no attempt at evangelising. This model of community, based in principles of monastic living adapted to a more modern age, has remained fundamentally constant since Pilsdon's inception. This book is in part an exploration of how this approach has been sustained over sixty-two years, what its benefits can be and how it offers an alternative to more familiar models of support for people in need.

The material for the book was generated by an oral history project, undertaken in 2018 to mark the 60th anniversary of the community's founding. Our aim is to open up the community to those who know nothing of it; to share experiences of and insights into a way of living that is very different from what is usually regarded as mainstream life, as well as to make visible the lives of some of those who have been part of the community throughout its history. There are many stories of the Pilsdon Community. In this book we tell some of them. We do so because we think the community is important in its own right, because of what it can help us understand about ways of living with others who are different, and ways of living together that can help us all accept our vulnerabilities and learn ways of dealing with our troubles.

We have written much of this book at a time when a global pandemic has made our interdependencies and our vulnerabilities visible in ways that have been described as unprecedented. This, in turn, has given rise to an equally unprecedented focus on the lives of those who give and receive care; on those who are seen as the 'essential workers' who sustain our lives, and on what is important to our own wellbeing and that of the planet on which we share our lives with those of other species. In 2021 it is not possible to think or write about fragility, vulnerability and interdependence without recognising how the impact of the coronavirus pandemic has affected all our lives. The lens through which we look is inevitably shaped by new awareness that there are things we do not control and which can cause us harm. Perhaps this, in turn, creates a new humility amongst human beings and a recognition of the way our lives intersect with the other than human world.

But most of the stories we tell here and the insights they offer pre-date the pandemic, its immediate consequences for our everyday lives and the, as yet unknown, long term consequences for us as individuals and our relationships with others. In the final chapter we record reflections of what the pandemic has meant for the community, as well as offering overall reflections on what this way of living together can offer in all times. The crisis has had an impact on Pilsdon as on everyone else. But it has survived this crisis as it has survived other, more localised crises throughout its history. Its unusual longevity itself is a reason to learn more about what the community means and has meant to those who have been part of it, and to reflect on what it can help us to learn about how we can live well together. So whilst others would tell different stories and emphasise different aspects of the Pilsdon Community, our aim is to both offer a view of a real place and the people who live there, and to suggest the potential of an alternative way of life that has a much broader significance.

ORIGINS

The origins of the community lie in the vision of one man, inspired both by his Christian faith and by the example of another man from a much earlier age. We tell this early story largely from the account offered by the woman, Gaynor Smith, who was a central part of its foundation and who contributed to the community's development over its first 20 years (Smith, 2008).

The Pilsdon Community has its unlikely sources in a 17th century religious retreat in Huntingdonshire, founded by a young City of London merchant with business interests in the new North American colonies, together with the experiences of an English priest and his wife in mid-20th century Hong Kong. Percy and Gaynor Smith lived and worked in Hong Kong for seven years from 1946 as Anglican priest and teacher respectively. Their daughter Ruth was born there in 1948. While Gaynor never felt truly happy in that very different culture, it seems that Percy, fascinated by China, assumed that their working lives would be spent there. However, their ambitions and expectations were changed dramatically by the chance reading of a book titled *Nicholas Ferrar of Little Gidding* (Smith, 2008: pp.21-23).

Nicholas Ferrar was the young London merchant who, in 1625, abandoned his career to move with his immediate family to a run-down manor house in the countryside. His aim was to establish a small community based on a life of simplicity and prayer, offering support to strangers in need of help. The community of Little Gidding lasted only 32 years but knowledge of it, and interest in and admiration for what it attempted to do, survived (and was to be an inspiration for TS Eliot in the last of his *Four Quartets*). The impact of Nicholas Ferrar's story on Percy and Gaynor Smith was profound. It appealed to their interest in community life and to their mission to help others. Most particularly, it appeared to offer a way of pursuing a monastic style of living, based in prayer, work and companionship, that was appropriate to a married couple with a small child. They fairly quickly made the decision that this was what they should try to do, and they returned to England in 1954 with the aim of finding an appropriate location in which they could realise their hopes.

This took time, and after considerable but fruitless searching for the right kind of place, they settled in Devon, near the boundary with Dorset, where Percy took a post as parish priest. It was then more than three years before they discovered that Pilsdon Manor House, with adjoining church and land, was for sale. Pilsdon was only six miles from where they were living, and their first visit convinced them that this was what they had been looking for. Gaynor later remembered that when they drove down the steep lane into the Marshwood Vale, "we rounded the bend and saw the little church with a steeple so incredibly like the one at Little Gidding there could be no doubt in our minds that this was to be the scene for the re-enacting of a long forgotten vision" (ibid: 25). A further wait followed while Percy and Gaynor embarked on fund raising, writing to friends and colleagues in a bid to supplement their own small amount of capital with sufficient funds to enable them to make what they hoped would be a successful offer. The property was sold at auction on 16th October 1958, and the couple found themselves the owners of a 17th century Manor House, the church, a cottage, various outbuildings and 9 ½ acres of farm land for the price of £5,000.

The Smith family began living at Pilsdon more or less immediately, together with the other members of the first community, some of whom were to stay at Pilsdon for many years. Apart from Little Gidding there does not seem to have been any particular example of communal living that they took as a model or source of learning, even though this was a time when communities or communes of one sort or another were springing up in the UK and elsewhere. Rather, guided by Percy's strong vision of a life grounded in prayer and work, they followed the one piece of clear advice they had been given: "Just plunge in and take what comes" (ibid: 27). It is clear that in those early days life for this small group was hard. Gaynor described it as "... tough and spartan. There was no central heating and no mains electricity. The rooms were cold and draughty in winter and the corridors even worse ... We had no amenities, no washing machine, no electric fires, no electric mixer, not even an electric kettle" (ibid: 27). But they gradually developed a level of self-sufficiency, with an increasing number of farm animals providing meat, milk and butter, and the garden and orchards producing fresh fruit and vegetables. There was also support from neighbours in the local area and from friends further away, in the form of donations of food, furniture and equipment which helped the community become established.

Percy put considerable energy into developing and maintaining contact with a wide circle of people, both through preaching in local churches and by communicating the vision he had for the community through talks and newsletters. He was evidently a man of considerable charisma and a fearless personality which enabled him to persuade people of the value of the Pilsdon experiment. This applied to those who would become direct supporters, perhaps even becoming community members; to the friends who gave support from a distance; and to those with particular needs who came to stay as 'guests'. The story is recounted of Percy standing at the gates of Portland Prison, some 20 miles from the community, and inviting any discharged prisoners who had nowhere to go to come and live at Pilsdon (Barnett, P & M in Vincent, J., 2011: p.98). As it became more widely known, so referrals began to be made through health and social services and the police, and the numbers of people coming for shorter or longer periods increased. The practice of offering meals and temporary accommodation to wayfarers – men, and the occasional woman, who lived 'on the road' – also became a regular feature of community life from very early on.

The community continued to consolidate and develop throughout the 1960s, with a routine becoming established that revolved around prayer times, coming together for meals, and working to sustain the animals, gardens and buildings. Gradual improvements to the living accommodation were made as money became available. Income came from contributions from the social security benefits that many of the guests received, or from the private resources that others possessed, although there was no fixed 'charge' for staying at Pilsdon and no-one was turned away because of lack of financial means. Gaynor noted that by 1966 life at Pilsdon had achieved "a framework of orderliness" (Smith, 2008: p.41), and in 1970 the community became a charitable trust, as it is today. Now, over 60 years since it was founded, the community continues to operate on the basis of the Christian faith of its members and in order to provide hospitality and a place of safety for people living with mental health problems, with addictions or other troubles that lead them to seek shelter there.

As Gaynor's account in her book *Pilsdon Morning* shows, the people who come to Pilsdon create the community, but the environment in which they live is also an integral part of this. The community includes the physical space and the animals, plants and buildings that it comprises. The interweaving of different lives within what is a distinctive and special place generates what some understand in Christian terms as 'Living the Kingdom': an expression of their faith through the way they live their lives together. For all those who come, believers and unbelievers, the intersection of place and people creates a space that is different from the more familiar context of most everyday lives. For many this offers the possibility of healing, although not all are able to make the transition into or out of the community successfully. The people who make up the community change over time, and the place changes according to seasons and the exigencies of old buildings and their need for renovation. What is possible in terms of the life of the community and what this generates comes from the interactions of an evolving collection of people, whilst the community's core ethos remains remarkably consistent with Percy and Gaynor's original vision.

THE ORAL HISTORY PROJECT

At the time of the 60th anniversary one of the community members was Mary Davies. Mary is a historian by background and she saw the possibilities of a project that would enable Pilsdon's story to be told by some of those who had known the community since it was founded. This would both feed into the anniversary celebration and enable an enduring record that would be accessible to others. The oral history project on which this book is based would have been unlikely if not impossible without Mary's imagination and enthusiasm.

Oral history emphasises the importance of personal recollections and accounts of those who have lived in a particular place, worked in a particular institution or have been part of a movement or project over a number of years (Abrams, 2016). It encourages people to tell their own stories that can then enable a rich, multi-perspectival insight into what the place, work or other activity has meant to those who are and have been directly involved. Sometimes there are differences of both fact and interpretation in the stories people tell. Not everyone talks about the same topics, but this in itself can contribute to a complex tapestry woven from different vantage points and drawing on different materials. Oral history is not research that seeks to address a specific question, nor to evaluate an experience, a practice or an institution. Oral history generates accounts that are open to different interpretations and other authors would offer different narratives from those we recount here. The interviews undertaken for this project have been lodged as both voice recordings and written transcripts in the Dorset Local History Archive. They are available for other researchers who might approach them using different lenses. Unlike most social science research, oral history interviews are often not conducted on the basis of confidentiality. Those who took part in this project knew that their words would not be anonymised and they agreed to take part on the basis that others could both listen to and read their interview.

The project involved 32 one-to-one interviews and 5 two-way conversations involving current and former guests, members, wardens, wayfarers, volunteers and friends of Pilsdon. All the interviewees could be regarded as experts with knowledge to contribute to a history of the community that comes from their personal experience at different times. Few of those who were part of Pilsdon in its early years are still alive, but it was possible to interview Gaynor Smith, who celebrated her 100th birthday in 2020 and died later that year, as well as her daughter Ruth.

The interviewers were also people who had been involved with the community at different points in its history. The two main authors of this book, Marian Barnes and David Prior, had just become day volunteers at Pilsdon as the project was getting underway. Although our knowledge of the community was very limited at that point we asked if we could contribute on the basis of our previous research experience. We have both been social researchers and Marian has a particular interest in the experiences of people who live with mental illness. For us it offered a rich insight into the community that encouraged us to want to stay involved with it. We have continued to volunteer and during 2020/21 spent periods as residential volunteers there.

Mary brought interviewers together twice to discuss how we would approach the project, to agree a broad structure for the interviews and to consider the ethical issues inherent in a project of this type. This was of particular significance since the interviews would become publicly available records. Initial contact was made via letter or email with follow up phone calls to explain the project and arrange to meet. Most of those contacted were keen to take part and only one person felt unable to do so. The interviews took place in people's homes or in a 'Memory Shed' established at Pilsdon for the project. The conversational style interviews took between one and three hours. The interviews also contributed to posters celebrating the anniversary and a play co-written and produced by current residents and a community theatre director. This was performed in the garden of Pilsdon at the anniversary event in October 2018 attended by about 200 people. In spite of cold winds that both chilled performers and blew over props, this prompted an outpouring of both recognition and joy.

WRITING THE BOOK

This book only exists because of the memories, stories and experiences recounted by many of the people who have known the Pilsdon Community during its 60 plus years. However, the results of selecting from and interpreting this vast collection of material, and attempting to shape it into a coherent and faithful account of the Pilsdon approach to 'living life in common', is the responsibility of the three authors.

Mary Davies has lived in the Pilsdon Community for 5 years, initially as a residential volunteer and for the last 3 years as a member. She came from a career as an academic historian, specialising in oral history and having undertaken substantial field research in a village community in Malawi. This professional background enabled her to plan and coordinate the project on which this book is based. Mary says more about her reasons for living in community and her wish to understand the significance of that way of life in chapter 8. Her perspective as a long-term member of the community for whom the Christian faith is fundamental to what the community means for her offers a different and distinctive contribution to the book. The daily realities of being a member at Pilsdon – described in later chapters – prevented Mary from contributing as much to the writing of other parts of the book as she would have liked. However, the book's development and ideas for its key themes have been generated in conversations over daily tasks within the community and more focussed conversations, reflecting very much the 'Pilsdon way' in terms of the intermingling of practical activity and thoughtful reflection.

The major part of writing the book has therefore been done by Marian Barnes and David Prior. They both worked in local government and in universities as social researchers and were both retired when they became involved with Pilsdon and with this project. We were introduced to the community by our neighbours, Alan and Maureen Frost. We had initially been reluctant to volunteer at Pilsdon because we do not share the Christian faith, but we were interested in the community's approach to offering a place of safety and support for people experiencing mental health difficulties. We have continued as day volunteers and in the wake of the coronavirus epidemic spent some time as residential volunteers. That experience of living and working in the community for several weeks at a time, playing a full part in the daily routines of communal life (thereby being able to add the skills of milking, muck-spreading and hedge-laying to our CVs) and developing much closer relationships with guests and members has been of enormous benefit in helping us better understand and appreciate what the Pilsdon Community is about. We hope it has also helped improve the quality of this book.

Our perspective thus stems from something of an outsider/insider status. We bring to this account a general understanding of how to work with rich qualitative data and the importance of enabling research to engage directly with lived experience. We also bring our interest in and knowledge of ideas of community; of mental health services and responses of people living with mental health problems to the way they have been treated, and a commitment to the necessity of care as both ethics and practice. We have brought these perspectives to the analysis and interpretation of the material generated by interviews. So whilst we tell different stories of those who have been part of the community based on their own accounts, we acknowledge that this is **our** telling of those stories. Others would tell them differently. And we understand that those who read this book will come to it looking for different things. Mary's chapter (chapter 8) speaks more directly to those whose interest in the community stems from a desire to understand how Pilsdon might offer a way of enacting their Christian faith. We all want to speak to people whose motivations for being interested in the Pilsdon Community have different starting points. Our hoped for audience is not only those interested in this particular community and others that, like them, are based in faith or alternative ways of living, but those with personal and/or professional interest in how we can better care for and support those who are troubled.

What we try to do in this book is describe the Pilsdon Community to those who know nothing of it as well as to offer an account that those who do know it will recognise. But we also seek to locate the community in relation to both other ways of thinking and doing community, and other ways of seeking to help those who live with addictions, mental illness or other troubles. Thus in chapters 2 to 5 what we offer is primarily a descriptive account: of why people come, what everyday life is like for those who live and work there, how people experience living with others and what is involved in running the place. But in chapters 6 and 7 we also offer a more analytic perspective. We reflect on how we might understand how care is done within the community, drawing on insights from care ethics to do so. And we consider both the spatial and temporal nature of the community in the context of things that endure and things that change. This means that the same material sometimes reappears at different points as we look at the community through different lenses. We have not sought to change what people said in interviews and conversations: the words you read in the material quoted are the words people used. We have, however, undertaken minimal editing of the material to improve clarity and comprehension.

Woven throughout the text is discussion of the enduring importance of faith to the members and some guests. Whilst David and Marian recognise and respect the importance of this and have tried to do justice to the centrality of the Christian religion in the origins and continuation of the community, we also recognise that we cannot write this from a shared faith perspective. In chapter 8, Mary offers a personal account of what commitment to a life in common means from the perspective of a member living their faith at Pilsdon. Both the language Mary uses and the traditions she draws on in offering her personal reflections are different from much of what we recount as we describe and discuss how Pilsdon works from the perspectives of those who were interviewed – although the significance of faith to many of those who have been part of the community is a theme throughout the book. We noted earlier that the telling of the Pilsdon story would be different from different perspectives; Mary's chapter, rooted in her personal values and experiences, provides a striking contrast to the approach we take in the preceding chapters but, we believe, complements and enriches it.

As we began to write this book we started to meet with current members and guests to discuss what we were

writing and invite responses to this. The intention was
to generate a text that was to some extent co-produced.
That was hard because the rhythms and priorities of the
community do not fit well with the discipline of writing,
or even of ordered deliberation. We remember a Sunday
afternoon early on in the process when a meeting to
discuss ideas for the book, which had been carefully
organised some time in advance, proved resistant to all
attempts at maintaining a consistent flow of discussion.
People came and went, someone would appear and throw
in a new thought then leave, someone else would be part
way through a lengthy suggestion then realise they had to
go and milk the cows, others arrived late on and had to
be brought up to speed. This was in itself an important
learning experience about how Pilsdon functions and
what is, and is not, possible. Nevertheless, we were able
to draw from many conversations and discussions as we
developed the text. Then came the lockdown imposed
as a result of Covid 19. We were no longer able to visit
Pilsdon. The idea of arranging Zoom meetings for book
discussions was not even up for consideration! So we have
not been able to do as much as we would have liked in
times of co-producing this text. But the shutdown invited
another perspective. Whilst this book is based primarily on
interviews conducted in 2018, the community's experience
of the lockdown in 2020/21 felt too important to ignore
as we seek to understand the community and what it can
help us learn. The lockdown was a real challenge to the
hospitality that is at the heart of the ethos. But it also
focuses key messages about creating a safe environment in
which people can live well together. So in the final chapter

we include reflections on the lockdown experience from the warden, a volunteer and several guests.

THE STORY TELLERS

The stories generated by this project contribute personal histories and different accounts of what the Pilsdon Community has meant to people over 60 years. It is an enormously rich resource that could provide the basis for different ways of narrating the nature and significance of the community. This book offers one such account that highlights its significance as a place where those experiencing the impact of mental health problems, addictions and other troubles can live alongside others who are seeking to express their Christian faith by living in community. Here we provide a brief introduction to those we quote in this book so that we do not have to repeat explanations of who they are whenever we quote or refer to them in the text that follows.

Members, wardens and their families

Gaynor Smith established the Pilsdon Community in 1958 with her husband Percy.

Ruth Thurgur is Gaynor and Percy's daughter and moved with them to Pilsdon when she was 10. She met her husband *Mike Thurgur* who lived nearby and started to visit the community in the 1960s.

Stuart Affleck took over from Percy as warden in 1980 and remained warden until 1994. He had first visited Pilsdon during a summer holiday when he was a child, had continued as a regular visitor, became ordained and then was approached by Percy Smith to become warden after he had decided to leave the community.

Dominic Affleck was born in 1972 and came to the community when his father became warden in 1980. He lived there until the mid 90s.

Peter Barnett was recruited as warden in 1994 and moved there with his wife *Mary* and some of their children. He had previously been a priest in inner city areas. Peter remained as warden for 10 years, leaving in 2004. *Mary Barnett* said she had visited Pilsdon to attend a service some time previously and had loved the place without thinking she would ever live there. She found it hard to leave the city and her work as a teacher of students with learning difficulties.

Jonathan Herbert first visited Pilsdon when he brought two young men from Liverpool to become guests there when Stuart was warden. He and his wife Suzie were friends of Peter and Mary Barnett who later encouraged him to stay at the community. Jonathan became a member but Suzie did not as she was training to be a nurse. He became warden following Peter's departure in 2004.

Adam Dickens and his wife Theresa joined the community as members in 2004. When Jonathan Herbert moved on in 2009, Adam took up the post of warden.

Michael Deegan was the warden of the community at the time of the 60th anniversary. He had taken on this role in 2012.

Annie Hardie's relationship with Pilsdon has continued over many years since her first contact in 1976. She first came to join her husband who had come to the community because of his problems with alcohol. She remained and became a member after her husband left the community.

Andrew Davey came to the community in 1994, when Stuart Affleck was about to leave and the community was looking for a new warden. Andrew decided not to apply for this post but was encouraged to join the community and he did so as a member. Subsequently he became a trustee, then chair of trustees.

Chris and Jan Renyard, a married couple, became members during Adam Dickens' time as warden.

Sue Langdon joined the community as a member in 1999 and stayed for 2 years before going to theological college. Sue continued to live locally and, as an ordained priest, retained contact with the community by offering spiritual guidance and mentorship to members and guests, and through occasionally leading services in the church. She returned to the community as a volunteer for 14 months in 2015. In 2019, the year after the 60th anniversary, she was appointed as the community's first woman warden.

Guests and wayfarers

Henry Thomas is a current resident at Pilsdon and has lived there since experiencing serious mental health problems over 30 years ago.

Rosemary Cortes came to Pilsdon for a break on the suggestion of her psychotherapist in 1984. She returned later that year to stay and then visited on and off both to stay and help out until she was 70 in the early 2010s.

Alex Kelly came to the Pilsdon Community during Michael Deegan's period as warden. He initially came as a wayfarer, then became a guest. He had a history of drug misuse and described a chaotic upbringing. During his time in the community he met *Rosie* and they subsequently married. Rosie had mental health problems. Alex and Rosie recorded a conversation for the oral history project and Alex took part in an individual interview.

Nick Hillyard came to Pilsdon in 1974 and was a guest, on and off for 3 years. In 2000, at the suggestion of Peter Barnett, he returned to teach pottery at the community.

Ann Davies came to Pilsdon in the mid 80s when she was in her late 30s. Her description of the way she came to the community indicated she felt she had no option but to come here, but also that she had little idea or expectation of what the community might be about.

Sarah Hallett arrived at Pilsdon in 1989 soon after her 21st birthday. She had experienced mental health problems, had been admitted to psychiatric hospital and had attempted suicide.

Bill Scanlon had continuing mental health problems following a breakdown in 1998, was sectioned and spent time in different mental health units. He came to Pilsdon as a guest in 2004 and has spent time at the community on and off since then. He now visits as a volunteer.

Emma Davison came to Pilsdon in 2016 as a guest. She was physically very unwell when she arrived and had a problem with alcohol.

Nicky Beresford was a guest at Pilsdon when Emma arrived. They developed a friendship which has continued since Nicky moved on. They recorded a conversation together for the project.

Daniel Kittow came to Pilsdon after his marriage had broken down and he was unable to have contact with his children. He had developed an addiction to alcohol. He was a guest when the oral history project took place and took part in a recorded conversation with Bob Edwards.

Michael O'Shaughnessy has been a regular visitor since 1967/8. As a young man he moved to London from Ireland and eventually got a job working on oil rigs in the North Sea. He married and had children. Problems in his marriage and his use of alcohol eventually led to a friend who knew the community suggesting he come to Pilsdon.

James Morris first came to Pilsdon as a wayfarer in the mid 1980s and has continued to visit. Stuart Affleck was warden at the time of his first visit.

Simon Norris is a wayfarer who has been visiting Pilsdon since the late 90s or early 2000s. He originally came as a result of encouragement from his mother.

Simon Smith heard about Pilsdon when he was living on the streets and spent time at Hilfield Friary. His first visit was in 2000. He visited every 6th weekend until he was rehoused. But then started coming again in 2005.

Trustees, volunteers and friends

John and Karen MacAuslan. Karen has known Pilsdon since she was a child in the mid 1960s – her father was a friend of Percy Smith. She took John to visit when they married in 1979 and they continued to visit together. He was invited to become a trustee by Stuart Affleck.

Hilary Joyce's first contact with Pilsdon was in 1987 when she joined the choir there. She has been in touch with the community ever since, became a trustee in 2008 and chair of trustees in 2013.

Shirley Edwards was in her 80s when the interview was conducted. She had spent time in different communities when she was young. She came to Dorset with her second husband feeling like she knew nobody. She cannot remember how she was introduced to Pilsdon but has been a friend of the community since 1974.

Jane Dibdin lived locally and heard about Pilsdon from her rector soon after it was established by Percy and Gaynor. When her sister had what Jane described as a breakdown she went to Pilsdon for the summer and had a positive experience. Jane was a regular attender at church services and events at Pilsdon, her children often visited when they were young. She became a trustee on behalf of the diocese during Peter Barnett's time.

Bob Edwards has been a residential volunteer at Pilsdon on numerous occasions since he first came in 2007.

Caroline Hillyard grew up near Pilsdon and her first memory is being taken there as a child. She regularly attended church services there and joined Gaynor's choir. She was invited to become a trustee during Stuart Affleck's time as warden.

Caroline's mother *Doreen Pinney* has known Pilsdon since it was founded and remains a friend of the community.

Rob Bailey was born in 1976 when his parents were living at Pilsdon. He lived in the community until he was three and continued to visit with his parents for holidays. After living in different places he has returned to live nearby and continues to visit regularly.

Alan Frost was the one paid employee of the community at the time of the project, having worked as the administrator there for almost 20 years.

In the final chapter we include material from interviews or conversations with a number of people who were resident at Pilsdon during the pandemic lockdowns of 2020/21. These interviews did not form part of the oral history project and are not contained in the resulting public archive. We are grateful to Craig, Eddie, Simon, Jack, Joni and Alex for their permission to use the material quoted in chapter 9.

As these brief introductions show, some people have long term relationships with the Pilsdon Community and during that time the nature of that relationship can change. Someone who is a guest at one point may return as a volunteer, a friend may become a trustee, a member become a warden. As we will see the fluidity of relationships is one dimension of Pilsdon's distinctiveness. But we start with the ways in which people first come to the community and what their initial reactions were to this unusual place.

CHAPTER 2

———

Coming to Pilsdon

In the first chapter we gave a brief introduction to the emergence and development of the Pilsdon Community. We now develop that account to enable others to understand what it is like to live and work at Pilsdon and to consider what the community has meant to people over the years. Pilsdon is a shifting coming together of people who share their lives for varied lengths of time. They do so for different reasons and in different circumstances. For some the encounter is a brief, one-off, stop on a road elsewhere, whilst for others it is home for many years. Often a first visit is the start of a continuing relationship with the community that may be intermittent but continues over a long time. As one person said, Pilsdon tends to 'get under your skin' and whilst the nature of the relationship might change, the community becomes an important part of many people's lives. They form deep-rooted connections which persist even when there is little or no physical contact with the place. This was an important factor in enabling the oral history project to take place – it was still possible to make contact with people whose initial involvement with the community had been decades previously.

In this chapter people talk about what brought them to Pilsdon. We distinguish those who come as members or wardens from those encountering the community as its guests, but we also discuss the way in which this is a place of fluidity rather than strict categorisation. A visitor to Pilsdon will initially find it hard to distinguish members from guests from volunteers. Conversations with new arrivals cannot assume a particular identity. Why people come does not always map on to the role people play within the community. All those who come to Pilsdon are seeking something, but this may not turn out to be what they anticipated when they first arrived.

LIVING THE FAITH

Pilsdon started and starts with people who have a Christian faith being drawn to give expression to that faith by living in community, and inviting others who are experiencing the impacts of mental ill health, addictions or other life problems to share their place of home and work. It is this that gives rise to the description of some of those who come to Pilsdon as *members* of the community and others as *guests*. Others come to Pilsdon as wayfarers, as residential or day volunteers. And there are others for whom the community becomes an important part of their lives who come to be known as friends. Still others take on the formal

25

role of trustees. As we will see throughout this book, whilst there are important distinctions arising from these different identities and consequent relationships with Pilsdon, one of the distinctive characteristics of the community is how an acceptance of others on the basis of shared humanity unsettles any firm demarcations in understanding what Pilsdon means to those who come into contact with it. We will also see that people can and do move from one identity to another at different times.

We start with the perspectives of members and wardens because without them the community would not exist. They carry the overall responsibility for ensuring it operates on a day-to-day basis and is sustained through the inevitable challenges and difficulties such a community experiences. The community is their home for whatever period they devote to it. In some cases an agreement is made for a specified time: three years, for example. In other cases they join without knowing or pre-determining when they will leave. There have been 6 wardens during its 60-year history with those holding this role staying in it for 3 to 22 years; two of these were community members for a number of years before becoming warden (the seventh and current warden was appointed a year after the 60th anniversary). Some wardens and members come on their own, others with a partner and some also with children. Pilsdon has been home to families on many occasions throughout its history. Whilst Pilsdon is also their place of work, community members are not paid staff, but neither are they volunteers. They receive a small payment, but this does not constitute a salary and a decision to become a member means a preparedness to live simply with few material possessions.

So what draws people to live in this way and take on the responsibilities associated with ensuring the safety and wellbeing of the people, animals and environment that constitute the Pilsdon community? We have called this section 'living the faith' because all those who become members share a Christian faith. Whilst they may talk about this in different ways, and some may feel more secure in their faith than others, without this they would not be at Pilsdon. Whilst trustees and residential volunteers are also usually people whose involvement is motivated in this way, neither guests nor wayfarers are expected to share the faith: some do and this will be evident in what follows, but Pilsdon is open to people of all faiths and none.

We have described how Pilsdon came to be founded and the role of faith in that. In her account of the community's early years Gaynor Smith wrote about her and Percy's personal histories and the importance of religion in their development and in their journey towards Pilsdon: "We both dreamed of religious communities, read the lives of those who had lived in them, and dedicated ourselves to the spiritual life. No knights of the Grail could have been more earnest in their quest." (Smith, 2008, p. 21). But she also reflected that, whilst its origins were in the ordered liturgy of the church, what became: "the major, and certainly both the most obvious and for many of us the most fulfilling, side of Pilsdon life was its concern with the welfare of 'guests', most of whom were men and women with a problem of one kind or another, who were battling to try and find a way out of their own particular mental and emotional jungles; people who had ground to a halt and needed a shortish or longish respite from the pressures of their daily lives." (ibid, p. 18).

In the interviews former wardens spoke of their journeys to Pilsdon and how this offered an opportunity to live their faith in a way that they had not been able to find in the established church. Since all are ordained priests becoming warden is a 'job' to a rather greater extent than is the case for other members, although it is a job with rather different appeals from many:

> I found it absolutely mind-blowing and so fascinating that actually, people could live the Gospel and not play at it. All sorts of things about it appealed to me as a teenager and continue to appeal to me. The slightly rebellious side of me links to Pilsdon quite easily and my confrontations with bishops and stuff has never bothered me, they're just men, and indeed now women. (Stuart Affleck)

Peter Barnett outlined his background in the church following ordination as a priest in 1972. He worked as a parish priest in Wolverhampton where he confronted:

> issues of multi-cultural, multi-faith and often the racist society, having been the constituency where Enoch Powell was the MP at the time of his 'Rivers of Blood' speech. And that had a profound influence on the rest of my ministry and the priorities that I had in ministry.

He subsequently worked in other multi-cultural and multi-ethnic areas of the Midlands and Bristol where he and his wife established community projects to address youth unemployment, supported diverse cultural activities and involved the church in community development. He rejoiced in working in areas of diversity where tensions were often high. He was initially reluctant to move to Pilsdon when approached by a member of the community to do so as he thought there was still work to do in Bristol. His decision to come was in part to do something completely different in a very different environment.

For Michael Deegan coming to Pilsdon involved not only a move from a city to a rural environment, but also a commitment to a change of country. He had worked on street homelessness projects and a food programme in Los Angeles before making a decision to become ordained. Michael felt he was not cut out to be a parish priest. But he worked at Salisbury Cathedral and the Bishop, who has oversight of Pilsdon for the Church of England, suggested to him that the community "was probably more what I was looking for" when a new warden was being sought in 2012. Michael was initially uncertain. On the one hand: "it actually presented a really compelling argument to me… it was sort of stunning that it was such a once in a lifetime vocation. It involved a lot of challenges, it was focusing on experiences I had had with people in Los Angeles, work that I really loved." But it was also challenging at a more personal level:

> I had always envisioned that I would have a nine to five job and go back home at the end of the day and I assumed it would be in a large city. So, the fact that it was on a farm and living in community were actually the two things <laughs> that were the challenges. It wasn't the challenge of working with people on the fringe of society or people struggling with life issues

around mental health or addiction or bereavements or homelessness. That wasn't my biggest challenge. The biggest challenge to come around was, 'How do I live in community? How do I take a life as a 50-something-year-old man who's always had autonomy and share my life in some way in community?' I had no real idea of how to do that, and living on a farm just presents obvious issues to someone moving from Los Angeles.

Jonathan Herbert was also uncertain that he was suited to life as a parish priest. But unlike Michael, for Jonathan living in community was a key attraction:

I remember sitting in a lecture when I was at Bristol University studying theology and drawing this big house with a big courtyard around it for some reason. I walked into that space, that courtyard at the back [*he is referring to Pilsdon Manor*], that house and I just thought, 'Yeah, this is a kingdom place.' In the parish I was in, I was always banging on about community, ... you know, community banks, credit unions, community associations. We did loads of community arts projects and I was always banging on about the church being a community and we had community services and I thought, 'Well, maybe I should go and live in a community.' I'd lived in community before. I'd been in Simon Community in London, working with the homeless, and loved that, lived on a kibbutz and lived in a group home in the mid-eighties with people with learning difficulties. So, I liked the community thing, that was always there for me, really.

Adam Dickens also spoke about being drawn to a way of living and working that linked faith with a form of ministry that included practical projects for people in need. He had been working in a city not too far away and had first found out about the community when he received information on behalf of someone considering going there as a guest. Adam's wife Theresa then heard Jonathan Herbert speak and they were struck by the fact that he:

> talked about Pilsdon as a place that held people. And I can't remember all of the details that Theresa recounted but there was something about prayer being something in which we are held, and it made reference to the physical nature of Pilsdon, that there's the manor house but then there's the yard with this arc of buildings that physically demonstrated in a sense what Pilsdon was trying to do with people's lives and it being a place where people felt held.

Like other wardens Adam had also sought to develop a church community that contributed to wellbeing. He saw in Pilsdon a way of counteracting the damage done by a:

> society where the individual is increasingly held up over and against a more communal or corporate expression of life, fine if you were gifted, you'd got plenty of resources and had got the confidence to use that; but if you weren't, then actually life was pretty tough for you really. And there wasn't that sense of a strong sense of a wider community that did the role of holding a lot of people. People easily fell out of the system.

Adam also recognised the significance of Pilsdon's approach to horticulture and caring for animals. It was: "somewhere that sought to value the environment", he said, and this was a further factor that attracted both him and his wife. He was uncertain that the "full on" nature of Pilsdon was something he could cope with, but he was also excited about the possibilities it offered.

As people spoke about their journey to Pilsdon there was often an indication of uncertainty, a need for a different direction without clarity over the road to take. Members as well as guests have often been looking for something that they had not found elsewhere in their lives. Pilsdon seemed to embody a sense that living the faith can be possible in a way that resonates with both spirituality and human justice.

Yet coming to Pilsdon can itself be unsettling. In their conversation Chris and Jane Renyard, who became members in 2012, reflected:

> Well, we said, didn't we, that the first six months were just... yeah, I think 'unsettling' is the right word for it. It wasn't anything terribly conscious, it was very sub-conscious but it took us those six months, really, to feel we had any root to hang on to. Yeah, I suppose it was a bit like being a tree or something that's uprooted from one place and you stick it somewhere else and you just feel very vulnerable and blown by every breeze until you set some roots down.

Mary Barnett, wife of former warden Peter, recognised that she had to adjust her expectations about what aspects of her former life and experiences would be valuable in this new context:

> Well, I was more thinking about all the things I was going to bring to Pilsdon because I had all kinds of skills and things I thought would be *amazingly* helpful and useful, and loved people and still love people, and was rather dismayed to find that actually all the things I thought I was bringing weren't really a great deal of use and I had to kind of accept, humbly, that actually I didn't really know anything about anything. And I had to start very much from a new person, just as everyone else arrives at Pilsdon, to find my way really which was quite hard ... and I did, at the beginning think, crikey, I don't know really what I'm doing here, I don't know if I'm in the right place.

John McAuslan first encountered Pilsdon through the woman who became his wife and who had lived locally. He subsequently became chair of trustees. In his interview he spoke of the way that Pilsdon could challenge people's sense of themselves:

> **JM:** Going to Pilsdon was always challenging. Whenever we went, and we went quite often, stayed for quite long periods sometimes... ... I was always slightly anxious before we got there and then, at the end, very sad to go away. Obviously got under my skin every time, reliably.

> **Int:** Do you remember what you were anxious about?

JM: That it exactly was not everything that I was used to. It didn't relate to any part of my life or my past. Being a person who is possibly less than ideally socially confident, the fact that I would be meeting an awful lot of strange people, who were obviously very different from me in many ways, probably was daunting.

These reflections highlight the alterity of Pilsdon, its distinctiveness from a way of life that most people are familiar with. Some of those who come are on a journey in which they are explicitly looking for a different way of life, a chance to follow a different path. Others come across Pilsdon, recognise its difference and find that this offers something they may not have known they were looking for. As Andrew Davey recalled: "I think I picked up this was a place where it was OK not to be OK. And so at another level in me, I felt drawn to being here, I thought, this is a safe place, this is a good place to be, for me."

From the start, the Pilsdon Community has attracted people who felt at odds with mainstream society. This was the case for Mike Thurgur, who lived locally and who met and later married Percy and Gaynor's daughter Ruth. He spoke of feeling: "quite an outsider and somewhat critical about the political structures, the system, etc., so I was always happy to escape, in a way." When he encountered Pilsdon through Ruth he rejoiced in its difference and felt comfortable there.

SEEKING A DIFFERENT WAY OF LIFE

So for some coming to live in community is a positive choice. Some see it as a challenge: it is not what they are used to and it questions aspects of self-identity. Community living can mean both embracing a tradition with deep roots in early Christianity and being part of a secular alternative culture. Peter Barnett's decision to take up the post of warden was influenced by his interest in monasticism:

> I had always toyed with the whole issue of monasticism: I tested my vocation to join a community as an ordinand for community resurrection in Mirfield, Yorkshire. I had been greatly influenced by the Franciscans and by the Taizé community in France as a young person, and I'd always kept in touch with communities, but while at college I had to make the decision about whether to be a celibate monk or marry the girl that I loved so I did the latter. And it seemed to be going to Pilsdon actually could perhaps kill two birds with one stone and after much thought and deliberation we decided that we'd up sticks and go there.

Sue Langdon had also been attracted to community life but had been uncertain about how to achieve this:

> I'd been looking to join a community but knew that, as a person who was married, and that's complicated, with grownup children, that joining as a novice to become a nun wasn't really, in terms of my own maturity, possible, I couldn't go back to being a novice. I still felt drawn to

community life but I didn't know where to begin to look, really.

Stepping out of the mainstream into an alternative way of life at Pilsdon is not about leaving behind tensions and challenges for members, wardens and volunteers who make a positive decision to spend time living there. Nevertheless, interviews conveyed a powerful sense that people want to commit themselves to living the faith in a way that provides a profound alternative to individualistic, materialistic and competitive cultures, and offers a safe space for others confronting significant difficulties in their lives. In doing so Pilsdon has met different needs for members, volunteers, trustees and friends. As well as enabling them to put values into practice, it has helped them at times of personal troubles. Thus for Bob Edwards, who has been a residential volunteer at different times over many years, the community offered a sense of companionship and value after his wife's death:

> I get the impression that Michael was glad to have me back 'cause he could see me as a pair of hands that would help. I wasn't thinking about that, I was thinking about me, <laughs>. I was thinking about a good place for me. Yes, there's stuff I can do and I can play my part but it wasn't Bob Edwards giving all this up for Pilsdon. I was gonna get what I get out of the place, which is companionship and doing something which I think is worthwhile.

A key purpose of the community is to offer hospitality and welcome to those who are seeking something they have been unable to find elsewhere, and those who are experiencing pain and troubles. A place that offers hospitality prompts a response. It is to this that we now turn.

PAIN, GRIEF AND UNCERTAINTY: BROKENNESS

Pilsdon is not a retreat: the work required to keep things going does not allow for that. But it does seek to be a place of repair. It is a place where new arrivals bring with them their troubles and their humanity and hope that they will find healing. For some of the guests and wayfarers those troubles derive from mental illness and its consequences. They may be the consequences of addictions that have led to breakdowns in close relationships, and/or are themselves consequences of existential crises. Disruptions to the lives of those who come often include homelessness and loss of many kinds. Some of those who come have found limited help from formal psychiatric or addiction services. Some have been imprisoned and are looking for routes out of the way of life that took them there. Others have found it hard to adjust after a period in the armed forces. Pilsdon can seem a last resort, but also an opportunity to pause, reflect and explore alternative ways of being.

There has been rather little change in these trajectories since the community's foundation. And arriving at Pilsdon does not mean the end of the pain people feel. The process of repair does not follow a linear path. In her interview Gaynor Smith recounted the story of two women who came in the early days of the community:

We had a lady called Elizabeth staying with us, she was a depressive, she was very tall, she was rather beautiful really, tall and slim, and very upper class. And she came in to stay with us because she was depressed. And one time, Evelyn, she was a member of the community, and she said, 'Gaynor, I don't know where Elizabeth is, can't find her.' I said, 'We best go and look for her.' So we went to look for her, we found her... There was a lot of hay outside, haystack, found her at the bottom of the haystack, drunk. And... well, drunk with drugs really, not so much drunk, but you know, she'd taken all her drugs, I think, and she was wet and dirty, it was raining and she was wet and dirty. So we had to half carry her back to the house, put her in a bath and get her to bed.

One of the worst things was a girl called Ella who cut herself, you know, she was a self-harmer, a very, very bad one, I mean she got cuts all over her arms, both arms, and I tried to befriend Ella but it was very difficult, but all I could do was just hug her, tight, as tight as I could, so that her arms were immobilised. I used to hug her tight ... I just felt very sad for her and a bit frightened that I couldn't do more for her, a bit frightened really. But mostly I just felt very sad for the ones who were sad, you know, I felt their sadness.

Interviews with guests revealed a combination of fear, despair, chaos and loss in their lives before coming to Pilsdon. Henry, now into his fourth decade of life in the community, recalled his arrival in his early 20s: "I was very much more scared than I am now because of the trauma of my mental illness and having spent a year in hospital, it was

very nice to get down there, to finally find somewhere else."
Others had experienced mental health services, had failed
to recover and had continued to look for an environment
that would hold them in safety. Ann Davies who came to
Pilsdon in the mid 80s said:

> I believe that there were no other options at the time. ...
> And a nurse called Frank had stayed here in the 1960s
> and he explained why he'd come and he just said to me,
> 'Come on, I'll take you to visit', and he said, 'It's a Christian
> community', and immediately I thought, 'Oh no, some
> kind of gothic building with a dour sort of bulldog faced
> priest' and just entrenched in a sort of cold comfort farm
> environment. I was very anxious when I came up but it
> was October, I'm not sure exactly what the year was but I
> remember it was October... and everything in my life had
> disappeared that had meaning at that time, just at that time.

Noting that she was very unwell at the time she came Ann
spoke more about her arrival:

> I don't know how I got here, I don't know who brought
> me here, ...there was a great sense of losing more by
> coming here, initially, rather than trying to hang onto
> what was and crawl back there was a sense of, 'Oh', and
> leaving it all behind. So, I felt quite, sort of light in a way,
> light but not in a good way, there was nothing that I had
> brought with me from a life that was very relevant to
> me. So, yeah, quite depressed at the time when I arrived.
> Very exhausted, really mentally, physically, spiritually
> and emotionally depleted.

Sarah Hallett also came in the late 1980s following psychiatric treatment. Her mental health problems started as she was finishing A-levels and prevented her from accompanying her contemporaries to university. She described how she felt at the time:

> I felt very isolated and very lonely, very left behind. Over time I felt a real failure because I wasn't away doing a degree like all my friends were, and also at that time there was a lot of stigma around people with mental health problems, so many of my friends didn't keep in touch with me, they didn't want to be my friend anymore.

She had not found mental health services helpful:

> And I think also at that time in the mental health services, there wasn't as much hope for people as there is nowadays, so it was more kind of lock the door and throw away the key. I think I felt really abandoned actually, whereas now I think there's more of an expectation that people will recover and have a meaningful life, whatever they choose to do, and basically I was so unhappy and I couldn't see any hope for my future, and I took an overdose in about October 1989.

Sarah's overdose led to an admission to another mental health unit where she encountered a psychiatrist she described as: "quite a progressive ... he wasn't a conventional psychiatrist." He encouraged her to resist the over protectiveness that was her family's response to her suicide attempt and which Sarah thought made her more isolated. It was at this point that she went to Pilsdon:

> I wasn't actually suicidal anymore in that I didn't want
> to end my life, but I couldn't see much of a future for
> myself, so it was as if the weather was very grey and
> overcast, and I can remember during that winter when I
> was initially at Pilsdon, I was so angry it felt as if I had
> like iron bands around my forehead and after Christmas
> West Dorset was cold and wet and muddy and sort of
> grey and brown, and it was actually quite a tough winter
> really. And I used to walk in the lanes a lot, I used to walk
> a lot from Pilsdon, and yes, I was still quite depressed
> really and I think it was with the changing of the seasons
> almost which my mood lifted, and possibly my favourite
> time of year in the West Country is the springtime, and I
> can remember seeing the primroses and the violets, wild
> violets in the hedgerows.

Sarah's story exemplifies what many of those who come
to Pilsdon experience – that there can be more than one
arrival. Sarah left the community and got a job in a hotel,
but then was sacked because of crying in front of guests:
"…somebody at the hotel, who might have been one of the
other members of staff, had a little baby and … for many
years of my life I desperately wanted to have a little baby,
and I haven't been able to fulfil that part of myself, the
maternal part of myself, and I cried, I started crying and
the manager didn't like me crying in front of people and so
I was sacked." She returned to Pilsdon for another couple
of months, but with the clear intention of recovering and
then moving on.

Bill Scanlon's story also illustrated how mainstream services were unable to offer help for some who subsequently found Pilsdon a place in which they could seek to repair broken lives. For Bill mental health problems followed a marriage breakdown. In 2003 his deteriorating mental health led his doctor to ask him to accept voluntary admission to psychiatric hospital. Although he initially agreed, he changed his mind when the ambulance came to take him and tried to run away when he arrived at the hospital. He was admitted and put on: "some pretty heavy duty drugs."

Bill discharged himself after 3 weeks, but had psychotic episodes and was eventually sectioned (compulsorily detained in hospital). He described being heavily medicated and eventually pleading to be discharged. He said being in hospital scared him more than anything he had ever experienced. Eventually a review tribunal did discharge him. In spite of his family's attempts to prevent him, he travelled to Australia to visit his sister. But his mental health remained poor and on his return to England when he was living in a shelter his community psychiatric nurse showed him information about Pilsdon and suggested he try it for a weekend. Bill described how this offered him an opportunity that transformed his life:

> **BS:** So anyway, I got here, Adam was in charge, that was on the Friday I got here, he picked me up on the Friday, I was due back on Monday, but on the Sunday I told him what I did for a living. He said, 'Really?' I said, 'Yeah, I'm qualified.' He said, 'Well, we've got lots of things need doing round here.' I said, 'Well, I'm your man.'

And he went, 'Right.' On the Sunday he said to me, 'Bill, would you like to come and stay with us for a little bit?' And I said, '*Yes, please,*' straightaway.

Int: So you immediately felt –

BS: Oh, *as soon as I got here*, I wasn't in a hospital, I wasn't looking at people, you know, the … Pilsdon Community saved my life, Mary. *No doubt about it,* no doubt, I wouldn't be here.

Pilsdon not only offered Bill a place of safety, but a place where he could offer his skills. Both contributed to the process of repair. He has continued to visit Pilsdon for short periods ever since and has been a volunteer at the community.

Not all those who come to Pilsdon have experienced formal interventions from mental health services. Nick was one of the earlier guests, arriving during Percy's period as warden. For him it offered the possibility of a new direction, facilitated by flexibility in the type of relationship he could have with the community:

I'd been teaching for, I don't know, four or five years and got totally depressed and incapable of doing anything. I was working for a cousin in Kent who grew apples and pears and he came by by chance one day and said, 'What are you going to do next, Nick?' and I said, 'I've got no idea.' He said, 'Well, I've got this friend who's coming. He knows these people down in Dorset who have cows <laughs>.' That's how I first heard about it. 'So, come and talk to him and see what he has to say.' From that moment, one thing led to another and I was soon ringing up Percy.... when I came, he said, 'Well, stay here for a few days, so you can look after the cows.' I said, 'Goodness, I've never had anything to do with cows.' 'That doesn't matter,' <laughs>. I stayed almost three years to the day and the staying or the going was never mentioned again until I ran out of sickness benefit and then I was obliged to move. I then went to the little village of Membury, just outside Axminster, and I borrowed a pottery for nothing because I'd started potting at Pilsdon. Then, I fell out with the people who owned it, Percy came out to Membury and he said, 'Nick, if you want to come back, come straight back to Pilsdon,' and it hadn't crossed my mind.

Nick subsequently returned as a volunteer to teach pottery in the community.

Relationship breakdowns associated with addictions, becoming unemployed or other crises can precipitate a move to Pilsdon. This was the case for James Morris who first heard about the community when he started going to Hilfield (a Franciscan Friary in Dorset that also offers temporary accommodation for people who are homeless) after: "coming out of a bit of a messy relationship, with children involved, and stuff like that, and I lost my job, I had a very good job and I lost it. My relationship had fallen apart." This was in the 1980s and James has been coming, on and off, ever since.

In their conversation Daniel and Bob, a guest and volunteer at the time of the interview, also shared their experiences of being: "estranged from our wives and our young children [are] being brought up away from us." Daniel said:

> It's just weird how it's all panned out. It's as if my journey to Pilsdon... I came in as a wayfarer and then it wasn't 'til I was sat in the horse box, praying and crying my eyes out... I had blisters on my feet from where I'd been walking the streets and I honestly thought, 'Life can't get any worse than this.' But I was so grateful just to have a warm bed and a roof over my head 'cause I could hear the rain lashing down.

Because guests and wayfarers come to Pilsdon at times of crisis or other major difficulty, their initial experience of arrival is important in terms of feeling, like Daniel, that this is a safe place that can provide a refuge. The response of other guests impacts this. Nicky had formerly been a guest at the time of the history project and her conversation with current guest Emma reflected a number of issues about their continuing relationship, starting with their initial encounter:

> I'd been at Pilsdon for a little while when Emma came, and I was determined that I was going to make her very welcome. I asked about her but nobody told me anything about you, they just said, 'Her name's Emma.' And I remember you arriving and I thought, 'She looks ill, and tired, and quite...' if I say rough, I don't mean it in a rude way, I mean, you look as though you'd been up against it in life.

Another conversation was between Rosie and Alex who met and fell in love at Pilsdon. Rosie said:

> I was in a really, really bad place when I came here. I was living from one tranquilizer to the next, just isolating myself and feeling absolutely just dreadful, I'd lost everything. Then I met Alex and he was funny and everybody liked him and he was vibrant. He was just this incredible guy that everybody just thought was so wonderful and he was in recovery. He made me realise that I could be in recovery but I could still be a good person and I could still have fun and I could still be normal.

In an individual interview Bob spoke more about the circumstances surrounding his initial arrival. His marriage had ended and his children were being brought up by his ex-wife. He had sold his business and decided to set off travelling. On his return journey, unclear where he was going back to or why, he heard a reading of Tobias Jones' book *'Utopian Dreams'* on the radio. Interested in this he found out more about Pilsdon through the internet, then emailed to inquire about becoming a volunteer. He spent a week at Pilsdon and then:

> Jonathan [Herbert] said, 'Can we meet in the chapel in the house for a chat?' So, I thought, 'This is it. Hopefully, he's gonna say yes, I can stay and then I can stay.' When we got in the chapel, Jonathan just said, 'How have you found it?' I just sort of dissolved, I became all tearful and we talked and he wanted to know about some of

my reasons for being there and such like. So, everything came out and we had a really good conversation and he ended by saying that yes, he thought I should be here but they weren't quite sure whether I should be a guest or volunteer. But he said I needed to be here, so I was gonna come back anyway. Then, I think if I remember rightly he said that I could come as a volunteer but it would be a month at a time, sort of thing. So, if anything were to happen or for reasons why, I probably wasn't emotionally stable enough to do the job, then things might change.

It is difficult to categorise the reasons people come to Pilsdon solely by reference to their identities as members, guests or volunteers. Some come without a clear designation, others return in a different capacity. This is particularly evident in the story of Annie Hardie. Annie first encountered Pilsdon when it was suggested that her husband, an ordained priest with a severe alcohol problem, should take a break from parish life in 1976. He spent a number of periods at Pilsdon over the next 4 years, but was not able to stop drinking and sustain a job after he left. Annie had not gone to Pilsdon with her husband during this period and was struggling to find a job and look after their two sons with very little money. She was trying to find a job that came with accommodation. At this point Stuart Affleck contacted her and suggested she come with her sons to join her husband. The initial suggestion was that she should come for 6 months and the boys could go to the local school. Annie saw this as a lifeline, coming completely out of the blue and offering an unanticipated solution to the problems the family was facing: "I hadn't even thought that that would be a possibility, so when Stuart phoned and said, 'Come and join us,' it was wonderful."

Annie described the move:

> So, we hired a van, loaded it up. The van was too small so we had to leave about a third of our possessions sitting in the hallway at Riversdale. No, never do a move with a man and a van if you don't know what the size of the van is, <laughs>. We came down here on the 16th May 1981 and we were met by Stuart and Ben, his middle son, at Crewkerne station and so started the adventure. Down the lane, past the Pilsdon Pen, cow parsley lanes full of red campion and bluebells and I thought, 'I don't believe it, this is quite amazing.' And there, at the bottom of the hill in the vale, was the manor house. So, we came and we were made very welcome and our first meal was all together. I think the boys were a bit kind of taken aback by the whole thing.

The family moved into a flat at the top of the house. They had no bathroom so had to use one on the first floor or go out to use the showers in the courtyard. It felt good to be reunited. Annie joined in the life of the community, doing a lot of cooking and helping out with driving. Numbers had declined in the aftermath of the transition from Percy to Stuart as warden. There appeared to be a role for Annie within the community and she slipped easily into that:

> I like having things to do, I like being busy, so that was easy. When there was fruit in summer, you just went out and you picked it and you topped and tailed and

you chopped up rhubarb and you put it in the freezer and you do all that. Took your turn at the laundry and the washing. There was always plenty to do 'cause we were quite a small community but it was important that everybody who came also did things as well.

Annie had arrived as the wife of a guest and effectively became a volunteer. She enjoyed the sociability she encountered, in particular because her husband's drinking had led to the loss of friends. So when her husband started drinking again and Stuart asked him to leave, Annie stayed. Two years later she formally became a member and stayed for fourteen years.

Annie's experience illustrates the flexibility and fluidity of identity that has been possible in people's relationships with Pilsdon. Her arrival was associated with the difficulties associated with her husband's alcoholism, uncertainty about jobs and accommodation, and the pain of what felt like rejection as her husband appeared unwilling or unable to put his wife and children before his addiction. But Annie spoke of the rightness she felt and her ease in fitting into the rhythms of the community. When, later, one of her sons was killed in a motor-cycle accident she experienced even more profoundly the pain she shared with many of the guests:

The guests come to Pilsdon, in all their sense of things having gone wrong and failed and broken and messed up and all the other words. I've felt... well, I was here as a member of the community, having come through failed and broken and messed up and homeless. So, I thought,

'Well, I can identify with you in some ways,' so I can also say, 'Look, things do get better.' When something happens, when the death of a child happens in the community <cries>, then we're all the same... So, all the other people's remembrances of pain and loss come out and they just hold you, literally hold you, until you stop crying and they're there. It was an awful summer because not only did Simon die and we had all that and then Stuart and Judy left, which they'd planned to do and you couldn't stop them because that wasn't the way of things. So, it was like a double bereavement in that summer <cries> and you just had to get on, you can't stop. You haven't got the luxury of saying, 'Oh, Pilsdon is going to close for two weeks until I regroup myself or sort myself out.'

Grief and loss are experiences we all share. Pilsdon has been a place to go when grief and pain become part of others' lives, not least because of it is a place of acceptance. Hilary Joyce, former trustee said:

my mother at that time was living in Beaminster and in due course she died, and my husband died four-and-a-half years ago and on both occasions ... the first place I went to when I was going out of the house, if you know what I mean, was Pilsdon. And my mother, I think I'd been to the hospital and done everything and then, then I actually went to Pilsdon and I was greeted with open arms by everybody. People were incredibly kind to me. Everybody. And partly I went there because I knew that if I burst into tears no one would bat an eyelid.

Sometimes people bring with them such a level of pain or trauma that they are unsuited to life in the community. This can lead to tragic events. Peter Barnett recounted two such stories, one involving an unfamiliar wayfarer who cut his face with a razor in the shared dormitory after having attended an Easter service. The other related to a woman priest who was subsequently discovered to have committed arson elsewhere. Peter recounted what happened in some detail:

I was taking compline with her in the house chapel and I left after the compline and just said, 'Please blow the candles out before you leave.' She was going to stay. …half-an-hour later I heard the fire alarm go and I thought, oh god, someone's burnt the toast again as that's the usual reason why it went. But fortunately I didn't just make that assumption and wait for it to stop but went down and looked to see where the alarm was coming from and to my horror it was coming from the store room not from the kitchen. …I said to the chief fire inspector, 'What caused that?' And he said, 'Oh, it's arson.' I said, 'How do you know that?' He said, 'Fires don't start in four places at once, they start in one place and then spread.' And so then, I don't know why, but I went and looked at the floor and lo and behold there was a trail of wax from the chapel all the way to the store room. So I went to see this priest in her room and she was in a catatonic state on her bed, could not be moved, roused or anything so I phoned the ambulance this time and they literally had to lift her up in a crouch position and take her to hospital …And her sister had her home and then she went somewhere else and there was another fire in which sadly she died.

Wayfarers and guests spoke of chaotic and complicated lives. Often this chaos is associated with heavy drinking or drug use. Michael O'Shaughnessy's first contact with Pilsdon came from a phone call with a mate:

It was getting worse, I didn't wanna go to work, I didn't wanna do nothing, I just completely… everything started upsetting me and I just couldn't cope with anything. I mean I was having rows with the gangerman every day and everything. … And this is why I got in touch with Danny Burns.… I said, 'Danny, I've got to get myself sorted out. I've been drinking very heavy', I said, 'I've got a nice girlfriend, got a nice place in Yarmouth but I've gotta get myself sorted out.' And then he said to me, 'Michael, I'll tell you a place to go', he said, 'for a few months. Go there for three months, six months, whatever.' He said, 'You've got money.' I said, 'Yeah.' He said, 'Well go there and spend a bit of time there', he said, 'that is the place to go to sort you out. If any place will sort you out that'll sort you.' So Pilsdon it was.

In the case of Alex Kelly it was chaotic drug use:

So, my life before coming to Pilsdon was absolutely chaotic. I had a very alternative upbringing, so my mum is sort of like a New Age traveller, my dad's a Glaswegian headcase. A very strange mix of people, so my upbringing was very varied, it was never really settled. It was chaotic and even in my early years, there was a lot of drug use ... around the ages of 12 to 15, I was doing a lot of ketamine and acid and stuff and hanging around on the New Age traveller scene. That progressed, by the time I got to 19, I'd started using crack and heroin on and off. That progressed, it was a really long addiction for me, especially the heroin. I'd have periods of clean time, very short periods. ... So, I'd just come off heroin again for I don't know the how many'th time. I'd done my Subutex detox and I think I'd managed half a year clean. ... I can't remember exactly what went wrong or whether anything did go wrong, I just started to use again over a period of three or four days. My step mum, who was a drugs worker, said, 'This has gotta stop. You're just going around in this endless cycle of getting on and off drugs and nothing's really changing.' So, she said, 'There's this place, Pilsdon. I'm gonna send you there as a wayfarer.'

Others who came as wayfarers told stories of violent incidents, significant health problems and the impact of homelessness. Simon Norris had been referred by a probation officer and spoke about frequent arrests and time in prison. Like many others he has returned to Pilsdon on more than one occasion.

I was quite badly assaulted and nearly died, actually. I was assaulted and I had bleeding from the brain and my behaviour really did change, from one punch. One punch can really kill you and it nearly did me and my behaviour did change, I was homeless... I stayed in night

53

shelters and I just couldn't cope with circumstances. I was asked to leave a night shelter and I didn't get all the possessions back.

He was angry about the failure to help him find accommodation on discharge from prison and recounted his campaign using local and national media and letters to his MP that all gave his address as a public toilet in Bournemouth. Simon's story, and that of others, reflects the hard lives of many of those who come to Pilsdon.

CONCLUSION

One of the things that is said about visiting Pilsdon is that you could find yourself sitting at lunch with a bishop on one side and an ex-prisoner on the other. In this geographically secluded space people from diverse backgrounds and facing different challenges come together to share aspects of their lives. They may have been drawn by desperation, hope or a sense of having been called or guided. All are, in some way, involved in a search for an alternative way of living. For some community is the attraction, for others the challenge. Faith is fundamental to what Pilsdon means for some and incidental for others. In many cases coming to Pilsdon is a consequence of acknowledging that the way they have been living has damaged themselves and others; people are looking to change themselves, to repair the brokenness they feel. Sometimes they are more straightforwardly looking for respite. For others, their relationship with Pilsdon is an opportunity to give expression to aspects of themselves that are suppressed in other contexts.

In this chapter we have started to hear some of the different voices of those for whom Pilsdon has offered a home, a place of work and of shelter for 60 years. In the next chapter we consider what it means to live in the Pilsdon community by describing what everyday life involves. And as we continue to look at what Pilsdon means from different perspectives throughout this book, we start to understand more about what is distinctive about this place of nurturing and why it has continued in this role for over 60 years.

CHAPTER 3

———

Everyday Life at Pilsdon

People often arrive at Pilsdon following times of trouble or even despair. Others come looking for a different way of living, one that enables them to give everyday expression to the values they hold or the faith that centres their lives. They may not know quite what to expect and it can take some time before many feel settled. Few will have experienced living in a community like this and both the rural setting and the people with whom they find themselves thrown together create an unfamiliar environment in which to try to find the healing that many are seeking.

In this chapter we describe what it is like to live at Pilsdon. Everyday life as described by people over the sixty years' life of the community points to aspects of community living that have changed in that time, but emphasises much that has remained essentially the same. Much of that is a consequence of the particular location of the community. So we start by considering the impact of the specific geographical, environmental and architectural settings which impact on how life is lived at Pilsdon. Within this place people live, work, establish relationships, struggle with their particular demons and worship their God. Here we discuss the social dimensions of everyday life, the fundamental significance of rhythms and routines in structuring day-to-day activities, and the key roles of prayer, work, communal meals and celebrations.

THE NATURAL ENVIRONMENT:
LIVING IN A PLACE OF BEAUTY

Pilsdon is situated in the Marshwood Vale, a rural and isolated part of West Dorset, criss-crossed by narrow lanes and bounded by high hills. It is some seven miles from the nearest town, Bridport, with no public transport connections. This location means that, while different people experience it in different ways, there is a general awareness of living in much closer proximity to the natural world than is the case in our predominantly urban society. Many of those we interviewed spoke of life at Pilsdon being directly shaped by factors such as the changing seasons, weather conditions, the appearance of the night sky, the impact of trees and flowers at different times of the year and a heightened sense of the aesthetic appeal of the surroundings. And for many people, these factors were bound up with a particular spiritual response to the place. In chapter 2 we introduced Sarah Hallett who arrived as a young woman in a state of extreme depression. She linked her changing mood with the natural environment:

I think it was with the changing of the seasons almost which my mood lifted, and possibly my favourite time of year in the West Country is the springtime, and I can remember seeing the primroses and the violets, wild violets in the hedgerows ... And gradually almost hope began to shoot and flower within me, because of the connectivity that I had to the natural world around me, which was so valuable. I still do value that greatly, but it's something which Pilsdon can offer, fortunately. Yes.

Mary Barnett also noted this capacity of the local environment to effect lasting change in people:

the beauty, the physical beauty of West Dorset is... you can't really describe it really. I think it changes people and I feel changed. <Laughs> I feel that I enjoyed my professional career, if you like, before but I think I left a bit of my heart at Pilsdon <laughs> really, I think everyone does.

People recalled different aspects of the environment and the way they responded to it. One recurring memory was of the clarity of the night sky and the sense of wonder in being able to observe the beauty of the stars:

There was no external light at night, which was beautiful, it was so beautiful. And I used to step outside and just stare at the stars for half an hour, particularly in the winter, they were so beautiful, and just be really in awe of that as well. Which, you know, mapped in with the faith that I was being here as well. (Ann Davies)

And I remember also coming out... it's a place where the stars come out in their brilliance at night, *absolute brilliance,* and I flitted out in me nightie with a shawl at about two in the morning to catch them. And unfortunately I bumped into one of members who I think thought I was on an assignation! <Laughter> Which I was *not,* nor ever was at Pilsdon! <Laughter> ...you used to see shooting stars and all, you never see it like that in town, it just doesn't happen. (Rosemary Cortes)

Not all experiences of being in close touch with nature were positive, and the weather in particular was a source of some less happy memories. Chris and Jane Renyard reflected that poor weather in their early days as new members was a factor that impeded their adjustment to life at Pilsdon:

JR: I remember the first day we came... Although it was May, it was a beautiful sunny day and I remember Adam saying, 'Oh, it looks beautiful but the weather's not always this good.'

CR: Yeah, I have to say for myself that the weather did affect me. The first summer here wasn't very good and of course, we were just trying to shake ourselves down and settle down. Of course whenever people start a new life, you want to get into a settled place and start feeling secure and the very unsettled summer we had didn't help. Very cold, very cold April.

But whilst cold, wet and mud can impair the everyday experience of the place, the natural environment plays a major role in shaping people's response to being at Pilsdon. This is often experienced spiritually and may be understood both within a framework of Christian faith, and within a system of less conventional religious beliefs:

> Geometrically, I think there's something special about the place, I'm absolutely sure of it. The way it lines up with the Pen [*a Neolithic hill fort*] and that church there, I'm sure there's a ley line or something running through it. I started reading about that while I was here so I'm pretty… I think anyone who's that way inclined or that way in touch with nature and the location and places knows that this is a special place. It's got a special energy about it, some kind of, without sounding too hoo-ha, healing energy here. You feel it and you know it, anyone who's, like I say, that way inclined or in touch with that. (Alex Kelly)

Sue Langdon also thought the community was set on a confluence of ley lines. She said:

> and I think there's a real sense of the energy of the place, the beauty of the place and the built environment of course all adds to the holding value of it and its capacity to hold the community, despite whoever's there at the time sometimes. There's a sense that the whole place is held by something much deeper than you can give words to. Of course, that church has held people's joys and sorrows for centuries.

As well as this intersection between physical beauty and spiritual energy, the relative physical isolation of the community offers a space in which to re-focus:

> it is sort of physically cut off. And so if one's trying to... I don't know when people are trying to deal with something, when something is being dealt with just organically, there's not things that are interfering or tempting you out of the rhythm of that, so I think that was probably helpful to a lot of people, though I'm sure there might be some people who would find it a pressure being in such a wild place. I mean I've come across people who just can't imagine the idea in normal life. (Mike Thurgur)

Mike's comment alludes to one particular way in which the relative remoteness of Pilsdon is helpful in sustaining it as a place of safety: there are few of the temptations that surround us in busy urban settings. For instance, the nearest pub is some distance away and not easily accessible, as is the nearest town – important considerations for guests with a history of alcohol or drug addiction.

THE BUILT ENVIRONMENT: LIVING SIMPLY

The church is the first thing you see from the road when approaching Pilsdon, and is the focal point of the community's spiritual life. By reminding them of the church at Little Gidding, it was a key source of inspiration for Percy and Gaynor Smith in creating the Pilsdon Community. The address of the community is 'Pilsdon Manor'. The house that Percy and Gaynor bought was a 17th century stone built manor house. The manor house is at the heart of community life, with its common room, dining room, library, large kitchen and separate Aga room, chapel and several flats and bedrooms. At the front of the house is an extensive garden with lawn, trees and flower beds. Behind the house is the separate east wing where many of the guests live, which was converted from former farm buildings. It also contains rooms used for specific purposes such as the pottery, an arts room, a 'boutique' of donated clothes, a games room and a TV room. Opposite, on the other side of a large courtyard with grazing for sheep and calves, are more living quarters; the loose boxes that originally housed horses, then became basic accommodation for residents in Pilsdon's early days and are now used by wayfarers for their short-term stays; and the dairy, laundry and a general activities room. At the far end of the courtyard are specific farm buildings like the main barn, workshop, cowsheds, milking parlour and pig sties. Elsewhere, separate buildings provide the community's administrative office, accommodation for short-term visitors and chalets for members.

Ruth Thurgur, Percy and Gaynor's daughter, recalled her first thoughts on realising that the family would be moving to Pilsdon Manor House: "I had a childlike excitement of going to live in this beautiful, big house in the middle of nowhere". However, whilst most people are impressed by their first view of the buildings, as with a number of aspects of everyday life at Pilsdon the nature of the accommodation can present simultaneously contrasting experiences:

In terms of the fabric of the place and the location, you can't help but be amazed, how nice the place is when you approach it. You come here and you think, 'Wow, this is good.' Then, I was put in the annex and there were big holes in the wall, somebody had punched through, and they'd been covered with newspaper, <laughs>. (Bob Edwards)

It was a summer's day, beautiful day, and I walked under the arch and stood... I had the manor house here and this beautiful yard, stables, all that, Daisy the goat standing the other side of the yard. ... Then I was given a single bed and about the same space again to live in. I think the walls were hardboard and a lovely, difficult, wonderful, irascible, fantastic guy called Harry Barlow lived next door to me, who's gone to play his harp now. I could hear Harry coughing and I could hear his radio. I didn't need a radio, I could listen to the news on Harry's radio. I had enough room for a few books and to go to the loo, I needed to go out into the yard in the middle of the night. (Sue Langdon)

However, like many others, Sue found the simplicity of the accommodation and the way this enabled a simple but satisfying lifestyle greatly appealing. This appreciation of the simplicity of life at Pilsdon, symbolised by the basic nature of the accommodation, has been shared by those who came as guests with little conception of what to expect, as well as by members who might have been attracted by monastic style living. And the fact that everybody shared in the hardship of the lifestyle, and could swap experiences, was another attraction. The following accounts are from people who knew Pilsdon in the 1980s:

> I lived in a loose box and I loved it, loved it. I loved the fact that the radiator was on, came on at a certain time in the loose box. I loved going to bed at maybe quarter to eleven and climbing under the sheet. It was blinking freezing, it was absolutely freezing, you wore thermals in bed with old baggy tracksuit bottoms and a big old fleece in bed and maybe a bobble hat as well, it was so cold. … and then the hum of the generator in the background was so lovely … the hum gradually going down and the lights just dimming slowly. Conducive to wonderful sleep, I felt. (Ann Davies)

> I can remember wearing my warmest pyjamas in bed and we had woollen blankets and I still needed an extra blanket. It was quite cold in the winter … and if you needed to go to the toilet in the middle of the night you had to walk all the way down the yard to where the toilets were. I was at the north end of the yard and it was a very cold walk to go to spend a penny in the winter! But I also remember very happy times because the Aga room, I think we used to have an emergency light in there and I think it might have also had access to some mains electricity, so there was always a light on over the Aga and so we used to sit in the kitchen round the Aga and drink tea and probably smoke cigarettes and talk until way after lights out. (Sarah Hallett)

Current guests have rather different experiences. Developments to the estate in the 1990s reflected both changing expectations and changing legal requirements for accommodation. Guest accommodation is now all *en suite*, with plentiful supplies of hot water and central heating. And those wanting to smoke are banned from the Aga room and instead have to go outside to the smoking shed. But one element of life at Pilsdon which continues to be influenced by the accommodation is the limited scope for accumulating personal possessions: another facet of the simplicity of everyday life there. This was reflected on by former member and warden, Adam Dickens:

> I think also there's something about simplicity because I was always very conscious of people who came to us, often they might come with a bag and that would be it. And they might leave with a bag. And also we were living in fairly tight accommodation really. ... So you learnt to live with less because there wasn't the space to put lots of stuff. ... you become aware of how your possessions provide a kind of protective layer around yourself and you go through the emotional process of letting go of all sorts of stuff, but then you become conscious of the fact that actually, I don't think I really needed that. What was that all about? So it becomes quite freeing.

THE SOCIAL ENVIRONMENT: ACTIVITIES OF EVERYDAY LIFE

Rhythms and Routines

A visitor to Pilsdon observing life in the community is likely to be struck by two seemingly contradictory impressions.

The first is of an apparently high degree of personal freedom enjoyed by guests: people appear and disappear throughout the day, some choosing to stay in their rooms for extended periods while others undertake work activities or sit reading in the library, some deciding to go for a walk or even a run in the countryside and others opting to take part in some form of art or craft activity. Some have their own patch of garden that they can cultivate as and when they like. In the evenings people may again choose to be on their own, or to join others in watching television or to get involved in games.

The second impression is of daily life being structured according to a well-established set of routines: the church bell rings four times a day for prayer services which people can choose to attend or not, the house bell is rung at fixed times for meals (which everyone is required to attend) and for morning and afternoon coffee and tea breaks. Certain work activities themselves involve a necessary routine, particularly those concerning the farm animals: feeding and mucking out must be done on a regular basis, the dairy cows must be milked morning and evening, the milk pasteurised, and eggs collected from the chickens. Laundry and house cleaning are constants, as is the preparation of three meals a day and the washing-up that follows them (done by hand). A weekly work rota assigns these various tasks to individuals, including members, guests and volunteers. Not everybody does everything: tasks are to an extent allocated according to preference and ability, and some guests take on specific regular responsibilities; but most people take their turn at a range of jobs. The timetable for these tasks, from morning milking at around 6 am through to kitchen floor cleaning after the evening meal is finished, mean that different people are engaged in work at different times of the day. In between these times, they are free to do what they wish.

The sense of a general air of informality in day-to-day life, even while the routines of work are pursued, is important: whilst there are certain rules governing how the community functions and certain limits to what people can do, it is not somewhere where guests are closely supervised or tightly regulated, and this is, for most people who live there, an attraction. But the message that emerges strongly from the interviews conducted for the oral history project is that what is most significant and most valued about Pilsdon is the consistency of the rhythms and routines that provide a structure to everyday life in the community.

This message was conveyed by someone who has been a frequent visitor to Pilsdon over a long period of time. Jane Dibden was also a trustee for some of that time but has never actually lived in the community; nevertheless, she recognises the significance of the 'Pilsdon rhythm':

> the fact that there is a definite rhythm of life, there's a timetable that, you know, that's terribly important, that bells go and things happen at certain times. The security, people knowing where they are, there's a definite pattern of life and people get up and get on with things, you know ... I think that's important for everybody because that helps. If there's a mess or muddle you've got to stick to this, the timetable helps keep things on an even keel, I think ... And the fact that the worship happens at the same time, the prayers before lunch, quarter to one or whatever, prayers in the evening.

This sense of a shared recognition of the importance of ensuring that everything is done to sustain the everyday functioning of people, animals and accommodation, becomes very evident to anyone who lives for even a short time in the community. The value of the set rhythm and its place in life at Pilsdon is appreciated even by someone whose lifestyle as a wayfarer is generally completely counter to an externally imposed routine:

> It's really funny really because I can't abide institutionalism and institutionalisation, I really hate it you know? But all communities have a rhythm, because you need that rhythm ... so long as they realise that it is just a rhythm and not an institu... and so they don't get more institutionalised, because that's when problems start to begin to happen. So to keep people who come here who are probably in a traumatic situation anyway, to stop them people from becoming even more traumatised, then is to remember, yes you need a routine. (James Morris)

The distinction that James draws between a daily rhythm and imposed institutional rules reflects the way in which the tasks necessary to the continuation of the community are shared between guests, wayfarers and members. The warden will take their turn at kitchen floor cleaning and volunteers and members cook and wash up. Whilst there are, as we will see, distinct responsibilities that members do not share with guests, the basis of the community in living and working together helps to minimise a sense that 'they' determine the rules which 'we' have to follow.

The centrality of rhythm to what Pilsdon is, to the experience of living there and to what it can offer people who may be in great personal need was emphasised by two of the former wardens:

> ... those rhythms, so important and we've lost them. In particularly urban society, people have lost that sense of rhythm. Each day was, in a sense, very contained. It's one of the things that made Pilsdon, I think, feel like a safe place; you had that routine, which held some of the pain, some of the fear, some of the anxiety, some of the madness there. Yeah, I loved that. I think the rhythm of prayer is a really hidden, understated thing at Pilsdon but I'm sure it's the glue that holds it all together. So, that going on all the time, the regular mealtimes. I've had 20 years of having lunch at 1 o'clock, tea and toast at half past 4 so I can tell the time by my stomach. (Jonathan Herbert)

> I think the daily rhythm was key actually. I think that was ... the rhythm of prayer, whether you were there for it or not, but you would hear the bell ring and you knew that it was happening, and the rhythm of the cows coming out to be milked 6 o'clock in the morning and half-past-five in the afternoon; the rhythm of meals and coffee time, I think was vital, or is a vital part of the holding that happens at Pilsdon. I think it's ... I certainly found it helpful and I think people who came to live at Pilsdon also value that rhythm and that routine, so there may have been challenges or difficulties but if people heard the bell they'd sort of go yeah, well, it's alright,

the meal's on the table. Out trot the cows, there's Henry, all's well kind of thing. And yeah, I think that was, and is, crucial. (Adam Dickens)

The Rhythm of Prayer

As is evident from the above quotes, the routine of four daily prayer services at fixed times, announced by the church bell, is regarded as fundamental to the rhythm of Pilsdon's life as a Christian community. For the members of the community, as well as for some guests and volunteers, the prayer times are an essential part of their everyday life, although this does not mean that they necessarily attend every service:

And there's the rhythm of prayer, that four times a day the chapel bell goes, and I personally found that very helpful, I rather loved the immediate mixing of being involved in something practical, and then being invited by the bell and the stop to enter a prayerful place, however you used it. To attend to another dimension of what we were about, and be reminded of that, and to think on it, and to pause. (Andrew Davey)

I mean, waking up early to go and milk the cows and sitting on a stool in the milking parlour on a chilly spring morning with the martins flying around the yard and the sun absolutely clear as a bell, there was no better way to start the day, really. Then, to go down to the church to have morning prayer or early morning eucharist was good … But what I enjoyed was, I guess, the opportunity for silence, really, in the church and would often find myself down there on my own. (Sue Langdon)

One of the interesting points about both of these quotes is the suggestion that while the prayer services do provide the opportunity for prayer in a formal liturgical sense, the times set aside for prayer may also be valuable as enabling personal reflection on everyday life and engagement with a different way of comprehending one's place in the world.

For many others, who do not share the Christian faith or do not wish to practise it in this particular way, prayer times provide a kind of backdrop to living at Pilsdon; as Jonathan Herbert said: "the glue that holds it all together". It is something which is recognised as foundational to what Pilsdon is, without requiring direct participation in it.

> The majority of people at Pilsdon don't participate in the prayers but I think there was a sense of this is part of the life and some people were really grateful that it was happening, whether they engaged with it or not. It's a bit like parish churches often function, it's kind of a vicarious religion that we do it on behalf of other people. They're glad you're doing it; they won't do it themselves, but they're glad that somebody's doing it... I never got the sense of anybody wanting to say, 'You should stop. We don't want you to spend all your time in the chapel. We want you to be out here doing stuff with us'. It felt an acknowledged part really of what made up Pilsdon. (Adam Dickens)

The notion that Christian faith is an essential part of Pilsdon that is acknowledged and accepted even by those who do not share the faith was spelled out by former guest, Alex Kelly:

It's vital at the heart, you have some kind of spiritual framework. The Christian ethos is what holds this place together. I mean, even though I'm not a Christian, I recognise that that is vital. Even though it's not really in my heart, the Christian thing, I would attend Compline some evenings because it became apparent to me... I'll be honest, it's not that important to me, religion, but it was really important to the people I was living with.

The Rhythm of Meals

Alongside the prayer services, the other great structuring routine at Pilsdon is mealtimes. It is a core principle that meals are taken communally. Breakfast, lunch and dinner are served every day in the large dining room, and everyone is expected to attend (although arrangements for breakfast are more flexible). This includes wayfarers, who may turn up unannounced, and casual visitors.

The requirement for participation in communal meals goes back to the very beginnings of Pilsdon, when it was seen as an important means of enabling barriers between people to be overcome and of preventing individuals becoming isolated.

I'll say about the early days. You couldn't baulk out of attending a meal, you had to be there, you had to be present, unless you were obviously ill, and that was part of the condition of you being there. You didn't have to eat but you had to be present. You could sit at the table and refuse to eat but you had to be present. That was part of the necessary routine for a lot of people, who probably came from chaotic backgrounds whether they either didn't know where their next meal was coming from or certainly didn't have a routine of meals. I think that built-in routine of life at Pilsdon is very important. (Caroline Hillyard)

Eating together has also, of course, an important symbolic meaning in a Christian community: the formal breaking and sharing of bread carries the message of the Eucharist into everyday life, although this is not given particular emphasis at Pilsdon.

For a long period of Pilsdon's history the social organisation of meals was quite closely managed, with people being directed where to sit; subsequently this arrangement changed, and people now make their own choice about where and with whom to sit. Jonathan Herbert reflected on the impact of changing norms in this context:

I remember once, we talked at a community meeting of changing things, 'cause in Percy's day, in Stuart's day, in Peter's day, people used to get directed where to sit in the dining room. Everyone had to queue up outside and we were beginning to think it was rather belittling of people. So, we discussed it once, as community members, and then the next day, somebody just said, 'Well, the community [wants you] to sit where you like. We've changed our mind,' <laughs>. And we had ... there was this sense of... it was like the headmaster or somebody. It just felt deeply patriarchal, I felt deeply uncomfortable about telling men who were 30 years, 40 years older than me where to sit. So, we got rid of that but we knew the other traditions, ways of doing things, the boundaries we set worked, really, so we were loath to change them.

Despite such changes, the value of prescribed meal times, of sharing food together with everyone participating on equal terms and of meals being an occasion for social interaction, remains central to life in the community.

Natural Rhythms

The daily routines of prayers and meals connect to other routines associated with Pilsdon's status as a working farm and more widely with its rural location, emphasising the significance of the changing seasons and the influence of the natural world. Together, these various routines make up the complex but regular rhythm of community life.

The rhythm is defined by the countryside and by the animals, by the needs of, not the humans, but the land and everything else. So there is a natural rhythm. And when we were there the generator would finish at nine o'clock and the lights would go out so the rhythm was actually quite defined because we didn't have exactly electricity in the bedrooms and things. So the actual earth's rhythms, along with the liturgical rhythms, the rhythms of people in their birthdays and those sort of things and the rhythm of the bell... (Mary Barnett)

I think there's a lot to be said for its geographical location. It has enormous benefit, of just being part of the animals, the landscape, that daily routine, the farm. It works because it's all centred around worship.

It's not just centred around the farm, it's a community that's centred around daily worship, which is centred around… I suppose they're a little bit like circles, aren't they? Then, you've got the routine of the farm, then the routine of feeding and eating together, and then relaxing together and doing things. (Annie Hardie)

Jonathan Herbert described the importance of the agricultural year:

… and the rhythms of that. Cleaning out the winter quarters, which was a great communal effort every January, every May when we'd have 15 wheelbarrows up and down the yard and three or four people digging out all the muck and another person at the other end, building the new muckheap. All those things. The lambs being born, planting in the vegetable garden. Then, the hay harvest, big one and then in the winter, going out collecting wood, chopping logs. Winter work, the big fires that would… lovely, coming in at half past 4 when it was already dark in December to see this great blaze going in the common room.

The suggestion in this comment by a former warden that there is a strong connection between the experience of seasonal change, the nature of the work needed and the positive impact on communal life, is echoed by former guest, Alex Kelly:

Like I say, in the winter, you get more cosy nights by the fire, more conversation as much as is measurable. Out working in the rain, it's really nice to come into the house and that sense of all being together and hunkered down in the warmth, or out pushing against the elements a bit, 'cause you have to push. Waterproofs on and sometimes, the rain's blowing in sideways and you have to go and muck out at six o'clock in the morning or whatever, or go and do the gardening. You don't get that in everyday life, do you? Here, you live in rhythm with the elements and the change of season.

And what you can get in everyday life outside the community may be in stark contrast with the security that comes from the routines of work at Pilsdon. This was emphasised by Simon Smith, who has known Pilsdon as both a wayfarer and a guest, when asked about the experience of moving on after a period of living in the community:

Bit scary. It's like a novelty when you first go out for the first day or two, it's a little bit like oh I'm free! Then you sort of get there and think, hmm what am I gonna do now? No dairy today, no milking today, no chain sawing today, no loading up the boiler today, no hoovering the corridors in the manor house, hmm what am I gonna do now? So yeah for a while it's a bit like that till you can engage in something, you're like, oh, just sort of sat there twiddling your thumbs. There's only so much reading and watching… well I don't watch much TV anyway, but you know, there's only so much of that you can do and you're just sat there like… staring into thin air.

WORK AND THE PILSDON ETHOS

Work, in which everyone is encouraged and expected to participate, is a key feature of everyday life and is a major aspect of the Pilsdon philosophy of living in community. This has at least two dimensions. First, as described above, certain work is necessary simply to enable the community to function on a day-to-day basis, to provide a place for people to live: the farm must be maintained as a source of food, meals must be prepared, rooms cleaned and buildings and grounds kept in reasonable repair.

Secondly, work is seen as a crucial component in helping guests who come to Pilsdon for personal recovery and renewal. It provides a form of therapy in providing the possibility of rediscovering meaning in life and building responsibility and self-respect. Since work is vital to the survival and well-being of the community, the opportunity to contribute by undertaking jobs that need to be done, however modest they may be, can be a significant way of enabling people to feel valued by others and worthwhile in themselves. People can develop skills that are valuable when they move on as well as bringing to the community skills from which the community benefits. Amongst the guests have been butchers, electricians, carpenters, cooks and housekeepers and others whose skills have been put to use in support of the community.

The interaction between these two dimensions of work is experienced as a real lived relationship; as Shirley Edwards put it:

> [Pilsdon] gives a place for people to work, the place needs them, that's important. The garden, the animals, very

important. It's something for people to be connected to that doesn't make demands on them – well, doesn't argue with them <laughs>. The house needs to be cleaned, the food needs to be cooked, so it's not artificial.

Pilsdon is, then, alongside its significance as a place of spiritual practice and as a place of safety and support, at its heart very much a *working* community. This was captured by a former guest, Rosemary Cortes, when she said: "But you were always expected to work, I mean people outside ask me about Pilsdon and they seemed to think it would be a long retreat, perhaps spending your time in the chapel. I'd say, 'It's not like that.'"

The central role of work in the way Pilsdon operates was one of the cornerstones of Percy Smith's original vision. Gaynor Smith recalled that:

everybody had to work, we all had breakfast at eight o'clock, then everybody had a job. Percy gave the jobs out at breakfast time and we all had a job to do, everybody worked, and Percy believed everybody *should* work, it was a therapy, but it wasn't a rule. They didn't *have* to work…

Although Percy was convinced that people needed to work and ought to work, he recognised that people had different capacities and that what they could be asked to do should be tailored accordingly; the key thing was that they should feel they were contributing something. According to Percy and Gaynor's daughter, Ruth, who spent much of her childhood and adolescence at Pilsdon, her father:

had a *huge* work ethic thing. He was quite a slave driver in some ways. Sometimes he gave people tiny, little jobs, 'cause he knew that they were either old or weak or recovering from something, so it was maybe something really quite small, but they still got given a job whatever it was, even if it was just polishing that brass pot or whatever, to give them all a meaning, to help with the running of the place, in a way, to be seen to be part of it.

This rather directive approach clearly reflected Percy's personality and also the era in which he lived and worked: Ruth described him elsewhere as "rather autocratic". In subsequent years and under different wardens, the importance attached to work remained but was managed in a more inclusive and less authoritarian manner.

There was always plenty to do 'cause we were quite a small community but it was important that everybody who came also did things as well. It was always pointed out to people coming that, unless in exceptional circumstances, it was not a place for a two-week holiday, it was very much a working holiday. Quite gentle working but it was not somewhere where you could just spend all day sitting in the library. And the community wasn't sitting back and directing operations and saying, 'You do that and you do that.' ..... It was a 'Come and help me do', nobody was sent off to do something that they couldn't do. (Annie Hardie)

The acceptance of variation in what different people might contribute through work has always been part of the Pilsdon philosophy, relating to the broader principle of accepting people as they are. Caroline Hillyard, a former member, reflected on this:

> You're never judged necessarily by how much you've done, but people work hard because they need to and people get away with it because they're not used to it or whatever. In the end, it all comes out, it's a sort of balance, isn't it? Yeah, I think that work ethos was very important in the early days.

It is also clear, however, that the strong expectation is that people will do what they can, and that a refusal to contribute without good reason is not likely to be tolerated. Simon Smith, a wayfarer who has visited Pilsdon over many years, recalls a particular incident when a couple of wayfarers tried to 'get away with it':

> And I was out there nine-thirty one Saturday morning waiting to start out with the wheelbarrow and shovelling everything and [the warden] went to the wayfarers and just said, 'Come on guys, we need a hand today, if you wanna stay here you've gotta give us a hand.' And I know two of 'em said they weren't gonna do nothing, and he run 'em back into Bridport ... It was a bit like 'work to stay' sort of thing; if you wanna come and stay here for a few days or a weekend, go out on the land and dig and put in drills or something, the veg, and just help out like that.

Thus wayfarers who stay at Pilsdon only for one night or for a weekend are expected to do some work in exchange for the board and lodging they receive and for which they do not pay any money. Most are both willing and pleased to have the opportunity to do this.

For longer term guests, work is both an integral part of the everyday life of the community and an opportunity to discuss issues and problems in a context far removed from conventional counselling situations. As Annie Hardie described it:

> You were offered the time and space to talk but nobody said, 'Monday morning at 11 o'clock, we'll talk,' or, 'You will come and see me.' We didn't have that kind of… if people said, 'Stuart, can I have a chat with you?' he'd say, 'Yes, after milking,' or, 'Come and help me in the garden. I'm going to do some digging so you can come and help.' That was a bit of a surprise for some people. I think they thought it would be a cosy chat in an armchair but it's much easier to talk while you're doing something.

The therapeutic benefits of work do not just arise from the satisfaction of undertaking some worthwhile activity or from the chance to discuss concerns while working alongside another person, but also from interaction with the farm animals (see chapter 6 for another perspective on this). Jonathan Herbert emphasised the value that he believed many guests gained from developing relationships with animals and which he himself had experienced:

> **JH:** They got a huge amount from looking after the pigs, huge amount of self-confidence, a huge amount of…

very, very therapeutic, going in and stroking a pig and having that responsibility, as well, for looking after an animal … Yeah, really powerful effect there. If you're looking after the chickens, you've got to get up to let 'em out, gives people a reason to get up.

Int: I suppose it's the same with milking?

JH: Yeah, yeah, with milking. Myself, I could be really stressed by 5 o'clock and then I'd go and sit under a cow for 20 minutes, get up and feel completely different. Amazing.

He illustrated the point further with a story about the experience of one particular guest:

We had one chap we asked to look after the donkeys. He described himself as having social phobia and when I asked him to look after the donkeys, he said in a tiny voice, 'Will they like me?' I said, 'Of course they'll like you. They'll love you, as long as you treat them right. As long as you muck 'em out, as long as you feed them, as long as you groom them properly. Just don't touch their ears.' And that young man was transformed by the [experience].

As Jonathan's comment about the benefit he obtained from milking a cow indicates, the Pilsdon approach to work is experienced as therapeutic by community members as well as guests. Adam Dickens, expanded on this in discussing the differences of life at Pilsdon from his previous role as a city-based parish priest:

I loved the physical stuff. I think, certainly for me, it provided a really good counterbalance to some of the pastoral and some of the emotional processing that you were having to do as part of living in that setting. It just provided a really good counterbalance ... the physical stuff of working off some of the stresses really, it felt it was a good challenge really to be able to chuck some bales of hay around or whatever, when you were feeling very angry about something or were angry with someone, rather than direct it at them. To be able to then work that through and then allow a much more, hopefully creative response to a relationship that might be quite difficult felt very important .... we're all human beings on a spectrum really and I guess our vulnerabilities were at different points on that spectrum, but actually the therapeutic dimension of Pilsdon was, I think, played a really important part for the wellbeing of the community members as much as for the guests.

There is here, then, a strong sense of what might be termed the *functional* and the *therapeutic* dimensions of work coming together. Work is not being undertaken solely for its benefits to individual psychological and physical well-being, it is being done because it is necessary if the community is to sustain itself: animals have to be looked after, the garden has to be tended, household chores have to be done, meals have to be prepared. And it is in the doing of these necessary tasks that therapeutic benefits are obtained. That is at the core of the Pilsdon ethos.

Work: Who Does What?

Maintaining Pilsdon as a place that is fit to live in and is welcoming to newcomers has been a major challenge throughout its sixty years. An important dimension to that challenge is the principle that the work required is shared between everyone resident in the community, including those who may be very unused to undertaking such work. Sue Langdon described one aspect of this:

> I was given cleaning to begin with and I learnt very quickly that you couldn't find everything you needed and if you found it and put it in a place while you went and looked for the next thing, by the time you got back it would have disappeared. I found it very amusing and a touch frustrating but I could see what was happening. I mean, some of the people who I worked alongside, inviting people to clean with me, because it's not about guests working for, it's about members and guests working equally alongside each other, was very good. Of course, they would wander off and forget to come back and you'd have to chase them up and you'd come back and you'd find all the stuff you'd collected to clean with having disappeared in the process.

Current residents at Pilsdon describe very similar experiences; indeed, searching for things that have gone missing is something of a standing joke within the community.

In the early days of the community there was a fairly strong gendered division of labour, with women undertaking the bulk of the domestic work while the men dealt with the animals, the garden and building maintenance:

Jill and I shared the cooking and the washing, I did the cooking one week and then the washing and she did the reverse, when I was cooking she was washing, when I was washing she was cooking. (Gaynor Smith)

Polish. Polish! Oh my god, polish! My morning job regularly was to clean the common room, so that involved top down cleaning once a week, thorough polishing and dusting of tables and then floor, and the floor was done by big long type of brooms with soft underbellies and big dusters and polish. .... And if anybody wore their wellies I would be like, 'Do not come in here with your wellies on!', so at least twice a week there would be a thorough polish, and then you'd go over it again once it had been polished the next day to bring it back up to scratch. So, that was my, if you like, designated daily job probably for about the last three years ... But it was good, it was that rhythm of the day and everyone, as far as I knew, was doing something else somewhere else. (Ann Davies)

This was seen as a natural arrangement reflecting the different skills and experience that it was assumed that women and men brought with them, even when the reality was more fluid:

I cooked there for nearly eight years and great fun it was, but I actually helped build the end barn at the back of the wayfarers' room and the craft room, the end barn, I helped build that. And, of course, it was with two chaps, one was called Bob ... But, of course, when it came to take the picture only the men appeared in it!

<Laughter> I disappeared miraculously into the ether, never acknowledged that actually I'd mixed cement like the best of them, under instruction, admittedly, help lay the slabs and everything, so it's always been Bob's shed but never mine! <Laughs> I mean it was just typical, they saw it as a man's thing, I don't know if anyone noticed that I was there doing it! (Rosemary Cortes)

Guests and members could be called on to carry out whatever task needed doing:

So, we started off life here, just joining in whatever I could. I like cooking so I started to cook, help out where I could there. There were all sorts of other things to do. … I think there were just two drivers then, I think Stuart and me. So, if I wasn't cooking, I was driving, jumping in from one vehicle to another, whether it was a Land Rover to go and pick something up or a beat-up old car to do something else and just thinking, 'I didn't think this was quite what community life was going to be like.' But you just do it, don't you, 'cause you have to. (Annie Hardie)

The distribution of work tasks is one thing that has changed over time. One aspect of the more authoritarian regime in the early days was some exclusivity in tasks:

Guests never milked the cows at all. It was just Gillian and Percy but after I'd looked after the cows for a month or two, I edged my way into position of relief milker <laughs>, or indeed regular milker. We were milking them by seven in the morning or a bit earlier, perhaps half past six, something like that. I don't know. Then, I had to scrub out the milking shed and somehow, I always missed a little bit of it. Gillian would come out and inspect it and infallibly see the bit I'd missed <laughs> and say, 'Look, there, Nick.' So, that had to be done absolutely to a top standard, of which you start to get a knack because, of course, it makes it much easier to do things to an exacting standard. (Nick Hillyard)

Guests now do any and all of the jobs that are required irrespective of gender, working alongside members and volunteers. Women work in the garden, muck out the animals, take part in hedge laying; men cook meals, take on responsibility for cleaning, look after the laundry. The way the work is managed has also changed from the early years when Percy Smith decided what needed to be done and allocated people to the tasks. Now, priorities are determined collectively by the warden and members, and the weekly and daily rotas and schedules of duties are drawn up taking account of the particular skills, interests and preferences of guests, volunteers and the members themselves.

Some decisions about what needs doing are taken in consultation between members and those guests who are interested. For example, weekly garden meetings are held when jobs are identified for the maintenance of the fruit, vegetable and flower gardens in the coming week, involving whichever members and guests are able to participate, and a list of those jobs is drawn up. The jobs are then done by whoever wants to take them on, and the list revised at the next meeting. These meetings involve considerable celebration of the work that has been done and the produce that has been generated! In contrast, some guests take on substantial individual responsibilities for specific areas of work as a regular commitment, requiring most if not all of their working time. Examples of this might include building maintenance or looking after the dining room or library.

Anyone arriving to live at Pilsdon for a period of time is likely to have to learn a number of new skills: for example, looking after animals; milking and pasteurising; growing vegetables; cooking for relatively large numbers. Some of these may be entirely new experiences: including for us as authors and volunteers. An important principle is that those who have the necessary skills and knowledge pass these on to those who need them, and this is the case regardless of individual status within the community. Thus, a new member or volunteer may find themselves being guided and instructed by a guest in how to do a particular task, while that new member or volunteer may themselves bring specific skills which they pass on to others. The recognition that everyone has things to learn, and that anyone may have the capacity to assist in that learning, is a key part of accepting people for who and what they are.

CELEBRATING

Living at Pilsdon can involve hard work. But, in common with other contemporary and historical places in which seasonal and natural rhythms are of real significance in shaping everyday life, festivals and other occasions for celebrations assume a particular importance. Religious festivals, such as Christmas and Easter, are celebrated with appropriate acts of Christian worship, but the more secular traditions associated with them are also carried on: Christmas is a time for enjoyment of food, with a full-scale Christmas dinner served, and for the giving of presents – everyone who is there on the day receives a carefully chosen gift. Easter features a proliferation of chocolate eggs as well as liturgical celebrations. Other national festivals like New Year, Shrove Tuesday (Pancake Day) and Bonfire Night are occasions for much laughter, with some traditions very specific to Pilsdon: wheelbarrow races involving the tossing of pancakes, and a contest to see if anyone can succeed in hurling a pancake over the roof of the manor house. Pilsdon also has its own annual celebration to mark the founding of the community by Percy and Gaynor Smith in October 1958. Caroline Hillyard recalled such events:

> We used to put on a concert after the church service and after supper and we did one year, I think it was either Joseph and his Amazing Technicoloured Dreamcoat... we did do that one year but it may have been, we also did one called Noah's Ark. I remember doing the stage thing for that, where we had a rotating reel of animals which were wound into this ark, so that was a sort of stage prop. It took us hours but that's what we did, we did productions, we put on music. It was a lot of time and a lot of effort but it was always buzzing and probably over 100 people used to come and it was just a fantastic atmosphere.

The 60th Anniversary in 2018 prompted the history project on which this book is based. As well as forming the core of this book the interviews provided source material for a play developed and performed by a large number of members, guests and volunteers. This sought to capture the spirit and history of Pilsdon. Around 200 people attended the event.

Anybody who has spent Christmas at Pilsdon remembers it as a special time. Ann Davies, who lived in the community for a number of years, had vivid recollections of it:

> It was such a big thing, Christmas here ... I remember going out one year to collect ivy and holly to wind and decorate down the posts and red ribbon around, so the church, which was regularly polished and cleaned, just looked so beautiful at Christmas, so lovely. And then the choir would be preparing. Every week anyway they would be preparing but for Christmas it was special, just amazing choir ... So, everyone had a present from the community under the tree, of course all the decorations everywhere else went up, the wayfarers' room where they gathered for teas and the fire there, there was a Christmas tree in there so all the wayfarers had socks for Christmas, so everyone had a present ... and then I remember, I don't know when I got into doing this but organising the games on Boxing Day, and there were all sorts of games, the hat game, which had us racing around, racing around downstairs, there were things that were really fun, you know.

And the celebrations continue after Christmas:

I used to always stay New Year's Eve, I used to stay for a few days and we always had the quiz. And there were fireworks and bits to eat and games and it was just so different from the drunken revelry that so frequently goes on. (Rosemary Cortes)

On a more personal level, everybody's birthday is remembered and marked with at least a specially baked cake and, where children are involved, a party.

There was this big table, we'd be sitting, whoever's birthday it was you'd be sitting there, everybody would be in, Dad would be, and then he'd come in through the door, inevitably cigarette in hand, and start singing Happy Birthday and the rest of the community would join in and it would just be riotous. And it was a great ... anybody whose birthday it was had the same experience and everybody came in. No one missed out on it. The word would go round, 'It's so-and-so's birthday,' so we'd all be there so this place would be full of 40 people. It was great! (Dominic Affleck)

I have no idea how it happened but I remember spending my 18th birthday at Pilsdon and Gillian asking me what I would like to eat. I asked for a lemon meringue pie and I think she thought I'd chosen one of the most difficult puddings to make but she very kindly gave me lemon meringue pie. I have a photograph of that, actually, sitting in front of that lemon meringue pie with a candle in it. (Caroline Hillyard)

Everyday life at Pilsdon thus includes a strong emphasis on fun and celebration and the positive aspects of community living: an important counter to the ever-present level of pain and distress which marks the lives of many of those resident there, and which is discussed in other chapters.

CONCLUSION

People come to Pilsdon as guests in response to an invitation to live alongside the community members and the existing guests and volunteers. This chapter has described core features of what it means to live alongside others in the sharing of a common life, taking collective responsibility for the well-being of the community. It has also shown how certain changes have occurred that shape everyday life at Pilsdon, reflecting changing norms and ways of living in wider society, so that the relationship between individuals and the community is not the same as it was over 60 years ago. But these changes are, arguably, superficial: the principle that the everyday life of the community is organized around the routines of prayer, work and meals, the needs of the farm animals, the importance of celebration and the rhythms of the natural world, has stayed constant. Communal life at Pilsdon is, fundamentally, lived much as it has always been. How people have experienced that way of living with people often very different from themselves and the ways in which it has influenced them are explored in the next chapter.

CHAPTER 4

———

Living with Others

At the heart of life within the Pilsdon Community is living with others: individuals you have not chosen to live with, but who have, for their own reasons taken the decision to live in community. So what does that mean for those who have made Pilsdon their home for whatever period of time they are there? In this chapter the focus is on how living in the community has been experienced by the people who come to Pilsdon; on the ways in which being 'in community' shapes the nature of social relationships; how different people have experienced those relationships, and how their experiences of life within the community have made a difference to them. During interviews people reflected on the positive outcomes of living communally: helping to deal with pain and vulnerability, and building bonds of friendship and trust. They also spoke about the anxieties and tensions that can occur in living with others and the implications for personal freedom and choice;

and on the opportunity for starting a new life outside the community.

DIFFERENT LIVES

Many of the interviews contain stories of individuals who have been part of the community at different points throughout its history. Sometimes these accounts reveal social and cultural changes over the 60 years, in particular those changes impacting on the travelling life and on people without paid employment or a regular home. But they also reveal ways in which difference or diversity is talked about and understood in this particular place. Recounting stories of people who have made up the community, of what they contributed, of how they behaved, and incidents both humorous and tragic, is part of what sustains the community. It is a feature of conversations over coffee in the common room or muck spreading in the garden. Those stories illustrate the way in which remembering the different individuals who have been part of Pilsdon is a means of nurturing the continuation of the communal life.

Many of the stories told of Pilsdon's early years were of wayfarers. Gaynor spoke of them as 'the cowboys' with their networks of information, sharing and support. She said: "all of them had been in prison, one place or another, 'cause they all got drunk when they weren't working and when they were working they usually quarrelled with other people in the hotel. They used to work in hotels in the summer, but they were very quarrelsome or could be, especially if they were drinking a bit, so they generally only stayed there for about a fortnight or so and then they'd be off on the roads again." But wayfarers also worked for the community, depending on their physical state when they came. Michael O'Shaughnessy identified the differences. He is describing a time when accommodation for wayfarers was in dormitories:

> Well, there was a couple of people upstairs, they were in the middle room, there was four beds in it and you never went in that middle room because people was very poorly in there. But they were alright, they could get around and that but work like, you know there was no such thing. And in the far room you had Les and a few older lads and they were alright, they done a bit of stuff, bit of work. And in the bottom room, everybody in the bottom room, they all worked, there was no messing – get up in the morning, come down, even in the snow, there was *always* something to be done and you'd just get on with it.

James Morris who described himself as having: "a little bit of Romany in me", spoke of changes in the travelling life:

> When I was younger I travelled about all over the place, like Europe and all over the United Kingdom. But as I've got older I tend to not travel as far as I used to. As I said, there's not so much farm work out there anymore. There's still a bit of work out there, but over the last ten years I've become a bit of a wheeler-dealer, really, in the sense of probably going to car boot sales, and that, and picking something up really cheap and then selling it on

to… because we live in the digital age now, we never had mobile phones and computers in them days.

Whilst there are fewer people living the travelling life of wayfarers on a permanent basis, Pilsdon still welcomes those for whom a fixed home is either not possible, or who it not does not suit. Particularly at weekends the community is joined by some of those looking for short term hospitality, a temporary stopping place on what is often a circuit of places offering shelter, food and perhaps a change of clothing.

Caroline Hillyard was one of those who remembered Seamus, a long-term guest. Seamus had been a soldier who, by the time he came to Pilsdon, was drinking heavily.

> CH: I've also got a photograph of this chap called Seamus, who was there for years, actually. Very, very kindly, he was very kind to my sister and my sister's friend Katia, who adored him, a bit like a sort of father figure…

> Int: What sort of thing did he do when he was at Pilsdon?)

> CH: Very little! <Laughter> He kind of cultivated being a man of leisure. He did do KP-ing in the kitchen and he charmed people, I think, <laughs>. But he got away with it…

If Seamus charmed people, Sidney was the source of considerable respect:

Sidney had cerebral palsy and it was very good to have Sidney here because pretty soon <laughs> a lot of people stopped moaning when they saw what Sidney did and what he could do and what he was prepared to do. Some guests might just go, 'Oh, I can't do that, it's too difficult,' then you'd see Sidney battling down from his loose box, as he did, through the wind and the rain with this thumb stick to support him... People would go, 'Oh, it's a bit wet to go outside,' and you'd say, 'Mm, I don't know, Sidney's managing it, really,'. Ah, yes. He was just a fount of wisdom and knowledge for farming. (Annie Hardie)

Particular individuals featured in accounts and peopled the stories of Pilsdon over the years. But the point that people were often making was to reflect on the mix of backgrounds of those coming to the community. Diversity at Pilsdon is not primarily thought about in terms of the social group categories most used by social scientists: gender, ethnicity, sexuality, for example. There has never been any attempt to ask about or record information that would enable data about ethnic or other identities to be analysed. Because of its location the number of Black people coming to the community is small. During the time that we have known the community the majority of guests have been men rather than women, and more have been in middle age rather than being young people. But acceptance of diversity has always been central to Pilsdon's ethos. We have seen in chapter 2 that people with very different social backgrounds find themselves living together in the community: experiencing the "thrown togetherness" that Doreen Massey has written of (Massey, 2005). Most are looking for a way of life that is different from that which they have previously experienced and many bring with them the impact of damaging addictions and problematic behaviours. Their socio-economic circumstances; education and employment histories; family circumstances, and place of origin mean that it would have been unlikely that they would have found themselves in such close proximity had they not come to Pilsdon. The mix of people that results can create a challenging environment in which learning to live well with others is key to experiencing the benefits of communal life.

Rob Bailey talked of this in terms of recognising people's capacity to change, and of the need to avoid drawing moral distinctions between people on the basis of past behaviours:

> People can say there are different sorts of behaviour that are valuable, like to be sober or to be morally or religiously upstanding or respectable, but actually I think what matters about Pilsdon is that feeling that even if your life is a complete mess you can still be yourself and then you find out in your own time, at least in theory! <Laughs> But I do think there's a huge, generative energy to Pilsdon as this kind of... it has the capacity to be and often is a place where people discover their own strengths and the strengths of other people, not necessarily in a smooth way but in a real way.

Ruth Thurgur, reflecting on her childhood and adolescence at Plsdon, commented that living in community is: "a tiring old business". And this sense of tiredness comes not so much from the demands of the physical work required to keep the community functioning, but from the pressure of living with a diverse range of people, and from the need to constantly manage and maintain social relationships. Many of the interviewees, both members and guests, spoke about the challenges involved in navigating relationships at Pilsdon:

> I couldn't actually live on a permanent basis in the community. It'd drive me nuts. I wouldn't be able to do it. ... You've got this sense of different people, with different personalities ... And having shared views, and shared ideas is really a good idea, but, living with people with different personalities can be very tiring and difficult. (James Morris)

> If you live in a community you've got to put up with people's idiosyncrasies and they've got to put up with yours and that can cause absolute near violence, as it did in my case, 'cause you've only gotta get one person who wants to rock the boat. It's the way of the world, so you have to be a certain type to live in a community, and I find it a lot easier for me now to do. (Bill Scanlon)

Here, Bill makes passing reference to an incident during one of his early stays when he got into a physical altercation with a fellow guest. Whilst physical exchanges are not a common occurrence, the potential for conflict between individuals is always present, and verbal disputes are quite frequent. Reflecting on this from his time as member and then warden, Adam Dickens noted the particular

characteristics of conflict at Pilsdon and what this meant
for how it had to be handled:

> There was a level of, I guess, intensity or concentration
> that you don't get in a parish setting. There wasn't the
> space for ... you get difficulties in parishes but people
> have got a little bit of space to think through their
> responses or to cool off or to avoid the people that they
> find difficult and that sort of thing, whereas in Pilsdon
> you know that you may well be sitting next to them at
> supper, and thinking, 'Oh golly, this feels agony!' And I
> think that was really difficult. The gift of it was that you
> thought, 'well, actually we're going to have to tackle this'.
> Because the process of not tackling it was more difficult
> than putting it off. So there was a way of thinking, 'OK,
> I just need to go to this person and either apologise or
> say to them "What's going on?" and see what's going
> to come at me.' And so it allowed for the possibility of
> quite quick resolutions to situations.

The proximity of life with others encourages recognition
of the importance of forgiveness. Like Adam and many
others, Ann Davies also came to realise through experience
that dealing with conflict in the community required a
different attitude and approach from what she was used to
in her former working life:

> There were a lot of very, very diverse people staying here
> and I think I quickly learnt not to be a teacher, I learnt
> within that three months to be aware that that was not
> necessary. And certainly, in attempting to negotiate with

someone who was here, staying as a guest, an incident where I thought, 'How can they say that to me? That was awful', and approaching them and saying, 'I wonder if we could have a chat?', and then having another barrage of verbal abuse thrown at me, I thought, 'Actually, everything that I think is going to work isn't necessarily going to work'. And I think it was that day when I was in floods of tears about it with one of the community members, I just remember thinking about it a week later, actually what worked for me out there isn't necessarily going to work for me here.

Even in the absence of overt conflicts, the demands of always being in a complex social environment could be difficult for some people. Shirley Edwards is a great enthusiast for Pilsdon, but she nonetheless recalled that:

So, for myself, I always found it difficult in the dining room because I didn't know the people, I hadn't lived the same sort of lifestyle as they did. You can't do social chat, which is a cover for people who are used to making social chat. My hearing was bad so often, people would answer me and I couldn't hear or they would have a very strong accent and I couldn't hear. So, just to go and to be there in the dining room was difficult … but if you want to be there, you have to let that make whatever demand on you it makes on you or don't, don't go.

Learning ways of being with people who are different, with whom you would not immediately feel you can get on, or more straightforwardly having to be around other people more often than you might expect to in other contexts, is fundamental to life at Pilsdon – and indeed other communities. At the same time, the ethos of acceptance encourages those who spend time in the community to recognise that they do not have to perform their identity in a particular way. The opportunity to 'be one's self' was identified by a number of interviewees, starting with Gaynor Smith:

> I think it represented a refuge of some kind, a place where people could just be themselves, where people didn't have to pretend, that was the main thing about it, I think. The people who came all said, 'We don't have to pretend any longer.' They didn't have to make up stories about themselves or pretend that they weren't depressed or that they hadn't been alcoholics or anything … they could just be what they were. And if they had a bad future or even were bad people in the normal sense of the word, it didn't matter at Pilsdon somehow. Everybody accepted everybody else and they accepted the other people's stories.

Hilary Joyce, who never lived at Pilsdon but who has known it since 1987 and who became a trustee then chair of trustees in 2007, spoke of experiencing the benefits of this acceptance in rather different circumstances from most of those coming to the community. She campaigned to become an MP:

> …during the year I was campaigning I used to go back to Pilsdon whenever I possibly could. I was there most Sundays for the services and I did find it a huge

emotional support ... and a place where I could just be me and I didn't have to be anything else, which when you're campaigning for parliament you do. A big feature of Pilsdon is that you can be yourself as a human being. You're not ever playing any kind of role. And that's unique in my experience. I don't know anywhere else I can go and do that. And I found that immensely comforting and supporting at the same time.

Rosemary Cortes talked about Pilsdon as a place in which small rebellions: walking barefoot in the fields and experimenting with dress, were not only accepted but also a part of an alternative culture: "it was a place where you could dare to wear what you wanted and I did!" This sense of Pilsdon as a place where 'being yourself' was possible unlike elsewhere has meant that people have wanted to sustain their connection with the community beyond those times when it has been a central part of their lives. And as these accounts demonstrate, that can apply to people whose lives are otherwise very different.

This includes those not experiencing poverty, homelessness or mental illness, but who are seeking to live a more sustainable way of life. Chris and Jane Renyard talked about the simplicity of life at Pilsdon, an experience reflected in Sue Langdon's sense of pleasure in being allocated a living space (a loose box) that had nothing more than the bare necessities within it. She saw being allocated this accommodation when she first arrived as a member in 1999 as a test of her ability to put to one side her previous leadership roles and to accept what she was given with humility. She said: "I loved it 'cause it was the most uncomplicated... I had everything I needed and nothing else, really, in that loose box. It was a wonderful way to live." And Karen McAuslan also observed that:

> What Pilsdon has really done is made me very comfortable without a lot of stuff, without a lot of earthly attachments to things. It has made me treasure relationships with people, knowing that they can be quite short-term and fragile and not life-long. Not everybody's going to be there forever but while you have them, it is to be cherished and held that way.

One aspect of the sense that Pilsdon is, in Rob Bailey's words, a place of "generative energy" through its valuing of diversity has been the presence of children within the community at certain times:

> And there were loads of kids around and I must say here and now, of all those children there, and thereafter, all of them turned out well. The environment seemed very friendly towards children in the final reckoning, in spite of the range of people, and that was again what struck me, the range of people. You know, there is an impression that Pilsdon is only alcoholics and drug addicts, that's rubbish. I mean there was a vicar, there were social workers, there was a woman who'd been a probation officer, there was nuns <laughs>. (Rosemary Cortes)

One of those children, Stuart Affleck's son Dominic, now an adult, spoke of the impact of Pilsdon on him:

I could tell you stories about different people in different places. I got an amazing flashback of a character called Gino when I went to the kitchen, who used to scare the hell out of us as boys 'cause he was this crazy Italian, and he would, if we irritated him, which we often did, he'd be half-shaven so he'd just grab us and just rub our faces against his stubbly chin. So yeah, people, that's the big thing for me. And just being curious about people and what they do and where they've been. I guess that's why I became a teacher.

It seems clear that for most of those who have experienced community life at Pilsdon, the business of living with others is a learning process. The knowledge of how to live alongside others is acquired through the *practice* of living alongside others. This is something recognised by those who have been members and those who have been guests of the community:

> ... the process of learning to live with other people provided an opportunity to grow as human beings, and whether you call that therapy or not, but I think that was what it was. Learning to accept the rough edges of other people in the same way that they were trying to come to terms with all of your rough edges, and that process of social engagement over a meal, which for some people was a massive challenge, actually sitting down and having a meal with other people was agony for some people and they came in and they couldn't wait for the meal to end ... For others that social setting was an easier environment but that actually those were hugely

important life skills of trying to be in the company of others. (Adam Dickens)

When you meet people in life, you make snap judgements. Crazy old man, quaint little couple. You don't always get to see the full person but when you live in a community of people, you really, really get to see them. When you wake up every morning and sit opposite someone at breakfast, you know exactly how they're feeling. You can tell by how they are and the people you surround yourself with, they become you, you become part of a collective. To be surrounded by these people, the members, your fellow guests, slowly but surely, the longer you stay here, the more those labels fade away. Suddenly, there are no members and guests anymore, they're just your friends, they're your community, they're the people you live with. You learn to love over a period of time. It takes time. (Alex Kelly)

At the heart of the process described by Alex is the building of trust, and if the experience of living in community is to be a positive one, even if this takes a long time, then becoming able to trust in others is essential both in building community and becoming fully a part of the community. Alex continued:

Here, you're sort of all the same 'cause of the way you live here. We all work the animals, the garden, we work the land. We're all just trying to help each other get by, that's it, and you do it. Help can come from the strangest places and the strangest people. If you're willing to accept it, it can come easily from anywhere … To me, what the members here wanna do, their objective, is just to walk beside you for a while 'til you get well. That's what they wanna do, they wanna walk beside you … You've got to be willing to let them, that's the first thing. It takes time to build trust, for them to trust you and you to trust them. I was thinking, you let them walk beside you for a while and then they become your friends. You let them walk beside you a little while longer and they seem to become something more important than friends, like family. That's just from my personal experience. Some people come here and they never really lose that mentality of 'us and them' and that can be harsh, that can be really harsh.

This building of trust between all those participating in community life is, necessarily, a continuous process; not least because there is a constant, although variable, turnover in the Pilsdon population. Established residents leave, new people arrive. The personal fragility and vulnerability that many residents experience, itself subject to fluctuation, also adds to the sense that trust is always a work in progress, in continual need of reinforcement and repair. This is something to which the warden and the members have constantly to be attentive, and is a key reason why much of their effort is devoted to maintaining the routines of everyday life. It is through these routines, through the sense that community at Pilsdon is structured by repetition, and that the certainty and predictability that this generates can be relied upon by guests whose life experiences to date have lacked these qualities, that makes this a place of safety, of holding and potentially of recovery.

BENEFITS AND COSTS OF LIVING IN COMMUNITY

The benefits experienced from living in community at Pilsdon applied across the different groups: members, guests and volunteers. These benefits might be to do with helping to overcome specific personal difficulties:

> ... it gave me a real boost in confidence that I could live with other people, I could get along with anybody really because you don't have a choice about who you're living with at Pilsdon. People come and go and you have to get along with different people. So I think from that point, I think in those aspects it was a very good stepping stone for me ... I'd been very nurtured at Pilsdon ... So I think yeah, that kind of, as I said before, that kind of holding which one receives at Pilsdon, you can't take that for granted in other walks of life really. But I think that yes, personally I do need emotional support, which is one of the reasons why Pilsdon was such a good place for me. (Sarah Hallett)

> You wobble from time to time but at the same time... even when Simon [Annie's son] died, it was just good to be here. <Crying>. Yes, very good to be here. That's, I think, when you realise the strength of the community and how good everybody was. That's not just community and that's not people... it's wayfarers, everybody, they were just amazing <crying>. Yeah, and it really, really helped. Really helped. (Annie Hardie)

Community living could also provide the opportunity for personal fulfilment or achieving a sense of one's proper place in the world:

> It's almost as if I knew that there was something about this place and these people that I could give my heart to, you know? I could really be me, whatever that was at that point in my life. (Sue Langdon)

> And also working was very rewarding because what one was doing was for the community and the people around, so it was immediate ... it was not to benefit some kind of entrepreneur or whatever, it was going directly into the community. I think it probably... It was not the only thing that changed my life but it had a *huge* impact on my approach. (Mike Thurgur)

These rewards intersect with the particular challenges that make the role of warden so demanding:

> I think it's the hardest way to live your life that I can find. For people to choose to live together for no other reason than they believe in something, and then they had to live with themselves and with other people, and that's very, very difficult. Pilsdon was not easy, it isn't easy to live in. It's hell at times. You talked about confrontations and things, we used to have those and I would be the one who had to deal with them, those moments, and try and draw people together. Sometimes, I was quite good at that and sometimes, I was so frustrated, it was easier just to simply say, 'Go and we'll see you again.' (Stuart Affleck)

For warden and members life at Pilsdon is demanding
not only in the need to be aware of and responsive to
the often acute levels of distress displayed by guests at
certain times (and sometimes by fellow members), and
in dealing with the conflicts that can arise, but also in the
psychological impact of giving oneself over to the reality
of living in community, of being one amongst a highly
diverse and vulnerable group of people. Of course, this
has been experienced by members in different ways, given
their different personalities. For some this has been felt in
terms of constraints on freedom of choice and action. Both
Adam Dickens and Andrew Davey talked of the restrictions
in terms of movement:

> ... other than your day off or your night away before and
> then the day itself, which we valued, highly prized really
> and was essential for sustaining it, you couldn't just go
> and do something. One, you needed to check who else
> was around and check in the diary, and needed to be on
> site most of the time unless you were taking a guest to
> the doctor's or going into Bridport with somebody or
> whatever ... I used to say to people, 'One of the things
> that you'll probably find difficult is that you do lose a
> lot of freedom here. You can't do your own thing. Or
> if you do, it's within fairly narrow parameters.' (Adam
> Dickens)

> And there's the frustration of, you couldn't go out of an
> evening regularly without feeling a bit guilty. We never
> mastered this in my time. We used to have conversations
> about this among the members, about saying, I would've

wanted a bit of a rota system so you knew which evenings you were off, so you could just go and do things without having to ask. And some others never saw it like that. So we never quite mastered how to solve that one. But yes it does restrict your social life. Not being able to have a drink. It's a funny thing, but that restricts you as well, a little bit. (Andrew Davey)

For others, the effects of community life were more psychological in the awareness that one's inner self was exposed to others:

I've learnt over time, really, what the difference between community and having a vocation in the outside world is: you do share a lot more of your life. Not necessarily your history or your private life but just more of you comes into play with people on a day-to-day basis. The same way that I would recognise people's moods or where they were that day, I'm now living with a group of people that I have to acknowledge know mine … I remember people challenging my coming here. Not in an unhealthy way but just saying, 'You're single and you're moving into community and there won't be a lot of space for a private life, for a personal life in that environment.' That's always been a bit of the challenge of it. You lose a bit of your personal, private self or your sense of that boundary, that safety, into the community. (Michael Deegan)

The emotional demands of the role are such that, although the commitment is described as "24/7", it is recognised that members need some regular respite from those demands. Thus, as Adam Dickens mentioned above, each member is entitled to one day off per week, as well as an annual holiday, and this is seen as essential for the community to be able to function. This does introduce a distinction between members and guests, although the latter are able, once they have been resident in the community for three months, to take a break in order to visit friends or family. The justification for the distinction is simply that, without the possibility of members being able to take some time out, the community would not survive for long. Whilst conscious that he was enjoying a privilege not available to guests, Jonathan Herbert's justification was: "This is what I need to do to sustain myself and be here for a few years".

CHANGING LIVES

The length of time people remain living at Pilsdon is hugely varied. But for most people, both members and guests, the experience of living in the community is a temporary one. Whatever the nature of those experiences has been, it is something that people take with them when they leave and set about living their life outside of the community environment. So what kinds of changes do different individuals experience at Pilsdon?

For some what happens to them is considered transformative:

I've known people whose lives have been literally turned round from utter desperation to eventually leaving

Pilsdon and setting out on their own and even having had families and everything else in due course. But at the time they were at Pilsdon life had come to a full stop and they didn't know where to go next. And it gives people the space to sort that out. And there are many, many hundreds of examples like that. (Hilary Joyce)

The community does not keep records that would quantify the impact of time spent there in terms of what might be considered to be positive or negative outcomes. The community does not work for everyone and people being asked to leave because of drug or alcohol use is an unwelcome but familiar experience. This can happen quite soon after arrival, but in some cases things blow up after a lengthy period (a year or more) living in the community. Others leave voluntarily, but struggle to keep going without turning once again to drugs or alcohol. There are cases of former guests unable to sustain a life free from alcohol after they leave – one of the men we got to know in the first year of our volunteering sadly died having lost that struggle. But as Hilary's comment suggests, what Pilsdon offers is a space to explore the possibility of change, and even if that does not provide a cure it does enable people to attend to things that have not been right in their lives and to explore ways of being and living differently. For some, as Emma and Bill commented, Pilsdon has literally saved their lives. For others it has had a radical impact on what matters to them, what is important and how they want to live their lives.

Alex and Rosie met and fell in love at Pilsdon, although their personal trajectories to the community were rather different. For Rosie mental health problems had resulted in losing care of her children. In her conversation with Alex, recorded in the community to which they had returned for the purpose of the oral history project, she said:

> Although I desperately missed my children and wanted to be back, Pilsdon gave me the time and the space that I needed at that time. At that time, here was where I needed to be. It's an experience I'll never get back and I'll be eternally grateful for everything that Pilsdon's given me and being able to come back now... I spoke to my psychologist and said, 'I'm really anxious about going, I'm not sure. I wanna be able to tell them that I'm doing OK.' They said, 'Well, does it matter?' I said, 'Well, yeah, to be honest. Yeah, to me, it does. It really does matter because these people walked this journey of recovery with us'.

After leaving the community she and Alex were able to build a life together with Rosie's children and to achieve a way of living that was very different from their pre-Pilsdon life. Alex said:

> Rosie's now actually really heavily involved in the church. She's up there every Sunday and does charity work with them. I work with the local vicar. He's the closest thing I've got to a friend there, the local vicar. Whereas before I came to Pilsdon, you would not catch me within ten feet of a church unless I was burgling it for the overhead projector or something.

114

In his individual interview Alex enlarged on the way in which he and Rosie sought to live a different life as a result of what they had experienced in the community:

> I've dedicated myself to a pacifistic lifestyle now where it's not just no violence but literally, no aggressive confrontation if I can help it. ..... I lived here for three years without hurting anyone, without damaging anyone, without doing it and that shows you it can be done. You can live a calm, quiet, placid life, pacifistic. It doesn't have to be like that and we just tried to take all that back with us. We don't always manage it, we don't always manage to live in perfect harmony with the world around us, but we try to and we are still trying to live that way.

For Bill, who, as we have seen in chapter 2 came at a time when his mental health was very fragile and who had rejected mainstream mental health services, spending time at Pilsdon provided a space for rethinking what was important to him:

> [My wife] was having an affair with my best friend, that was the start of my mental illness. When you go from having a four-bedroomed house with a workshop, a double garage, two cars, massive bank account and you're in a bedsit, going to the pub every night for your dinner, it just... my world fell apart. But now I just... I was very sort of... I wouldn't say materialistic, but I liked having money all the time and I liked being able to do what I want to whenever I want to do it and now

it doesn't mean anything to me. I mean *it doesn't mean anything to me* …But it took Pilsdon and coming back down to Earth and what really matters and values to make me realise that my life was a bit… quite shallow before that.

The community does not evangelise or seek to persuade those who become guests to adopt a different value system. But for Bill and others, one consequence of life within the community is that recovery includes a shift in the way they think of themselves and others, and this can also involve a change in values. Bill still takes anti-depressants and continues to visit the community, at the time of writing he was spending periods volunteering there, but he was convinced that both his mental health and the context in which that had been problematic had undergone a profound shift.

Others have experienced Pilsdon as a place where they might sufficiently get on top of problems to re-establish family relationships. This was the focus for a conversation between residential volunteer Bob and guest Daniel. After his marriage breakdown Bob's children visited him at Pilsdon and were able to see him in an environment where he felt grounded and able to make a contribution. This was important for him and offered an example for Daniel as he sought to rebuild his relationship with his children. Daniel said:

Pilsdon has given me trust and self-worth. I've trusted the people here and for the first time, I've actually managed to correspond with the mother of my children, directly rather than going through a third party. Just that on its own merit and to be able to converse via email with her in a safe environment where everything that I thought was absolutely massive, Pilsdon has shown me is really rather small. The worries of general day-to-day things... which I fully respect. I've had jobs and money and all those things but to focus on yourself and then to let Pilsdon gradually embed itself into you, it does take you back to your core roots.

The separate space that Pilsdon provides can thus enable relationships beyond the community to be improved. It can also help people benefit from therapy that takes place beyond the community itself. It is a space in which people feel safe and, for a time, freed from many of the practical problems that accompany addictions and mental illness. Alex Kelly:

What's great about going from Pilsdon to drug counselling is you go there, you talk about it. When you come out of drug counselling, come back here, you have time to sort of process what you've learnt, you have time to put it into action. Because you're not dealing with the daily grind of life, you can solely deal with the problems of addiction, which all start and end with you. You can blame life circumstance or all that stuff but it starts and ends with you, which is what you've got here. You go away, you do the work and then you've got time here to process it, put it into action and really understand it. You've got time and space here to work it all out...

One of the key messages from survivors and other users of mental health services has been the value of peer support and learning. Expertise that comes from lived experience is shared in relationships that do not carry the weight of unequal power associated with professional/client relationships. Alex talked of this from his experience of Pilsdon:

> The other thing is, there are other addicts and stuff living here, you're living with other addicts and you pick up bits and pieces. There's a guy who's been here for a while who's helped me no end. He's sort of the best friend I ever had. He'd been clean a while when I got here and then he sort of took me under his wing as well and talked me through the processes of addiction and working out your problems.

The relationships that people have formed within the community, both with other guests and with members, have been key to positive changes. Emma provided a vivid illustration of how relationships between guests can be life-saving. She is talking to Nicky, a guest who became a friend whilst at Pilsdon:

> I says 'I fucked up at Pilsdon, I'm gonna have a drink.' I went to do that and Nicky text us. I got a text through. It was quite surreal, that. And I saved that on my phone. For months and months. It was, 'Hope to see you soon,' and all the rest. And I was about to do it. I chased her out the flat, you know, had a big argument about it. You know. But I thought, 'Oh bollocks to it, don't like Pilsdon.' And

I had the bottle in my hand, and I was about to go. But, see, you were my star, my little hero here. But it was life or death for me. Definitely. I was vomiting blood, I was urinating blood, quite a bit. So my kidneys were going.

These relationships sometimes endure after people move on. In this conversation between Nicky, who had left the community, and Emma who was still a guest, they spoke about what their emerging friendship meant to them. Emma talked about learning patience from Nicky:

I am stronger, and Nicky's made me realise I am stronger, and I can do this. When I've been hitting that brick wall, thinking, you know, banged my head against it, wanting a drink, Nicky's showed me how to calm myself down, and to get myself away from people in the community, just to step back, and like if I go in the TV room, I just walk round the yard, or go up the church, or whatever, on my own. Just to take that step back, and that calms myself down. And I don't have to engage.

Her words illustrate the interaction between human relationships and the physical space of the community that enables separation as well as closeness. And the reciprocity in their relationship is evident in this further exchange. Emma is anticipating her subsequent move to live in a flat in the same town as Nicky:

E: And hopefully I don't have to move on again. I might have to, but, it's a new page, if I get another year, to get myself motivated in my head, to plan. 'cause I don't want to just plan for six months, I want to plan for a few years. I don't want to move again, when I leave Pilsdon. I need to settle down.

N: You've got to take care of me.

E: Yeah.

As we write this, Emma was living in her own flat and has been caring for Nicky following an accident that left her with restricted mobility.

Learning to care at Pilsdon can enable caring relationships to be sustained beyond the time people spend there (see chapter 6). And for those whose lack of self-confidence and self-esteem had meant any relationships were difficult, the community provided a space in which learning to live with others was important in its own right. The changes people experienced often come gradually:

> Because you're you, you don't see it happen. The thing is at Pilsdon, it happens so gradually. You chip away at it a bit at a time, it happens so gradually, you don't notice it. You don't wake up one morning enlightened and say, 'Oh wow, I've really changed.' It just happens very gradually. (Alex Kelly)

People are not expected to set objectives to work towards in pre-determined time periods. In response to a question about how long she had expected to stay in the community, Ann Davies spoke of how different this was from what she was used to:

I didn't know, six months maybe. But I was always worried about how long I had and how long … And Stuart would always reassure me, 'No, no, you stay as long as you need to stay'. So, I'd ask for the reassurance quite often, once every two or three months, 'Do I have to go yet?', 'No, no'. I think that was all the way through, the whole time. And that was all about learning to be day by day, and that was a slow thing for me because I'd been in education where times and projecting ahead and all of that was so hugely important, so it was lovely to leave that behind.

Ann ended up staying at Pilsdon for 4 years. In time she was able to take on some of the responsibilities of a volunteer: driving people to appointments for example, and that was important to her in terms of building self-esteem.

Time enables relationships to develop that underpin behavioural change that is, in turn, grounded in a shift in understanding of self, and self in relation to others. In Alex's case what he described as a shift from screaming and shouting matches with Michael, warden at the time of his stay there, to a trusting friendship, enabled him to shake off the influence of a: "culture of violence and intimidation" that meant he threatened other guests. The change was in himself as well as his relations with others:

The plan was… when I got here, I thought, 'Great, if I can get a bit of clean time under my belt, if I can just hang out here for a couple of weeks and convince my family that I'm gonna make an effort to change, I can get back out there and get back on it as quickly as possible.

If I can just blag them all into believing that I'm trying to get clean and that I'm doing something, hopefully they start giving me money again and...'

Being at Pilsdon when he received the news that his best friend had died from an overdose provided the context in which reflection away from the immediate temptations of using drugs enabled him to build the relationships that saved him.

Sustaining the changes that guests experience after leaving the community can be hard. Some spoke with regret about the closure of a half-way house that had provided a space to move on to without having to take on the challenge of establishing their own home base and occupation. The capacity to cope when they leave can be related to the point in their lives at which they come to Pilsdon. Sarah Hallett, coming to the community as she embarked on young adulthood, felt able to take her experiences with her and benefit from them:

I think I felt quite well equipped to be working, because as I said, the dining room job at Pilsdon carries quite some responsibility, and you certainly need to be aware of time keeping, how you present your work, how you present yourself to other people, as well as doing the actual physical job, and I think that dining room job gave me confidence and I think the fact that the community had entrusted the dining room, they did entrust the dining room to me really ... I did take on responsibility for it, and I think that was actually very empowering. It was hard work, it was tiring, it was demanding, but ... I think in terms of preparing me for doing a job outside of Pilsdon it was very good preparation.

In contrast Nicky thought that it was because she had had the experience of being a mother and setting up a home *before* going to Pilsdon that enabled her to cope after it. And it was this as well as her experience of the community that she drew on in supporting Emma as she, in turn, prepared to move on.

For wayfarers time spent at Pilsdon is brief, but may be a part of a regular routine sustained over a period of years. In these cases the issue is less one of whether the community enables long term changes in people's lives, than how it can sustain those whose lifestyle can make them vulnerable to physical health problems as well as the detrimental impact of excessive alcohol use.

Simon Norris experienced a brain injury that meant he finds being in crowded places difficult. For him Pilsdon offered a different environment that enabled respite:

> where I live in Bournemouth is a very busy place. I can cope with it now but I was there on the recent bank holiday and it was just crazy, the amount of people there. I think a lot of these are triggers for me to drink. I like coming here because you're away from all that environment, aren't you? It's like, when I leave here on a Monday, I think, 'I know what I'm going back into.' I like the journey but it's when you get there and what you've gotta go through. It might not mean a lot to a lot of people but it's... Well, normal people wouldn't do it. That's why I like to come here, for a sort of break, 'cause

it gets me from that situation to a very quiet, relaxed situation where I don't really have to do much for three days.

Michael O'Shaughnessy's story of his initial contact with Pilsdon (chapter 2) marked the start of an ongoing relationship with the community. He had not settled down to a regular job after his initial contact with the community, but for him Pilsdon remained a key part of his life:

> But what Pilsdon done for me, you know personally for me, that's what I love about Pilsdon, and what it's done for a lot of other people, that is beautiful as well, what they do for other people … it gave me hope and chances that I never thought I'd ever get.

For Simon Smith Pilsdon is a place to get away from the temptations of drinking: "and not so much better myself but be at ease with myself, help others as well as others help you." Whilst James Morris recognised the longer-term value of Pilsdon for some whilst acknowledging that for him it was only short stays that would work:

> Well I think the Pilsdon community's fantastic, because I've been seeing there are people with many stories and obviously with different sorts of problems and backgrounds and I think communities like Pilsdon are fantastic to give people a rest, and guide people in certain directions, and give something to occupy their minds, and stuff like that. And a sort of healing space for people who've had traumatic lives and backgrounds,

which is really fantastic, I think, and that's wonderful. So for me to come here for weekends is really lovely, it's a break for me really, I love it. But as for living here, I couldn't do it. It'd kill me. It really would. I do get a little bit of depression but I try and deal with it, you know? In a positive sense.

Members have a different relationship with Pilsdon from that of guests and wayfarers. But their time within the community can also be a transformative experience:

Leaving Pilsdon, you don't leave, well, you leave Pilsdon but Pilsdon doesn't leave you and that's why people return when they have left, because you are changed because of all the experiences and all the things that have happened. (Mary Barnett)

As well as the "things that happen," for Mary it was also the nature of the place that created this impact and she reflected on the possibility of a similar impact from another place:

it's a bit away from things, very grounded in the environment really. And I don't think that can ever be, well, I don't think it probably should be recreated anywhere else. But the womb-like structure of Pilsdon, the fact that it's at the bottom, you're held, because people have to mean to go there, they don't actually just pass it, you don't really pass it. And everyone comes with some kind of intention, whether it be to wash their socks and warm their feet or whether it's a more grandiose intention. I'm just very grateful I had that time really. And I can't imagine it could ever be recreated anywhere else really, and it changes people.

We reflect more on the significance of the particular location and environment of Pilsdon in chapter 7. Here we can note that the intersection between the physical space, the routine of everyday life and the spiritual life of the community creates for many people a distinctive context in which they undergo different kinds of transformation. In Adam Dickens' case this:

> ... changed my perception of a lot of things! <Laughter> And therefore by nature of that really, impacted on how I understand myself as a priest. I think I would say that I feel ... felt both blessed and battered by Pilsdon really. I think amongst the blessings are ... something about the whole process of learning to ... a sort of dynamic of learning to accept yourself with all of your wounds and edges and all of that sort of thing, and also embody the process of doing that for other people and there's a kind of as you learn to accept others and their difficulties.

Jonathan Herbert reflected on what he had learnt in terms of the interconnectedness of life there and how this links to much broader connections:

> A sense of that ... that integrated life where things... I think that probably comes the deeper you get into prayer, maybe, but that sense of... you get up, you experience walking across a field, experience the stars

if it's winter, experience the sunlight if it's summer and then doing something very hands-on. Then, going into the chapel, then going for breakfast, then meeting some people, doing some people stuff, then going out and doing another job. So, to be able to do lots of different things but see them all as being part of the whole, where everything belongs, so that sense of belonging. The need to just accept people for where they are, understanding I can't save the world, it's not me. I think I got that fairly early on at Pilsdon. To just rejoice in people but also the landscape and the land and creation, how that shapes people. To have a solid rhythm to life, really important for me, I liked that. Just to learn from people who themselves have been very marginalised but have a huge amount of wisdom.

Jonathan took his learning from Pilsdon into his future role as a priest based at the Hilfield Friary working with traveller communities, and developed his understanding in a book focused on the value of 'accompanying' others (Herbert 2020).

CONCLUSION

Whilst members and wardens may talk about the changes they go through in a different way from the way in which guests talk about this, what is key to both is how living with others requires being open to relating to people in different ways, and that also requires being open to what might be considered more personal transformations. Experiencing

Pilsdon means learning to live well with others who may be very different from oneself and who have their own demons to confront. Being in a space that is physically separate from other places, that has its own needs for attention and nurture, and that contributes its own source of calm and joy helps the transformations that many experience – and may be necessary to them. But this does not mean that the community exists beyond any influence from the outside world. People bring with them what has happened to them before Pilsdon, and they return to a way of life that has different challenges. Some are unable to meet those challenges, while others find they can meet them in unexpected ways and are able to move on with their lives. But, as Mary Barnett suggested, very few leave Pilsdon without taking something of their experience there with them.

CHAPTER 5

———

Running the Community

Everyday life at Pilsdon involves many and varied types of work to maintain and sustain the people, the buildings, the animals and the gardens. Those who might come here expecting a retreat in which they can spend their time in contemplation, or a place in which recovery can be achieved through being looked after by others, will be disappointed. The Pilsdon Community can be understood in many different ways: as a place to practice Christian faith and values; as a place of refuge and recovery for those experiencing crisis in their lives; as a home for individuals and families; as a working farm; as an alternative way of living. Importantly, however, it also needs to be understood as a place that requires organisation and management to achieve its aims and to continue to function safely. It has to be managed in order to ensure that the necessities of daily living – food, accommodation, warmth, medical needs, etc – are provided. It has to be organised so that a large and highly diverse group of people with multiple needs are able to live together in close proximity. It has to be administered in accordance with both charity law and the changing policies of national and local government in respect of the welfare status of its guests and of regulations such as those concerning health and safety. These tasks add up to a considerable, if often somewhat hidden, responsibility carried by the members and in particular the warden, supported by the trustees.

But these responsibilities are exercised within a culture that is very different from that found in most work contexts. Andrew Davey described this from the perspective of members and warden who carry the responsibility for ensuring that work gets done, noting that while these roles bring a lot of freedom from many of the demands of conventional life, the responsibility is:

> demanding in time, it's demanding in commitment, but it's not demanding in that you've got to come up to meet a standard. You don't have a boss who's looking at your performance, which I imagine in some jobs, is a stress. And you are in a kindly environment here. Which is quite different to a lot of other working environments. So all of those I see as very big pluses, so I don't see it as a cost, it's just an exchange.

Such responsibilities are not, of course, unique to the Pilsdon Community. All registered charities in the UK have to conform to a range of formal administrative requirements. The UK Government guidance issued under the heading 'Managing Your Charity' lists twelve items of what it refers to as 'essential reading' for people involved in running a charity, covering topics such as the role of trustees, decisions and voting at trustee board meetings, governance and finance issues, the employment of paid workers, risk management and safeguarding and protecting people (www.gov.uk: 'Setting up and running a charity'). This is only a small part of the substantial volume of official government guidance on managing a charity, and beyond that there is a wealth of literature regarding management in voluntary or third sector organisations generally. Thus, the National Council for Voluntary Organisations offers detailed guidance on matters such as strategy and planning, financial management, quality and improvement, managing day-to-day operations, and others. There are then numerous textbooks on voluntary organisation management and university courses in the subject including at post-graduate level. This concern with management, and the importance of effective management practices, has grown enormously in recent decades as many parts of the voluntary sector have become increasingly integrated into the delivery of public services. Management in the voluntary sector has become a professionalised occupation in its own right and an attractive career choice for many people.

Talking about the Pilsdon Community in this context can induce a kind of cognitive dissonance. Many of those involved in running Pilsdon over the years would express – and have expressed – a profound antipathy to the idea that their role should be understood within a framework of organisational management principles and techniques, or that the community itself should be seen as a place where professional management is a priority. Alan Frost, who came to the post of administrator (the only paid 'post' in the community) from working in a bank, rejoiced in the absence of the bureaucratic procedures and performance measures:

> In the bank, every time you do something you have to sign, you know, sign on, sign off, sign for this, sign for that, and none of this happened here, and I found the best thing about the job was there was no targets.

Yet it is obvious that elements of management, administration and organisation are necessary for the community to function. This is clear from the experiences recounted by Tobias Jones, who, having visited and been inspired by Pilsdon, created a new community at Windsor Hill Wood in Somerset and subsequently wrote an account of it (Jones, 2015). Jones and his wife established and tried to maintain their community with an absolute minimum of administration or organisation and a maximum of informality. But even though it operated on a much smaller scale than Pilsdon it became apparent through painful experience that explicit elements of management, including issues of authority and control; of finance; of time management, and of external relations, were required if it was not to collapse. On the considerably broader and more complex canvas of Pilsdon, such requirements are unavoidable.

So here we focus on the need for Pilsdon to be managed; for organisational systems to be established and maintained and decisions to be taken and implemented over and above the daily routines of work and leisure; and on the longer-term requirement for planning to ensure the continued survival and development of the community. It includes the management and maintenance of the estate (buildings and land); the management of relationships with wider society, including national and local government agencies and voluntary organizations; the management of Pilsdon's finances, and the administration of the community, including upholding the community's values and rules, and ensuring appropriate admission procedures in relation to new guests and arrangements for people moving on. Questions of leadership and authority within the community are therefore a key theme in this chapter, including accounts of the tensions and disagreements that can arise.

A publication aimed at trustees of charities from the Wales Council for Voluntary Action is entitled 'Faith and hope don't run charities' (WCVA, 2012). Percy and Gaynor Smith founded and ran the Pilsdon Community largely on the basis of faith and hope, and Toby Jones believed the same principles would be sufficient at Windsor Hill Wood. Faith and hope remain central to the Pilsdon ethos, and this chapter is in part an exploration of the relationship between 'living by faith', as some respondents referred to it, and 'planning and managing'.

HOW THE COMMUNITY IS RUN

It might be assumed that in a community like Pilsdon, which brings together people of widely different social backgrounds and ages with a range of often profound psychological, behavioural and emotional issues, the management of those people would be a major preoccupation. While maintaining the safety and well-being of both individuals and the collective is indeed the chief responsibility of the warden and the members, this is not achieved through formal processes such as individual or group supervision, or systems for monitoring and regulating behaviour that are found in most institutional settings, whether therapeutic communities, traditional psychiatric establishments or some religious communities. Responsibilities such as fulfilling the duty of care, ensuring individual welfare, maintaining positive social relationships, can be seen more as integral to the ways that life within the community is lived rather than being the subject of specific management actions. Two significant exceptions to this, where explicit 'people management' action does occur, concern decisions over who will be invited to spend time at Pilsdon (whether as members, guests or volunteers), and decisions relating to the enforcement of the 'no alcohol or drugs' rule.

In interviews people talked about how the practical mechanisms and processes through which the community functions reflect its philosophy. They talked of how leadership is exercised and decisions taken, how the roles of warden and members are enacted and perceived, the role of trustees, the significance of rules and how they are applied. They talked of what was necessary to sustain relationships within the community, the contribution of volunteers and other external people, and the extent to which these arrangements have changed over time.

Strictly speaking, the Pilsdon Community consists of its members: a small group of people, rarely more than 7 in number, sometimes less, who make a commitment to living and working in the community for a period of years and who are collectively responsible for its day-to-day running, its organisation and the safety and well-being of guests. The team of members is headed by a warden who carries overall responsibility for the leadership of the community. In a wider practical sense, however, the community is made up of all the people who are living and/or working there at any one time. The community also encompasses other than human members: the animals and the physical environment that are part of the interdependent network that comprises Pilsdon. The largest group of people is the guests, who are fully resident and may number up to 25, and some of whom have lived in the community for many years. There may also be wayfarers present for a single night or for weekends; volunteers, who may be residential for a period of weeks or months or who come on certain days, and visitors, who might include trainee priests on week-long placements. There is also one salaried employee who deals with much of the routine administration on behalf of the warden. Thus it is possible on some days to find over 30 people present within the community; and this number rises considerably on special occasions such as Christmas and Easter.

While the principles of openness and acceptance are fundamental to Pilsdon's ethos of hospitality, decisions do have to be made about who comes to the community. Processes for dealing with this have evolved over the years. People who wish to come as guests now have to make a formal written application and, if they are then assessed as suitable, asked to complete a trial week as residents before a final decision is made. This arrangement also, of course, gives the prospective guest the opportunity to decide if they want to proceed. The reasoning behind this was explained by Michael Deegan in terms of the need to ensure a balance of people with different kinds of needs and capacities, and offering different contributions to the community. The critical decision in relation to new applicants is:

> whether their needs can be more than we can manage. We may have too many. We send our letter, it just says, 'The mix of the community is very important in order for it to run harmoniously. The mix is off and we'll have to put you on a waiting list for now.'

Whilst there is a reluctance to formalise and individualise the basis on which people are not accepted, experiences such as that recounted in chapter 2 when a guest set fire to part of the house have resulted in a decision to refuse people with a history of arson or of aggressive behaviour. A similar process of application and trial period exists with regard to applications from people wanting to become members, although here the process is more extended involving interviews and usually a number of visits over a period of months to ensure mutual compatibility.

AUTHORITY AND STATUS

Pilsdon is not a provider of residential services and people are not identified as staff or service users. Relationships between different groups are more fluid than in most places established to offer mental health or addiction services. Nevertheless, the different groups who constitute the wider Pilsdon community do carry different kinds of status and responsibility. An understanding of the distinct status of members has existed since the early days of Pilsdon, as Percy and Gaynor's daughter Ruth recalled:

> Obviously one never thought of Pilsdon in sort of institutional terms, so they were never called staff or anything like that, but they were people who had given up their lives to work for the cause of Pilsdon, so they were *members* of the community, quite distinct from those who were coming to stay for whatever reason. Yes, so it was quite an obvious distinction really.

In her thoughts on this issue, Shirley Edwards captured an important aspect of the Pilsdon approach to running a community in the sense that there has to be an acceptance that while roles and statuses may be different, people are all equal and all have need of care and support:

> The fact that it's called an intentional community, that means that the actual community members are intentionally together and that is a commitment for however long it is. That brings, as I understand it, a responsibility to their commitment but I think people aren't there long before they realise, on a personal level, they are equal with everybody else in the place. There's a difference, I think, between holding a role on behalf of everybody else and thinking you're different from everybody else. The warden holds the role of warden on

behalf of everybody else but the warden needs as much support as the latest wayfarer because he has a role to do that and the place wouldn't function, I don't think, successfully without some leadership. I think it's easy for people to feel, 'Oh, them at the top, they have...' whatever they think they have, rather than to realise that people hold a role on behalf of others. It's important for the people who hold the roles also to realise that they're holding a role and they have as much need as everybody else and it may take some people longer than others to realise that.

Recognition of the responsibility carried by members raises the obvious question of how authority is handled within the community's fundamental ethos. This is an issue that is particularly pertinent for those who take on the role of warden. They have to learn to exercise those responsibilities in ways that recognise both individual and community needs:

I think when I said a benign dictatorship is preferable to a democracy, it meant that decisions could be made and I would make them and I would direct. I do remember there was a lot of directing ... Oddly enough, the men of the road needed someone to be there, telling them what to do, and they respected that. That's how they'd worked, there's a foreman. The boss tells them what to do ... and even if I was asking them to do the impossible, if I was working with them while we were trying to do the impossible, then that was OK. I didn't stay in my office and just dish out the jobs and then never be seen.

So, that was, I think, what created the sense of safety.
(Stuart Affleck)

I was aware that the warden was very powerful and
sometimes I would tell, when I gave talks and so on,
I said some of my decisions actually could be seen as
life and death decisions. And that was frightening. But
I saw it was a necessary part of, a) being the leader of
a community, and b) sustaining a sense of stability and
trustworthiness in the community. (Peter Barnett)

The style of leadership adopted by wardens has varied.
Jonathan Herbert described what he saw as the multiple
dimensions of the leadership role:

For me, priority was supporting the community
members. Then, probably supporting the guests. Even
before supporting the guests, creating a safe place, a
loving... a dynamic place for people to be. So, those were
two key things and then you have to take responsibility
for managing the land and the buildings. There was the
spiritual health of the community, trying to maintain
it as a place of prayer. Then, there was the public face,
going out and talking about the community, writing
about it.

All those who have been wardens have seen leadership as
involving the maintenance of discipline: a sense that, in
a social environment with a high potential for disruption
because of the backgrounds of many of the people there,
things are under control. Percy Smith adopted a very strong

leadership style during the community's first twenty years and this established the principle that explicit leadership was essential if the community was to survive.

> I also think that for whatever one thought of my father as an autocrat, and sometimes he was infuriating, because sometimes it just felt like he was going a bit over-the-top, I think it was absolutely essential, actually. And his discipline was essential, because it created the structures that have carried on through. And I think when the discipline has got a bit sloppy, which it may have done at times, it has suffered... (Ruth Thurgur)

One of the very few cast-iron rules governing life at Pilsdon is the 'no alcohol or drugs' rule. Anyone found drinking or using illegal drugs, or obviously under the influence of drink or drugs, is required to leave immediately in order to maintain the safety of the whole community. Several of the ex-wardens talked about how hard it was to impose this rule. Peter Barnett told a story about how, early in his tenure, he had found someone drinking at night but had sent them to bed with a warning and the promise that: "we'll say no more about it". The next day he realised that everyone knew what had happened and that his kindness towards an individual was perceived as failure to take the proper action and had left the community as a whole feeling vulnerable and their sense of safety compromised.

For those who move from being a community member to becoming warden, having to accept responsibility as the ultimate authority in imposing discipline can require difficult adjustment:

I think one of the big challenges was that I guess by nature, and certainly as a community member, there's a strong sense of living alongside people and being with them, and when you're warden I guess, although decisions were made amongst the team members, the buck sort of stops with you and I think there's quite a tension about trying to support somebody but also having the power to say, 'You need to leave.' And that was difficult I think. I was very conscious of having that on one level ... having that level of power, but on another level of being very conscious that that power could be misused and therefore actually being quite reluctant to use it at all unless the situation really demanded it. (Adam Dickens)

But there is also recognition that the capacity to exercise authority when it is required and to insist that the basic rules of community life are adhered to, is one of the foundations for the kind of social environment that Pilsdon aims to be:

I think within the first month I was here, I walked a guest out because they had been regularly drinking, so I discovered. Once I did that, there was a whole crowd of people here that exhaled and felt safer for it because they knew what had been going on but they wouldn't say anything. You sort of think, 'Oh, that's where safety comes from.' Safety comes from having rules and sticking to them and actually taking actions. If you say, 'It's a safe place for these reasons and if you do this, you're out,' but no-one ever gets thrown out for it, then it's really not a safe place. (Michael Deegan)

Michael had worked in a corporate management position earlier in his life and was able to draw on that experience in speaking more generally about the specific challenge for the warden of maintaining appropriate authority in a community founded on the principle of living alongside each other. For Michael this reflected his understanding of being seen as a father figure:

> If you are in a work environment and you're the guy in charge, you have a different kind of authority because what you say goes or bad things can really happen … When you're in community, the thing I've learnt, and it took a while, is when you sit down to supper in the dining room, you have to be in relationship with every person in the dining room. You cannot fire people, you cannot treat them with disrespect, you cannot be manipulative. There are so many things that you cannot be. You can be hard and you can be truthful and you can do those things in love but you have to remain in relationship in order to sit in the dining room. The other thing that someone pointed out is, 'If this were a therapeutic relationship, you would never, ever, ever want to be perceived as a parent.' In community, there's no other way, so I accept the fact that for many people, I am simply a really strong father figure who holds a line around behaviour <laughs>.

A guest's view on the role of the warden in exercising authority and maintaining discipline within the community is provided by Alex Kelly, who experienced very considerable personal change and development while at Pilsdon. He told how in his early days there:

I could be a bit of a bully. The way I treated some other guests sometimes could be quite intimidating. I come from a culture of violence and intimidation, that's the truth of it, and Michael would not stand for that in any way, shape or form. Everyone's got a right to feel safe here and there were a few points where I was making quite a few people feel decidedly unsafe, through intimidation or just generally aggressive behaviour. ... Michael let me know in no uncertain terms exactly what I'm not gonna get away with, <laughs>. We had our moments but after conversations and various stuff had happened in my life, I learnt to go and talk to him and listen to him. As much of a rocky start as it was, again, it was that thing. His authoritative presence sort of faded away and it's just like, 'This guy cares about you. He really does care and he wants you to do well.'

While most guests accept and understand the specific status of warden and members, even if, as in Alex's case, this takes time, there are those who find it uncomfortable. An ex-guest, Rosemary Cortes, when asked if there were ever problems arising from this differential status, said:

Surprisingly few. I mean I can think of a person who wanted to see it as 'us and them', they didn't last long, to be honest. I mean if one sees it in those terms it's not going too well and I think there were others who wanted to invent hierarchies but they weren't there necessarily at all. In fact, there was huge care on the side of the warden and members not to impose their will violently, they would impose it when very strictly necessary, for the sake of health, safety and the good of the community, but not arbitrarily.

And a regular resident as both wayfarer and guest, Simon Smith, expressed a similar view:

> I didn't really see it like that, I mean I was conscious of it because in a lot of places I've been or other people go and I see other people's, what they tell me, experiences of, 'Oh he's a warden, he's higher up than us', like authority, but I never really saw it like that. I mean obviously I know members are more authorised over, sort of over us, if that sounds right to a degree … Yeah, there's a lot of people saying, 'Oh I couldn't live there with a warden and people like that over you all the time', I said, 'Well they're not, they're just human.' I can talk to them like I can talk to other people there…

It is, however, evident – and perhaps inevitable – that some guests found the differences in status and authority difficult even though their overall experience of life at Pilsdon was very positive. This could be because of factors around age, gender and previous family relationships. Sarah Hallett experienced the consequence of the warden being perceived as occupying the role of stern father:

> Stuart was quite … I was quite scared of him really. I mean he was probably about the same age as my own father, and I think he probably … well I don't know, whether this was how I experienced him or whether objectively he was quite authoritarian, I don't know …

I'm a similar age to Stuart's children, you see, so I didn't find him particularly easy to confide in. I know that some of the guests with mental health problems, they would go and talk to him for hours and they found him a very good counsellor and listener. I didn't really have that experience of Stuart but that's equally probably because of my relationship with my own father, he was … my own father was quite old-fashioned and … definitely my father was the head of the household, and I was always a bit scared of him, so in a way I brought that to Pilsdon and how I related to Stuart. The female community members, Annie and Judy, I think I found them easier … although there was definitely a distinction between community members and guests.

Sarah's very personal expression of her experience of relationships at Pilsdon reflects the idea voiced by a number of interviewees that Pilsdon can be understood as functioning like a large family, with all the volatility, subtlety and tensions of relationships that characterise family life.

WORKING AS A TEAM

Alongside all the other pressures of running a community like Pilsdon, dealing with the sometimes extremely difficult behaviour or emotional problems of guests means that the demands on the warden can be intense. Living alongside means that it is not possible to switch off overnight or at the weekend. The personal impact of this is something that

John McAuslan became conscious of during his time as chair of trustees:

> I also became aware of the price that was exacted from the warden, and community members as well, but particularly from the warden. It's a very lonely position and I gradually became aware of the way in which both Percy and Stuart were suffering from these burdens, the loneliness, the stress and the damage that that was doing.

For Jonathan Herbert, the pressures of carrying the leadership role after he had stepped up from member to warden eventually shaped his decision to leave, albeit reluctantly.

> I knew the warden had to exercise that authority and the place wouldn't work without me doing that. I didn't feel particularly comfortable about it; not that I thought it was particularly wrong it should be in the hands of one person, but it just didn't fit me very well. I don't enjoy being the boss. I can give good leadership, I can be clear, I can be firm, I can be just, I hope. I think I was. But no, I didn't enjoy it, really. It did me in, actually. I would've stayed longer, I think, if I hadn't been warden. Who knows, I might still be there.

For Jonathan, a key to being able to survive as warden, and to overcoming the loneliness described by John McAuslan, was the support of the other members, and he therefore saw a vital part of his role as being to develop trust and a sense of collective management responsibility among the members and himself:

As warden, I saw my role change a bit from supporting the guests to supporting the other community members. So, they in turn would support the guests and create... it was all about creating that reasonably healthy community. I felt if I could get a really good team of community members working well and feeling valued and listened to and try and inspire them a bit, then it would spread out in the rest of the community. For me, I had to build trust with them 'cause that was so key in Pilsdon anyway, the issue of trust. Occasionally, you could really have your backs to the wall, a difficult situation, somebody turns up drunk, starts breaking windows, you've got to know your other community members are gonna back you.

One means of building trust among the members and developing a culture in which they can rely on each other for support is through regular meetings to discuss current issues and priorities. These have evolved over the years and under different wardens, from being fairly *ad hoc* and infrequent to becoming much more systematic and embedded in the way Pilsdon is run. Michael Deegan described the system of team meetings in giving his view of the relationship between warden and members:

I sometimes think that it's more like the Archbishop of Canterbury, which is just simply 'first among equals'. We are all members and as the warden, I try to collegially act upon our combined interest and intelligence. That's why we have a meeting every morning, to settle the schedule, talk about anything that came up the day before and to hash out a bit certain things that need to be done. Whether they're about a person or a project or an expense or something, we all get to voice those things and then decide the way forward. I may, in many cases, be the person that's executing that but I'm not necessarily executing my take on it. We try to hold that together as a team. There are times when it is my decision because that's just the way it is sometimes, it has to be.

During Michael's period as warden, these daily meetings were supplemented by quarterly awaydays when the warden and members could get together away from Pilsdon for an extended period to reflect on their work and to give each other spiritual and personal support.

But support comes not only from within the group of members. It can come from those who volunteer their time at Pilsdon, and who thereby become part of the broader community, and it can come from long-established guests:

And also the local volunteers brought something of the wider community and the wider world into Pilsdon because otherwise I always felt there was a danger of things becoming too insular really and that our horizons just stopped at the gate or the end of the field ... Yeah, they felt like important people in giving some sort of stability and continuity amongst the changes of the membership team. And of course the other key people in the whole process of stability are the long-stay guests, which is a bit of a misnomer really because they've been living there for longer than the members, but obviously Henry and Trevor have been there a long time, and now there are people who I think are still there who started when we were community members ... And they help the place because they just get on with things really in their own predictable way, which when you've got a group of people whose lives have been unpredictable, actually to have a seam of predictability in the midst of it feels important. (Adam Dickens)

Judging when and how to draw on the wider sources of support available within the wider Pilsdon community is thus a significant, if perhaps rather under-appreciated, aspect of sustaining the community.

THE ROLE OF TRUSTEES

Given Pilsdon's legal status as a registered charity, the Board of Trustees constitutes an important and necessary part of the management structure of the community. This was not always the case, and in the first phase of the community's existence under Percy Smith's leadership there were no trustees. Moreover, when trustees were first appointed, in the 1990s, their role was not well-defined or understood:

Stuart asked me, and others I'm sure, to be trustees. I don't know whether there were trustees before then and when he asked me, he gave me the impression that it didn't mean anything, it was purely formal. Anyway, I was obviously going to say 'yes' but gradually, it became obvious, I can't remember exactly when, that it was not purely formal at all; that Pilsdon as a charity had to fulfil charity law and that meant there had to be trustees. (John McAuslan)

The role of trustees, however, extends beyond simply fulfilling charity law requirements. A key responsibility of trustees, albeit one that is called upon very infrequently, is the recruitment of a new warden. Given the demands of the role and the minimal material rewards attached to it, finding a new warden is a major challenge. Even if people are initially attracted, they may be put off once the reality of the position becomes apparent, as Alan Frost recounted:

> There aren't people queueing up to become wardens, and when we were advertising for the last warden, which was the position Michael took, we had only three or four applications come in ... We had a Baptist minister, he and his wife, and they came for a week to see what the place was all about and they decided that they would be working here far harder than they were working in their parish and they were actually looking for somewhere nice to wind down, nice big country house in the middle of the countryside, it's a nice last five years before I retire. Well, it's not like that <laughs> because you can be firefighting all the time with something blowing up...

Trustees oversee both the process of advertising for the warden post, which will include use of formal and informal networks, and the fairly lengthy process of interviewing and assessing applicants. And once the appointment has been made, the trustees play a broader supportive function in relation to the individual warden, the members and the community as a whole:

To support the community, to hold the vision. Because there are so many pressures, especially the pressure of money. That whole question of money and government grants is a whole big chapter in Pilsdon, a big thing to think around and talk around. So, to help to hold the vision, support the warden, support the community. (Shirley Edwards)

Being a trustee for Pilsdon involves all the normal things like deciding on large expenditure and that sort of thing, and keeping to the ethos of the community, but it also involves a general remit, which is the most difficult one of all, which is to make sure that everything's OK and is working according to Christian principles. (Hilary Joyce)

The development of this support function took time, however, and the initial introduction of trustees clearly brought a new and potentially unsettling dynamic to the way the community was run, and particularly to the decision-making autonomy of the members. For John McAuslan, who became the chair of the board, this created

a serious awkwardness, which only gradually dawned on me. It meant that under charity law, community members could not be trustees because they were beneficiaries, in the charity law sense. That meant that Pilsdon was going to be run, in a formal sense, by people who were not the community and that was very awkward. In the first place, the trustees had to be the responsible supervisory body and that was a very serious clash with the nature of the community, where it's the community who should be taking the decisions and should be the heart of the community. I thought they felt frustrated and baffled because it wasn't what they were used to and they didn't understand it completely.

Although John saw the role of the board as, in part, freeing up the members from bureaucratic responsibilities and leaving them to focus on the core purposes of the community, he experienced tensions resulting from both the division of responsibilities between trustees and members and the duty of trustees to ensure that certain legally required measures affecting the culture of the community were implemented.

I did feel that serious clash between the responsibilities of trustees and the nature of a place which had a community at its heart. I also felt the clash between the institutional requirements of health and safety and of social care and a community where we are not talking about 'workers' and 'clients'. We had a very sharp issue about minimum wage legislation when the law obviously needed to make sure that people didn't escape the legislation by pretending to be things when they were actually employers employing employees.

This issue was resolved through a campaign involving Pilsdon and a number of other communities eventually resulting in the legal definition and recognition of 'intentional communities', in which the members are officially exempt from categorisation as employees of the charity and thus not subject to minimum wage legislation.

Pilsdon Manor House, the heart of the community

The church, Pilsdon's spiritual centre

The farmyard, dairy block and looseboxes on the left

The Marshwood Vale

Percy, Gaynor and Ruth Smith outside Pilsdon Manor House

Christmas dinner – 1970s

Les, Sue, Seamus & Gino – early residents

Planting cob nut trees in 2021

Greeting after the spring release from winter stalls.

In the milking parlour

The herb garden

Harvest in the church

But there were more mundane aspects of change that trustees had to ensure were effected, which impacted on the culture that Pilsdon wanted to maintain:

> the place is not exactly like a home but like a family house, rather than like an institution. People, I think, are very susceptible, and all sorts of things that any place, Pilsdon included, has to do detract from that. Fire Exit signs. Nobody has that in their homes but every institution has it. Any signs in the kitchen or anywhere else that insist on health and safety. They may be necessary but they all detract from the sense of it being home, everything that makes it institutional.

Over time the relationship between trustees and members has settled down and, through both regular formal meetings and informal visits by trustees, individually and collectively, has established a clear understanding of their distinctive roles and enabled open channels of communication and dialogue. Nonetheless, the status of the two groups is different and preserving that difference is necessary. A recent chair of trustees, Hilary Joyce, reflected:

> And you mustn't ever get too close. You have to keep a certain distance between you and everybody else, which is again quite a difficult feat to … and also the level of involvement, because the warden and the members have the remit to run the place on a day-to-day basis and can spend up to a certain amount of money and all that kind of thing, and basically they have to do that on a day-to-day basis. And so it's not up to me to go in and

say, 'I don't like this brand of coffee. You should have something else' or 'Do you think you were right to get rid of so-and-so' or whatever.

Guests at Pilsdon do have a right of appeal to trustees if they feel aggrieved at the way they have been treated by the warden or members, for instance if they believe they have been asked to leave unjustifiably. But, while the existence of that right again illustrates the difference in status of trustees and members, it is a right that has been exercised very rarely.

MANAGING THE ESTATE

Looking after the physical infrastructure of Pilsdon – the manor house, the ancillary accommodation, farm buildings and land – is a very significant element in the task of managing the community. Interviewees told stories of major repairs and renovations required over the years, and the management challenges that they posed. But in addition there is the need to deal with more minor issues, the everyday things that, as in any household, get broken or become worn out and need repair or replacement. In the case of Pilsdon, given the age, scale and range of the physical property, this is an ever-present demand which as far as possible is handled within the community itself: there are usually one or more guests with knowledge and experience of building maintenance who are willing to take responsibility for a level of repair and renovation, and individual members also bring with them specific skills or are able to develop them – sometimes under the guidance of a guest. This can be an important context in which status differences can be blurred and working together can involve guests taking the lead. Alan Frost reflected on the pros and cons of this 'DIY' approach:

> there are periods when it's been a total shambles because, by the very nature of the people coming in, you can only do what those people have the skills for. We've got a brilliant chippy and general purpose chap, Eddie, and he – previously we had the chap who was virtually doing the same job was a Royal Navy trained electrician, whereas Eddie isn't, so Steve Hodge would do the electrics and other things, you'd just go to either of them and say, 'This is broken', and they'll fix it somehow, but obviously Eddie's not a sparky so we need to get professionals in for that. We've had builders in who've put up walls and then we've had people who say they're builders and they put up walls which don't stay up very long <laughs>.

As Alan's comment indicates, some problems can only be dealt with by external specialists, such as the central heating system breaking down or the telephone and internet system failing, thus generating a further administrative task for the warden and office administrator. A good proportion of the administrator's time is spent in dealing with external firms hired to carry out repair and maintenance work for the community.

> We've had problems with the new sewage system and then, when the machinery stops and the stuff goes into

the stream then the environment authority get on your back and then the local authority come in and test your other water from the reservoir and that's failed, you know, so why has that gone wrong? So, yeah, it can get a bit involved. And I try to field as much as I can from the members and the warden, certainly the warden's got enough on his plate so if I can shield him from some of that.

Large-scale changes and improvements to the physical infrastructure may be the result of specific plans for development, which will include provisions for financing them, but others are unplanned, resulting from something unexpectedly going wrong and requiring major work to put it right with no immediately available source of finance. Peter Barnett recounted two examples of major work during his time as warden. They began with a sudden urgent need for substantial remedial work and led to a very large-scale planned renovation project:

I had just finished compline one February night and there was an almighty bang! And I looked out of the window over towards the pottery and there used to be an electricity cable that ran from the corner of the house to feed the pottery kiln so it was a high voltage cable. And this suddenly burst into flames and looked like a firework sprinkling down sparks and all the rest of it. All the lights went out, the electricity went and there was nothing in the house at all, and I thought, crikey now what's happened? ...So the electricity board came ... he said, 'The source of the problem is this wiring is lethal!' <Laughs>

This resulted in the complete rewiring of the property at a cost of £120,000. However, the process of rewiring the manor house revealed a need for major structural renovation:

> And so then started a major restoration project that involved a second application to the Lottery Fund, and I got in an architect and a surveyor and all the rest of it who drew up then the plans for the whole of the Manor House and then also contingency plans for the buildings round the yards which were going to be done in phases. And that started in about 1997 and was finished three years later with a new roof and new windows, which was the best thing about the whole development was the windows. And we used the Lottery Fund as the main source but also our supporters were incredibly generous, I mean we got about half-a-million from the Lottery and then another half-million from other sources. And we never had to borrow which was very fortunate.

While major developments sometimes happen in an unforeseen way, as in these examples, generally substantial works required to maintain or improve the physical infrastructure of Pilsdon are discussed and planned in formal meetings between the warden and the trustees.

MANAGING MONEY

Ensuring that Pilsdon is financially viable is a constant challenge, in relation to both the day-to-day expenditure required to meet the costs of food, fuel and farm supplies, and the occasional major expenditures needed for repairs and renovation of buildings and equipment or for new investment. Interviewees recounted examples of this challenge throughout the community's history. Several reflected on one of the particular dilemmas of sustaining the kind of community that Pilsdon aims to be: the balance to be struck between, on the one hand, explicit financial planning and fund-raising and, on the other hand, 'living by faith'.

Both Ruth Thurgur and Caroline Hillyard commented on Percy Smith's approach to money in the early days of the community:

> Actually I think dad was pretty hopeless about money really, he didn't think about it either, and yet, somehow… I mean he probably wasn't as organised about it as he should have been but it still survived, didn't it? (Ruth)

> He survived and his attitude to how they were kept going was one of faith and it seemed to work. People gave very generously. (Caroline)

An example of what could happen through living by faith, albeit a rather tragic story, was provided by Stuart Affleck. An inspection for insurance purposes revealed that the boilers were unsafe. Once again the community needed to find a substantial amount of money.

> The usual things happened. 'Let's start having fetes,' and I said, 'No, no, no, no, no. We can't do that, it just doesn't feel Pilsdon. Maybe what you need to do is

pray, and pray very hard because we are on the point of extinction.' And we'd had a guy staying with us called Alan ... Immensely bright guy but terribly depressed and his family lived in the Vale somewhere. He committed suicide while he was with us, went up on to the Pen and cut his throat ... So, some time after that had happened there was a letter from his parents, in which they said... he was a very wealthy young man and obviously he had a wealthy family. So, we were given all his shares, a lump sum and something else, anyway, which covered the boilers. That was pure providence...

Over time, however, as the need for refurbishment and improvement grew and the possibility of new external sources of funding, such as the National Lottery, became apparent, wardens had to go beyond faith in providence:

I basically said fundraising is now going to be dramatically rejigged in this country because of this fund, no one will be able to compete with it and it'll be huge and I think we ought to be part of it. Fortunately I managed to persuade the trustees just to that way of thinking. The *coup de grace* in some respects was when I asked the guests how they felt about it, they said, 'Well, we have a lottery ticket every week and we want it to come to Pilsdon.' <Laughs> So I thought well yes, I hadn't really thought of it that way 'cause I had never bought a lottery ticket in my life! (Peter Barnett)

As we saw in the previous section, successful applications for Lottery funding were crucially important in enabling essential renovation and substantial new development at Pilsdon. However, this brought with it an increased requirement for both expertise and relevant systems of planning and management. Similar pressures arose with changes in the way money in the form of state benefits relevant to Pilsdon's guests was allocated and administered through central and local government. Tensions were created about the extent to which the community should get drawn into formal welfare systems, with their inevitable bureaucratic requirements for audit and accountability, as against the wish to continue to offer open hospitality to whoever was in need of it without worrying about external rules and regulations:

> We were being asked to account for the money that was coming from the county council much more explicitly than had ever happened before. There was the 'Supporting People' scheme that came in. And prior to that I think support for housing and day-to-day support was just given to the community and there was a sense of do with it what you like really, and it became much more tailored under Supporting People[1]. (Adam Dickens)

> We were always a little bit cautious of taking money from social services. We could have had pots of money for some people. We were cautious of becoming an institution. When I first became warden, we were under huge pressure from 'Supporting People'. We had a big

---

1   Supporting People was an initiative designed to allocate individual funding to people eligible for social care services. It marked a shift from funding for services to personalised support packages.

debate, whether we'd take their money or not, and we ended up writing I think 13 policies in six months – health and safety for vulnerable adults, for children, policies about gifts, policies about you name it, there were so many of them. (Jonathan Herbert)

One problem in deciding to become more integrated into government funding systems and thereby subject to official policies is that those policies and systems can radically change, and in the years of austerity, from 2010 onwards, Pilsdon experienced profound changes in its financial situation as government expenditure on welfare was drastically reduced.

It wasn't that many years ago that, apart from the guest housing benefit and their top up, we were getting £140,000 a year from the government. That has now gone down to nothing except that West Dorset District Council have, because we are the only open access refuge in the county, they realise what our value is and they managed to find £10,000 for us. In the previous year it was £20,000 so that's going down. So, that's going to be the issue, is where the money comes from. (Alan Frost)

In response to this major loss of income, a number of decisions were made about how Pilsdon would operate in future. These included decisions to eliminate certain areas of significant expenditure, such as in 2014 the closure of Brook House, the 'half-way' establishment for guests who were moving on from their time at Pilsdon and which was leased by the community from a housing association. A more wide-ranging decision was to change the nature of the relationship between the Pilsdon Community and government, in order to end any financial dependency together with the bureaucracy and requirement to follow externally imposed rules that entailed. Michael Deegan explained the thinking behind this:

> So, we made a decision as a membership, probably four years ago, maybe a little more than four, that we would do our very best to run the community without government money. So, the money had been going down and I couldn't look out into the future and see that ever changing. The money came with lots and lots of strings and requirements. We were keeping notes on conversations with guests, we had to have move-on plans. It was just totally against the pastoral side of Pilsdon, we don't do those things. When you cook a meal with a guest for three hours in the kitchen, you don't run to the office and make notes. So, we sort of made the decision that we would do our best to operate the community and move away from government money so that we could move in the directions that we felt were necessary, as Pilsdon Community, to embrace the ethos that we believe is the right thing to do and not become a government agency.

It remains the case that guests, as individuals, receive welfare benefits, generally in the form of housing benefit, from which they pay the cost of their accommodation at Pilsdon. This in itself generates a significant administrative demand, as Alan Frost described:

I obviously deal a lot with the local authority housing department in respect of rents, housing benefits, and if issues come up with a guest, because quite often the first time we know there's an issue is when the housing benefit stops and we've had guests here who've just, with the ostrich syndrome, they get a letter from the housing department, they bury their head in the sand and stick the letter under their bed and hope that it will go away and because they haven't provided the information that the housing department are asking for, the housing benefit stops. So, then I need to phone them up and say, 'What's going on and how do we resolve this?'

But beyond that, Pilsdon has endeavoured to move back to a form of living by faith in developing and sustaining a large network of supporters who both provide regular donations and make legacy provisions in their wills. As Alan put it:

we are a charity of faith, people are and have been extremely generous with legacies coming in, we're just amazed at how the donations seem to keep on coming in. You'd think that people die off and so their donations stop but people sort of come in below them and keep us going.

CONCLUSION: MANAGING THROUGH FAITH?

This chapter has discussed in some detail the range and depth of the need for the Pilsdon Community to be managed in order to survive as a legally constituted organisation within the changing economic, social and cultural norms of the wider society. We have also suggested that there is a subtle relationship between this need for management and the way it is exercised through formal roles, structures and systems, and the fundamental ethos underpinning the community of the Christian faith in unconditional hospitality, acceptance of others and mutual trust. There is a constant requirement on trustees, warden and members, and to some extent others including volunteers and long-term guests, to work to ensure that the balance between management and faith as contrasting organising principles becomes tilted towards neither a stultifying dominance of bureaucratic systems, nor a potentially negligent culture of assuming that 'God will provide'.

One way in which management and faith are woven together is by the active development and maintenance of a wide range of external supporters of the community. As Alan Frost noted, Pilsdon is kept afloat financially by external donations and this source of funding has grown considerably in recent years. Donations come from people who share the explicit Christian faith of Pilsdon's members, but also from people who may not hold that religious faith but who have faith in what it is that Pilsdon is trying to do and how it does it. Developing and sustaining a sizeable network of people who make a regular financial contribution and/or make provision for a legacy to Pilsdon in their wills is itself a substantial management task, requiring both regular communication with existing donors and promoting information about Pilsdon to potential new donors. Communicating and engaging with the outside world to tell people about the community, what it has achieved and what it aims to do, and encouraging them to become part of the dispersed network of 'friends', has always been a key element of the warden's role. This ranges from preaching in other churches, to giving talks to various organisations or groups, to the issuing of regular newsletters, to the maintenance of a website, Facebook page and Twitter feed, and the publishing of occasional articles and other materials, including this book. There are in addition events organised at Pilsdon which external people attend, including religious celebrations at Christmas and Easter and the annual anniversary celebration of Pilsdon's founding in October.

An important concept within Pilsdon's faith-based ethos is that of 'holding': a fundamental element in what the community does is to hold people in safety, understanding and compassion to help them to cope with difficult and threatening life experiences. When they are operating in an effective and balanced way, the management arrangements at Pilsdon can be seen as an essential infrastructure to enable this holding to take place, as a means of enabling the community's particular approach to faith to be practised. Thus, for example, as Michael Deegan explained, it is through the mechanism of appropriately exercised authority and discipline that safety, and therefore the possibility of holding, can be achieved. And more broadly, the management of Pilsdon's public relations, using methods common to most other types of organisation, helps to generate an infrastructure of external support in which the community itself can be held. While there may be, and have been, times when the demands for greater management of how aspects of the community are run is experienced as conflicting with the community's core faith-based values and beliefs, it is also possible to see how faith can be a resource through which effective management is achieved.

* * *

We now take a rather different tack from the previous four chapters that have described Pilsdon and discussed how people respond to it. In the next three chapters we reflect on the significance of the Pilsdon community from different perspectives. We still draw from direct experience and use the words of those interviewed for the history project to illustrate what we think this particular example of community life can offer to a better understanding of good ways of living together, but we also draw on wider literatures to place this in a broader context. In chapter 6 we reflect on Pilsdon as a place of care. In doing so we draw from a body of work on the ethics of care to understand both how care is practised and what Pilsdon contributes to an understanding of the complexity and diversity of care. In chapter 7 we locate Pilsdon in space and time, and consider the meaning of 'community' as it is enacted there. We look at what has changed in Pilsdon and in the world beyond that is of most relevance to understanding it as a place of refuge for people who are troubled that has endured for over 60 years. Chapter 8 provides a personal perspective from Mary Davies, as a current member of the community, on the nature of the faith-based commitment to 'live life in common' and on the distinctive way that such commitment is practised at Pilsdon.

CHAPTER 6

———

A Place of Care

Our descriptions of the Pilsdon Community, based on memories of some of those who have lived there and been part of the community's wider network during its 60 year history, have sought to communicate why people come, what it is like to live and work within the community and what is involved in ensuring its survival. Underpinning much of what people told us during interviews was the question of its longevity – what is it about Pilsdon that has meant this community has survived and flourished when many attempts at communal living have not outlived the enthusiasm of their founders. Some people reflected directly on this question. Others reflected on this indirectly in the way they spoke about its impact on their lives and the lives of others. If we are to go beyond understanding the Pilsdon community as an interesting project in its own right, we need to reflect beyond its capacity to balance effectively the diverse needs of those who live there with the regular demands of running a farm and old house, and the need for financial stability with faith to its founding ethos. In this and the following two chapters we pose some broader questions that we hope can offer inspiration from the way in which this small community in West Dorset has enabled people to live well together for over six decades. We start with its significance as a place of care.

BEING HUMAN

One of the characteristics of what it is to be human is that we can all be vulnerable and that we all need to be cared for. We are all likely to feel pain and experience losses that leave us exposed and fragile. How others respond to us at those times affects how we experience both pain and vulnerability, whether we survive and grow through this or are broken by it. The most intense joys of life come from our relationships with others. Friendships, love and the capacity to both give and receive care are necessary to individual wellbeing and to solidarity amongst those who seek to live well together. Looking at Pilsdon from this perspective is important to understanding its significance – and why it has survived for as long as it has.

As we have seen, many arrive at times in their lives when they feel hopeless, despairing or broken. Whilst the language we use may have changed, and both the contributing causes and the models of intervention may have undergone important shifts over the last 60 years, mental illness, addictions, loss and frailty remain constant dimensions of human experience. Gaynor wrote in the preface to the second edition of her book about Pilsdon's early years that it became a: "unique experience of friendship", involving sharing lives and developing friendships with:

> ...men and women from behind prison bars, from the locked wards of mental hospitals, from the streets and from doss houses, from every occupation – and unoccupation – and class and creed in society. (Smith, 2008, p.9)

Gaynor starts this preface with vignettes that capture the hidden and visible pain of guests she knew in her time at Pilsdon. Our interviewees recounted other stories of lives characterised by complex interactions between mental health problems, addictions, failed marriages, poverty, homelessness and, in some cases, imprisonment. Some people felt they had reached the end of the line, that Pilsdon represented their only option for survival. The "unlikely" friendships between members who have chosen to live in community and express their faith through living with others in this way, and those who come to the community for shelter, recovery and to find a way forward out of chaotic lives, are core to Pilsdon's purpose:

> We all came to know friendship not just as a spontaneous affinitive eruption between two people but as a way of life the basis of which was an unconditional acceptance. All of us, whether nominally Christian or not, were concerned with this ideal and with trying to break down, or through, the barriers so often created by wealth, status, education, culture, and even the barrier implicit in the word Christian. (Smith, 2008, p. 10)

Another barrier can be a belief that people can be divided into those who are, and those who are not vulnerable; those who need, and those who do not need care, and those who give and those who receive care. Living alongside people whose journeys to Pilsdon have followed different trajectories exposes the error of that view:

> I think when people are carrying a lot of pain… they can
> expose your own vulnerabilities, that pain can expose
> your own vulnerabilities so you become aware not only
> of their struggles but also of your own. (Adam Dickens)

In this chapter we explore how friendship and love offer responses to vulnerability and pain through everyday life at Pilsdon. And in doing so we talk also about 'care'. Some interviewees used this word, others did not. We do so because we think a care perspective enables us to highlight what is distinctive about how this community shelters and nurtures the people who live and work there. It is a perspective that enables us to make connections between what happens at Pilsdon and the way we think more broadly about collective responsibilities for justice and wellbeing.

THE ETHICS OF CARE

Pilsdon has never sought to offer care services, but care encompasses broader ways of thinking about relationships than the term 'care services' invokes. Care is one of those simple words that can cause a lot of difficulties. In everyday life it is generally associated with a positive idea or quality:

someone who is 'careful' or 'caring' is considered to demonstrate good qualities. But 'care' can also have more negative connotations when, for example, we talk about 'the cares of the world' to indicate that someone may be suffering burdens that weigh them down. Care has specific meanings when attached to other terms such as 'health care', 'nursing care' or 'social care'. In these guises it is the subject of public policies that are often disputed or subject to anxieties that care has failed or is too expensive. For those who may be described as needing care, care can be associated with infantilisation or even oppression. Being 'needy' can deny moral agency. Family members or friends who give care unpaid can find care a burden, hard work, a demand too far. So care can be resisted, both by those who receive it and those who give it.

One consequence of this is that the word care has, at times, been banned from the official discourse of agencies that have responsibilities for care. Users of social care services were encouraged to exercise choice and exert control over personal support services. For some in the disabled people's movement 'rights not care' became a campaign slogan because of resistance to being defined by dependency resulting from disabling environments (Barnes, 2012). We need to take seriously the reasons why care has been resisted, resented and rejected. We need to look more closely at what care means and at its significance in all our lives. And we need to consider the very different ways in which care can be practised and what we can learn from these.

In the early 1980s a feminist psychologist called Carol Gilligan published a book that became hugely influential.

In a Different Voice was a response to the realisation that theories of human development, including the capacity to make moral choices, were based on research carried out exclusively with boys (Gilligan, 1982). Gilligan's research with girls and boys, young women and men, enabled her to hear different ways of talking about moral decision making. The capacity to apply abstract moral principles to different circumstances in order to decide 'right' or 'good' actions had been seen to constitute mature, adult development. Gilligan refers to this as an 'ethic of justice.' Key principles here are rights and rules. But her research uncovered a different moral voice that both girls and boys, women and men, often struggled to express and which they had learnt to silence. This voice focussed on the specific circumstances and contexts of a situation and prioritised the relational implications of different actions. She referred to the latter mode of decision making as based in an 'ethic of care'. Its key principles are relationships and responsibilities.

The relationship between care and justice has continued to concern scholars of moral and political philosophy (Held, 2006). Some have argued care and justice cannot be reconciled, others have sought to argue that one or other principle should take precedence. Most scholars working in this area today seek to understand how care and justice intersect to create the conditions in which people in diverse circumstances can avoid or resist oppression and live well together. Work on the ethics of care has blossomed over the last two decades. As well as informing thinking about moral philosophy, policies and practices relating to how we help people who are ill, disabled or in situations of vulnerability, care ethics has been recognised as raising significant questions for both the substance and practice of politics (Tronto, 2013). Recognition of the interconnectedness of human and beyond human 'matters of concern' have taken care ethics into science and technology studies and to academic and activist responses to impending environmental disasters (Puig della Bellacasa, 2017). Care for other animals, for soil, plants and landscapes is necessary for human survival and those entities need care in their own right.

The ethics of care starts from a recognition that human individuals are relational beings who are dependent on others for their survival, growth and nurture. There are times in people's lives: childhood, if people became frail in old age, for example, when those dependencies are particularly evident. And for some people chronic illness or significant disabilities mean a more obvious dependency on others throughout their lives. But we all need care. Interdependency not independence best describes the human condition. We all receive care and all are likely to give care – at the same or different times. Care ethics highlights the necessity to promote caring relationships.

What is care?

Joan Tronto and her colleague Berenice Fisher offered the following way of thinking about what care is:

> On the most general level, we suggest that caring be viewed as a species activity that includes everything that we do to maintain, continue, and repair our 'world' so that we can live in it as well as possible. That world includes our bodies, our selves, and our environment,

all of which we seek to interweave in a complex, life-sustaining web. (cited in Tronto, 1993, p. 103)

This definition prompts us to think well beyond the provision of specific services designed to treat old or frail bodies, or to respond to those considered vulnerable because of learning disability or mental distress. Caring relationships include the intense, intimate and personal relationships associated with giving and receiving care in those circumstances. But they can also encompass friendships or work relationships, relationships generated by political activity or through encounters at work. They include the way we relate to ourselves: looking after our bodies and our emotional and social well-being. And care includes the world beyond the human: animals, plants, soil and other elements of the world need to exist in interdependent webs of care.

Care is more than an attitude towards others or towards the world in which we live. It requires action that needs to be determined within specific contexts. Whilst emotionality is an important part of care, a compassionate attitude towards others does not of itself deliver care. Tronto (1993, 2013) has elaborated five phases of care, each associated with a related principle. Care starts with 'caring about' – being *attentive* to others and noticing the need for care. Accepting *responsibility* and acting to meet the identified need is necessary if this awareness is to become 'taking care of' and then enabling 'caring for' – the hands-on work of care giving. In order for such actions to embody care they need to be undertaken *competently*. But care is not complete unless it is received. So we also need to include 'care receiving' – the *responsiveness* of the person being cared for, within a holistic understanding of care. How care receivers respond to the actions of care givers offers important information that feeds back to the attentiveness necessary for care to start. And 'caring with' – caring with others, including recipients, builds *solidarity*, a confidence that care is available when needed and a shared experience of the process of care.

The subjects of care

Care includes care of self and of known and unknown others. Those who are unknown may be distant geographically or generationally. Those involved in personal caring relationships can include people paid to care and those for whom care is part of a close personal relationship. Care givers also need to receive care – both in their own right and to enable them to care (Kittay, 1999). One of the problems of care is that it has been seen as 'women's work'. The majority of those paid to care and caring unpaid are women, but it is a problem if care is seen as a feminine virtue or female responsibility.

Caring relationships often involve more than two people: how caring networks operate impacts the way care is received and experienced (Barnes, 2015). A failure to care for care givers (both paid and unpaid) can undermine good care and represent a moral failure. Care receivers can also be care givers (consider the situation of adults with learning disabilities caring for elderly relatives). Care amongst those considered 'vulnerable' or 'needy' can reflect particular insights into what this means and 'collective care' can develop amongst groups often defined as care receivers: self-advocacy groups of people with mental health problems, for example.

And we also need to encompass non-human animals as well as our physical environment as subjects of care.

Care is political

Noticing the importance of care impacts political decision making, the recognition given to those involved in caring relationships and the substance of public policies. Policy analysis from an ethic of care enables not only critique, but renewal: what would policy based in caring principles look like? This can help avoid 'blame' for the failures of care being laid upon those who are least powerful. Deliberative policy making involving care givers and care receivers that is conducted 'with care' can help promote the values of care and avoid an association between receiving care and incompetence (Barnes, 2012).

The ethics of care thus offers a perspective that links the personal and often intimate practices of care to the organisational and political context within which social relations develop. It provides a language which helps us talk about the often invisible work of care and enables a critical and transformative analysis of policies and practices impacting experiences of justice/injustice. Looking at what Pilsdon does and how people talk about its significance in their lives from this perspective can help a creative reflection on its achievements and challenges.

DOING CARE AT PILSDON

Ruth Thurgur referred to 'the love thing' as key to what Pilsdon is all about. Acceptance, regardless of background or circumstance, underpins the welcome and hospitality offered to those who seek shelter there. Gaynor and Ruth's observations about the centrality of friendship and love to Pilsdon's ethos is reflected in the words of others interviewed for the history project. In responding to a question about why Pilsdon has endured Mary Barnett said it:

... expresses humanity, compassion, love in its many forms, the love of people, love of security, love of a place. It's a place of sanctuary, of grief, of pain, happiness, security, but it is that place that I think we all long for within ourselves, to have that place which we may get from our parents in our childhood, which we may not, but everyone really deserves to have that place sometime. And I think Pilsdon can be that place or is that place.

Whilst Sarah Hallet said:

I think there is something of God in it, I think it is important that it's a place of faith where people have faith, but I think it's also about our faith in humanity, our faith in each other ... I think it has to do with vision and the ability to see the potential in people, even when they're very broken and at a point of crisis in their lives.

Pilsdon is seen here as embodying and expressing human compassion for ourselves and others. For members, wardens and others, like Sarah, who profess a Christian faith, that human compassion and love reflects and is sustained by religious faith. Those who made this connection spoke about it in different ways. Andrew Davey said:

I think I can only really speak from a member's view, I think that the Christian faith, the Christian understanding of, well certainly for me, Christ and his welcome however we understand that, I think that powerfully sustains a sort of energy to do this sort of work, because one feels carried by a story that's bigger than us. And I think within Christianity there's that, I can't remember how it comes, but the idea of welcoming angels unawares, this idea of seeing beyond the surface of whoever rolls up through the gate, that sort of expectation of encounter, with another, and what that might mean on a profound level.

Stuart Affleck recounted being approached by a group of social workers who were interested in establishing a community similar to Pilsdon. He asked them where the church would be. When they said it would not have any religious life within it, his response was uncompromising: "I said, 'Then it won't work.'" This begs a number of questions. For those of us schooled in social research we might suggest that this is an empirical question – is there evidence of communities established with similar objectives relating to the support of people in difficulty that are not based on Christian faith that have been successful? If Stuart is right, what are the implications of this? A religious life can obviously mean faiths other than Christianity, but since Pilsdon is an Anglican community to what extent would a multi faith foundation both motivate and sustain commitments to this way of living alongside others? And if this way of living is dependent on religious faith, if only those who feel themselves sustained by a faith, as Hilary

Joyce put it "which catches them when they've had enough. And they say OK, I've had enough of this but I'll give it one more time", does the Pilsdon experience have anything to offer those who do not share that faith? Is it possible to find a way to be alongside people and care for them in a comparable way without the sustenance that Stuart and other interviewees spoke of? Humanism, for instance, offers a secular ethical framework and a set of practical principles for living well with others that seem to map closely on to the values and principles that sustain Pilsdon (Norman, 2012).

Acceptance

In Tronto's analysis of care ethics, attentiveness, noticing a need, is the starting point for care. This is necessary both at a collective and individual level. It is what lies behind actions to establish institutions such as the National Health Service as well as the immediate response to an individual in need. Percy and Gaynor's decision to live in community with others who were experiencing difficulty came, in part, from attentiveness to need. But the word used to summon the basis for care in many interviews was not attentiveness but acceptance. Core to the ethos and practice of life at Pilsdon is that people who come to the community are not judged, but welcomed and accepted on the basis of a shared humanity.

> It's just that acceptance, really, and I don't at all feel that my connection with it is to 'do good'. I think that's the worst phrase you can possibly... (Caroline Hillyard)

Peter Barnett decided that acceptance meant it would be a mistake to share too much information about people's histories with other members: "So that actually, when the person arrived, they could be welcomed and there wouldn't be a little voice in their head, going, '<Tuts> but they set fire to buildings,' or whatever." Experience caused practices to change, but the underlying ethos remains.

This acceptance can be unfamiliar for some. Alex Kelly struggled at first to think this was genuine:

> People seemed nice enough and because of my background, I wasn't actually buying it, I thought it was all a big act. 'Sooner or later, they're gonna want something from you, ...' I wasn't used to people being nice to you or trying to help you, just for the sake of... well, genuinely that. That they wanna help you. I was very, very, very, very wary.

But if care is a practice as well as an attitude how is acceptance enacted?

Care in practice

Pilsdon does not offer personal care, it does not provide therapy, nor carry out individual assessments and develop personal independence plans. So what does it do? What does the help Alex spoke of consist of and how is it expressed? Tronto and Fisher's definition of care provides a helpful perspective from which to consider this. The concept of 'repair' in this definition seems particularly appropriate for many of those who come to Pilsdon at time when they feel broken. Repair is a necessary precursor to transformation.

That often starts with the body:

> …Sister Anne [former member] I was talking to her and I said 'Anne I'm in a terrible state. I'm really in a bad state.' She said 'Where are you Michael?" I said 'Bournemouth. I've let myself go so bad it's unbelievable.' And she said 'I can get someone to pick you up Michael.' She did. She came herself…'Oh Michael' she said 'what happened to you, you look awful.' She said 'Get in the car.' She drove me straight back here and I came out in these bloody hives and everything, my body was just… it was terrible. And she nursed me through it and she got me back on my feet again.

Michael O' Shaughnessy's story of being taken to the community after a physical collapse illustrates a response to basic bodily needs that is fundamental to the hospitality Pilsdon offers:

> it's taking care of the very mundane parts of life that are actually so important … It's a place where they will be fed, they will be housed, they can get clean, they can be safe. We don't try to do anything more than that. Or set ourselves up to do more than that. But actually that's a huge amount, because when you offer that with kindness and as far as you can, an unconditionality about who comes, I think amazing things can happen and change happens. (Andrew Davey)

A wayfarer described his initial visit. Arriving after a long walk he was offered a change of clothes from the 'boutique'

– a store of donated clothing: "a lady came out and she said, 'Let me show you the boutique.' I'm thinking, 'Boutique? Is she off her rocker?' I said, 'I need a drink 'cause I am…' not that sort of drink. 'I need a cup of tea and take this rucksack off,' which she was quite obliging and she did take me to the boutique, which was in a poxy caravan." These responses demonstrate the importance of a welcome that encompasses an immediate focus on bodily needs, but which also communicates acceptance. This moment is important in communicating a recognition of basic needs that will be met without requiring any engagement with formal processes of assessment, diagnosis, or considerations of whether criteria are met. It is not only members who offer that welcome:

> usually, whoever's in the kitchen makes that first welcome happen because quite often that's the first place people come into, and so, there would be a warm welcome and a tea or a coffee and a scone and jam or whatever was available … Yeah, people would come at any time of day or night and we were able to put together a meal of some sort, even if it was 11 o'clock at night. So, that welcome, I think, was really important. (Ann Davies)

A focus on a, literal, embodiment of care through the provision of food was a common theme in interviews:

> I did a lot of cooking… every meal it was a way of caring for people in a practical way, in a physical way. I loved going in the garden and getting stuff, when it appeared I loved thinking, well, Henry grew the beans … I loved

the way everybody's place in the making of the meal, it's not the person who cooks but everybody who had a role in it appearing. ... I wanted people to be healthy and whole, but sometimes they'd been so neglected and neglectful of themselves that actually that kind of caring is a very uplifting thing... because Pilsdon is a very generous place and you're lavishing this bounty which is created around you. And I think it makes people stronger because they're worth it, they are worth all the effort that everybody puts in to help them to heal really, to become strong. (Mary Barnett)

Mary's words embrace many aspects of care at Pilsdon. Valuing people through the provision of food receives similar expression through baking cakes for people's birthdays and offering a good meal and gifts at Christmas. At its most basic Pilsdon provides shelter for people who have no other space to be, or for whom getting away from 'home' is necessary for themselves or required by others. In a very literal way the practical and value based nature of care is embodied in actions that contribute to healing of body and soul – to repair.

Being alongside

I think I'd assumed that somehow, we were supposed to fix people and I knew I was totally inadequate to the job of fixing anybody. So, it took a bit of time to realise actually, that wasn't what Pilsdon was about. Pilsdon's about walking alongside somebody, not thinking you can actually fix people. (Jane Renyard)

Jane's realisation that it was not a question of fixing people suggests that repair does not come from a technical intervention. Members are not therapists or counsellors. If they have therapeutic skills these are not exercised in the context of any particular model of intervention. But the absence of formal interventions does not imply that nothing happens in terms of actively offering help. Being or walking alongside people means living and working together, being attentive to pain and difficulty and demonstrating a willingness to talk at times and in contexts that work for the person concerned. Those who spend time at Pilsdon quickly realise that some guests do not want to talk about their lives or find it very hard to do so. Others seem used to recounting their stories, perhaps as a result of being required to do so in professional health or welfare settings. As relationships develop so do conversations about past lives and hopes for the future. In all cases listening and being available come before talk. Through being alongside, attentiveness is deepened and enables understanding of the way in which people are responding to their experiences in the community, and how this may help them address the troubles that brought them there.

Time for talk is often not distinct from time spent in other ways.

> ...if people said, 'Stuart, can I have a chat with you?' he'd say, 'Yes, after milking,' or, 'Come and help me in the garden. I'm going to do some digging so you can come and help.' That was a bit of a surprise for some people. I think they thought it would be a cosy chat in an

armchair but it's much easier to talk while you're doing something. (Annie Hardie)

The importance of talk has been consistent throughout Pilsdon's history:

> You might talk to Gillian or Gaynor was a very good listener and then later, by then I was on a more even keel, I would discuss things with Sid 'til the cows came home. There was always somebody to notice and pick up those moments. (Nick Hillyard)

> ...sometimes you just need somebody to talk to even just to talk to or make sure you're ... clarify things a bit more. ...I could talk to Michael Deegan, he'd say, 'You OK?' I'd say, 'Can I have a chat Michael?' And I'd feel really like rough situation and ten minutes I'd walk out there and you're crying 'cause I'm like, well I feel better now, it's like whoa! It's just like 'Thank you Michael', and he does what he does. (Simon Norris)

Beyond the human

We have seen that work in the garden, with the animals, and in maintaining the house are not only necessary practical activities, but also provide a purpose and a routine that holds people. Care and work intersect. Conversations offering opportunities to reflect and engage in processes of repair often take place as people work alongside each other. Whether it be preparing lunch, muckspreading or working together to lay hedges, members, volunteers and guests may intersperse requests to pass tools or how to plant seeds, with conversations about how people came to be there and what they hope for in terms of moving on. Showing interest and concern, and demonstrating understanding in this context can be enough. It can also lead to more extended conversations and opportunities to talk about hopes and fears and to offer encouragement and suggestions.

But there is more to it than this. Caring for the animals, for the land and for the house is a way in which residents of the community can give as well as receive care. Living alongside the other than human world prompts attentiveness to the needs of other entities and their place within webs of care. The necessity for these practices of care to be sustained whatever the weather or whatever else is happening in people's lives is hard, but provides a grounding that can sustain connections when these might otherwise become unsettled or disrupted. Developing an understanding of the interdependencies between the animals, the land and the people can provide a basis on which a broader understanding of interdependency can develop. Mary Barnett's reflection on the significance of offering food reflects that this is not only about nurturing people who have lacked nourishment. It is also an embodiment of the work of others in preparing the land, planting and looking after the crops and preparing the meal. The food that is put on the table comes from the collective contribution of guests, members and volunteers who have worked together. Some may no longer be there at the time the food is presented. But being able to care through the provision of food comes from a collective effort.

Whilst Percy Smith believed that encouraging people to work was an important way of countering depression, a care perspective enables us to recognise its broader significance. It is not only (or even necessarily) a way of 'working through' low mood, but of being part of a process of interweaving and creating what Tronto and Fisher call a "life sustaining web." We can hear a related way of thinking in a metaphor that embodied connections between the way of life at Pilsdon and the healing that many seek:

> And to engage with the land as well and the rhythms of life and death and new life emerging and how that reflected some of the things that were happening for people in terms of what did they have to let go of or die to and where might new life emerge for them, and we often made quite a bit of manure really, because it's a great metaphor that, how manure can be a source of life and how we work with the crap of people's lives and how that can somehow generate new life really. (Adam Dickens)

Sarah Hallett's account of the impact on her of the gardens and animals also spoke of healing:

> And later, when it was summer, I used to really like the chickens and I find their crooning noise really soothing … and I can remember being sent down into the gardens where the chickens lived, to pick blackcurrants with a fork, I was popping all the blackcurrants off their stems with a fork, and listening to this lovely maternal crooning off the chickens and I really liked that. …I was happy then. I was happy then and I wanted to live then.

The land and the animals are active participants in the processes of care. They both need to be cared for and are a source of nurturing for the human members of the community. Care giving and receiving is integrated into the everyday life of the community. This can mean that care is invisible, but this reinforces rather than reduces the importance of understanding how it works.

CARE GIVERS, CARE RECEIVERS

Throughout this book we have indicated that those who live at Pilsdon are referred to in different ways. Those who commit to making Pilsdon their home and to taking responsibility for its operation are 'members' of the community. They offer hospitality to people described as 'guests', although some thus described end up living there for longer than their hosts. Wayfarers are people, usually men, who have made a decision to live without a permanent home base, but for whom Pilsdon offers an occasional short stopover on a well frequented route. Volunteers come to the community as residents and as day visitors to help out. Newcomers find it hard to distinguish who's who during early encounters. Greater familiarity gives more indication of the differences, but initial responses to a new arrival need to avoid any assumptions. What does this contribute to an understanding of care giving and care receiving in this context?

Simon, a wayfarer who has been visiting for many years, showed the interviewer a letter he had received from one of the members thanking him for his kindness in having bought Easter eggs for her children. For Simon this recognition of an act of kindness on his part was very moving. It illustrates the opportunities Pilsdon offers for those who might be seen as care receivers to offer care to others.

Caring relationships can and do develop amongst guests and wayfarers. This was evident in conversations we have already quoted. These conversations expressed care for the other based in shared and different histories. Bob and Daniel focussed on the shared experience of failed marriages and loss of access to their children. Bob had been able to re-build a relationship with his teenage children and offered both recognition of the pain Daniel was experiencing and support for the way he was trying to change his behaviour and re-establish contact. Emma and Nicky talked about what both saw as an unlikely friendship developing when Emma moved in next to Nicky. In spite of being like "chalk and cheese" Nicky recognised that Emma's aggression hid a need for support and this was given and received in a way that continues following Nicky moving on. This is some of what they said in conversation with each other:

> Nicky: I mean to begin with I think I was so focused on trying to get through my practical situational issues that I didn't actually want anybody, and... but I don't know, you got through my defences, completely. You did.

> Emma: I wouldn't give up on you. I saw something in you Nicky, and I quite admired you in a way, so...

Nicky: Ooh.

Emma: Yeah. You were a pain in the arse sometimes, but I love you to bits really.

Nicky: I'll take that as a Geordie compliment <laughs>.

Emma: Nah, I do. There's something about Nicky, she's a little star, you're a star in my eyes.

People were more likely to talk about friendship than to refer directly to care. Friendships can be difficult amongst people who are dealing with difficult stuff in their lives. But accounts of friendships demonstrate that care is integral to this. For Alex this was part of what it meant to strip away: "all that stuff and all that nonsense" and "get to friendship with the people you live with, good food, a warm fire."

With some encouragement members also acknowledged their own vulnerabilities and recognised that relationships within the community could enable them to feel cared for. In response to a direct question about whether he had ever felt vulnerable Andrew Davey replied:

> I don't think I remember feeling in a sense at a loss, where I needed help. Well though actually, now, as I say that, I think there were one or two guests who actually helped me a lot, who drew closer, and were more willing to talk, because perhaps one had more time to talk with the guests than I did with the other members.

Stuart Affleck reflected on the tension between acknowledging that we are all vulnerable, and recognising the particular pain that leads to people becoming guests:

> I think that the struggle is not to say that you're not vulnerable, 'cause then that makes you really quite arrogant, that, 'Somehow, my life is different from yours.' It's actually, somehow keeping the balance and saying, 'Actually, my life is just like yours. It's different but it's just like yours and I have my vulnerabilities and my brokenness. It can never be the same as yours…' but I do believe that… I think that's what happened… sorry if I'm now… you're making me think while I'm speaking, which is interesting.

It *is* interesting that both Andrew and Stuart found themselves somewhat surprised as they were prompted to reflect on being on the receiving end of care from guests, and on the possibility of their own vulnerabilities. Their responses suggest that neither had previously considered these issues in quite this way. But one incident provided a focus for reflections from a number of people on how living together in community can unsettle the care giver, care receiver distinction. This was the experience of a young death in the community.

We have recounted Annie Hardie's story of coming to the community because her husband had a serious problem with alcohol. During her time there one of her teenage sons was killed in a motorcycle accident. Andrew arrived just after this event and described the community as being in: "an awful state of grief and trauma. Everybody, all the guests had shared in this trauma." He had a temporary leadership role in an interregnum between wardens and felt he had a role to help the community to "carry on living and whatever you do, to get through that."

Annie herself talked about what this meant to her, in the process acknowledging that loss is something that many who come to Pilsdon have experienced:

> When something happens, when the death of a child happens in the community <crying>, then we're all the same ... So, all the other people's remembrances of pain and loss come out and they just hold you, literally hold you, until you stop crying and they're there...You haven't got the luxury of saying, 'Oh, Pilsdon is going to close for two weeks until I regroup myself or sort myself out.' You can't because you've got everybody here and that would be so wrong, you could not do that... The easiest thing, the best thing to do, is just to be here and work through it. But all the people who would see that you were struggling sometimes and just step up and say, 'I'll finish making the bread,' or, 'Do you want me to do that? Do you want me to do the town run today?' or, 'I'll do the doctor's trip.' It made people step up, in a way, and help out and find resources perhaps they didn't know they had.

These different accounts highlight reciprocity in care giving and receiving. Everyone is exposed to both the strengths and vulnerabilities of others. Living alongside each other creates challenges and tensions, but also spaces in which it is possible to give and receive care regardless of the formal status of individuals concerned. Both guests and members may need to learn how to receive care and to care for themselves and, as we develop below, status differences are not completely erased. But an absence of any activity that is defined as a 'service' contributes to a practice of care that renders unhelpful an identity distinction based on whether one gives or receives care.

Receiving care

Care is not completed unless it is received. Care receiving is linked to the principle of *responsiveness* – how the person receiving care responds to the actions of the care giver. People's responses indicate whether the way in which care has been offered works for them and can help enhance attentiveness to the other. Sometimes people find it hard to receive care. This can make it harder to give. But care will be both more effective and more satisfying if there is a dialogue about how people feel and if both are able to contribute to the process of care. This builds a caring relationship.

Ann Davies offered an example of this:

Int: So, you talked a little bit about Stuart, going to see Stuart, getting support from him, advice from him or just chatting to him. What was the relationship but how did you experience the relationship between the warden and the guests in a sense? And what was important about that, what was difficult about it or what was your experience of that?

Ann: Well, I guess every guest and every member would probably experience it individually, obviously, but I don't know, Stuart was always very warm and kind and human and had a delicious smile and sense of humour and lit up. Extremely vocational, really his vocation was extraordinary. He sort of walked the walk, he walked the walk and yeah, so it was good to be alongside him, yeah.

Simon said of being invited to attend a leaving event for members that he felt: 'Just like a king on a throne I think, you know? I felt really privileged, like emotional, humble...' And Michael followed up his story of arriving in a really bad physical state with how things changed as a result of the bodily care he received:

> But it was the food you see, 'cause I was eating nothing and I found it hard to eat food. Once I started eating a dinner, getting a dinner down me I felt getting good again, you know what I mean? Sister Anne said to me once, 'Oh Michael, I've got a nice pair of boots for you.' I said, 'Oh lovely, thank you.' My feet were... well, they were as sore as anything as well. So she gave me a nice pair of boots, brand new socks and all that, brand new boots and oh I thought that was great, they were really comfortable.

Guests and wayfarers spoke of feeling healed and changed by the time they spent at Pilsdon. This doesn't mean it worked for everyone and that all relationships were experienced positively. Ruth reflected on some of the problems associated with the lack of care some people had experienced before coming:

I will just say that I quite often observed relationships, sort of, going wrong there and I think the reason was because a lot of people were very, very vulnerable and needy and maybe hadn't had anybody taking much notice of them since goodness knows when.

And Rosemary Cortes responded to a question about whether she and others felt cared for at Pilsdon:

I think some people would never feel cared for enough. <Laughs> I had my due share of attention, let's put it that way, and if I ever wanted more, that's probably something to do with me, not them. <Laughs> The attention seeker looms large in a lot of people and of course, in Pilsdon one person can't loom too large, it's got to be a shared thing, a shared community.

This suggestion that the need to receive care is associated with attention seeking perhaps reflects the way that to receive care can be linked with a deficit. Others recognise that it can be hard to ask for help:

And the thing is, we may be living in community but it doesn't mean you have to like everybody, or always be open to everybody, 'cause we're all struggling, we all have our own demons, and whatever they are, and if it's a bad time... I'm really bad about bottling things up, and then they come out at force, at whoever's around. Because I find it very difficult to ask for help, and when it's refused I find that an absolute slap in the face. (Emma and Nicky conversation)

A similar point was made in the conversation between Bob and Daniel:

> … before, I've shared personal things and I've made mistakes and I've automatically gone into a defence mode where I'm waiting for everybody to attack me or come out with some sarcastic comment. In Pilsdon, that's not the case. It's a very loving, kind place where you can just roll with it.

Learning how to receive care is part of the task for those who seek shelter there. Alex:

> To me, what the members here wanna do, their objective, is just to walk beside you for a while 'til you get well. … That is all they wanna do, is walk beside you and make sure you're alright.' You've got to be willing to let them, that's the first thing. It takes time to build trust, for them to trust you and you to trust them

Self Care

Learning to both give and receive care also involves caring for one's self. And caring for one's self requires recognising you are worth caring for. Simon said:

> I had this sort of argument with a Jesuit priest and he said, 'Do you love yourself, Simon?' I said, 'No, not really.' He said, 'Well, if you don't love yourself, how can you love someone else?' That made me think.

It can be difficult to care for yourself at the same time as confronting the impact of selfish, addictive behaviour on others. Working out how to balance necessary care for oneself at the same time as how to care for others is, perhaps, one of the major challenges for those who spend part of their lives at Pilsdon – members as well as guests. Daniel said:

> Pilsdon doesn't hold anything against you if you just say, 'Look, I just need a break,' or, 'I don't feel like doing that today.' This is a unique opportunity to look after myself and I've learnt to love myself. Now, that's a massive statement. People said that to me in the past, saying, 'All you do is care about yourself.' Well, in a selfish way, yeah, I did but now, selflessly, I try to care for myself in a better way.

The acceptance offered to those who come as guests needs to be turned inwards and this can be hard. Again, Alex spoke about the significance of enabling a realisation of self before being able to confront more deep-rooted problems:

> I was just sort of here and not really quite knowing why or what I'm doing. Michael always said to me, 'Just stay. There doesn't really have to be a reason.' He said, 'Just stay and look after yourself.' When all the drugs thing had subsided, I'm sure there was a certain amount of psychosis and stuff there from the drugs I was doing. … You have to get through all the psychoses left by drugs to work out what's actually, genuinely your mental problems and what are the side effects of years of drug abuse. Yeah, so it took a while to get to those, and we did.

Some guests recognised the need to get away from the constant demands of being with others in order to care for themselves. The physical environment enabled this: Ann Davis talked of going to lie in the meadow and "just have breathing space". For members whose role is more obviously associated with a responsibility to care for others recognising their own vulnerabilities and their needs to care for themselves often requires conscious cultivation. Care ethicist Eva Kittay (1999) writes of "nested dependencies" and the necessity for care givers also to receive care. Those who do not care for themselves are poorly placed to care for others. This is one way of understanding the significance of their faith for members. People have expressed this in different ways, but fundamentally faith provides a source of sustenance that can be internalised as well as offering a point of reference beyond themselves.

In practical terms an allowance for spending time at a retreat and access to spiritual directors have been designed to provide a space and time during which members can renew themselves. Mary Barnett spoke of the "magical space" offered by retreats run by a Methodist minister that offered her sustenance. But she also recognised that key to the way Pilsdon works is to enable members to feel that they are not alone in holding others' pain: "everyone is holding everybody as it were." Thus while, as Sue Langdon reflected, members take "quite a lot of responsibility for our own emotional housekeeping", facilitated away days and other opportunities for members to reflect together enable individual members to meet their own needs for care. Some suggested that living with a partner at Pilsdon offered more opportunity to experience personal support.

But Mary Barnett also wondered whether she and Peter had been able to focus as much on themselves as they needed to whilst they were there. Sue Langdon was concerned that Michael Deegan did not have the opportunity offered by a partner to take time out and had deliberately invited him to have a meal with her from time to time in order to get away from the community.

Underpinning most of the reflection of members and wardens on the issue of self-care is the question of time. Time to take a regular break during their working life there. And time in terms of how long it is possible to live in the intense and demanding manner this life requires.

RESPONSIBILITY

Living in close relationship to others is essential to the meaning and practice of community. But what do these stories suggest about how responsibility is understood and enacted in this context? In Tronto's analysis of the phases of care, taking care of, responsibility, underpins the shift from attentiveness towards the active practice of care. At its most basic, there is no point in feeling concerned about someone and not doing anything about it. Accepting the implications of caring about necessitates an acceptance of responsibility to act, often in ways that require putting to one side one's own concerns. This is challenging, not least because both self-care and care for those who give care are also necessary to a care ethical way of living. Care ethics requires us to hold, at the same time, an ability and preparedness to act in response to the needs of others, to recognise and respond to our own needs for care, and to accept care from others.

In professional contexts caring responsibilities are often enshrined in professional ethical codes. For unpaid care givers, family members or friends, a sense of responsibility comes from personal relationship and a broader awareness of societal expectations. A tension between societal expectations, personal desires and interpersonal relationships can often mean decisions about providing hands on care can be a significant source of individual troubles and family conflict. The situation at Pilsdon is different. Whilst it is sometimes described as a family, relationships within the community are not kin relationships. Our consideration of Pilsdon as a place of care needs a different perspective on responsibility from both family care and professional service provision.

It is helpful to look at other types of collective living and working to understand how responsibility is felt and enacted. For example, research into relationships amongst young people in residential care has demonstrated attentiveness to others who are experiencing similar troubles and responses based in shared knowledge (Emond, 2003). Collective action amongst disabled people and in mental health service user groups demonstrates the value of shared experiences in sustaining both caring relationships and political action (Barnes, 2007). Friendships amongst women with mental health problems and amongst young people with learning disabilities using collective services illustrate how such spaces can enable a caring solidarity even when the service itself is considered to be patronising. But how do we think about peer responsibilities in these types of context? This is a question that has received little attention. It is an issue to which the Pilsdon interviews can make an important contribution.

Responsibility featured in interviews from different perspectives. Responsibility was a specific focus for discussion with wardens because of the distinctiveness of their role. That included discussion about responsibilities for the maintenance of the fabric of the buildings, for external relationships and for financial management. But wardens also spoke of their roles in sustaining an environment in which people could be cared for (chapter 5) and a key focus for discussion of responsibility in wardens' interviews related to decisions about requiring guests to leave if they were using alcohol or drugs. We cited Peter Barnett who described a situation soon after his arrival when he agreed to overlook an instance of this and the disruptive impact this had on others.

Adam Dickens also spoke of his attempts to hold a situation and find an alternative place for someone to move to rather than simply asking them to leave. That took a toll on both the warden and members. The warden at the time of the history project, Michael Deegan, also emphasised the importance of maintaining a safe environment for people and that can require members to undertake advocacy roles that constitute expressions of responsibility going beyond the space of the community itself. Peter cited an example of action to obtain appropriate help for a woman experiencing many difficulties and not making any progress at Pilsdon. That involved taking her to a London hospital for assessment, then lobbying MPs, the NHS, and social care services to find her an appropriate service.

Members spoke about responsibilities for ensuring a safe space for all who come to the community, including the animals that live there. Guests and wayfarers also recognised responsibilities to act in ways that would not be damaging to others. Ann Davies for example, talked of the importance of ensuring rules regarding alcohol, drugs and aggressive behaviour were applied:

> ...if somebody got very drunk and very aggressive verbally, I mean I remember a few of us women, I remember Helen and I heading to the chapel because we just didn't want to be anywhere near that and just waiting until it was over and that person was removed.

Michael O'Shaughnessy, approvingly, told a story of the local bishop being asked to leave early in the community's history because he had come for lunch with alcohol on his breath. Michael also criticised people he thought took advantage of Pilsdon when they did not really need it:

> there's some wayfarers coming here ... they really get me down because they're coming here for years and years and years ... and they've got flats and they're getting social security and they're getting this and they're getting that and they never turn around and say, 'Well, thanks very much for a long weekend, here's 20 quid.' See that goes a long way towards Pilsdon, but they're not worried about Pilsdon really, a lot of them, they're not, they don't care about Pilsdon but they want it when they want a lie down, you know what I mean?

Most recognised that living in community with others whose lives are difficult and chaotic creates challenges. For that to work people have to play by the rules and if they don't no one will feel safe and cared for. There is an awareness not only of responsibilities to specific others, but also to the community as a whole – both now and in the future. In Michael's words, people need to 'care about' the community. Bill Scanlon reflected on the way in which responsibility to the community could also involve leaving it:

> I get a bit confused because I get the whole ethos of being a community, you're in a community, you wanna be in a community, you wanna live in a community, that's what you wanna do. And on the flipside of that coin people come here, they are very ill, mental health problems, alcohol problems, drug problems or all three ...Right, this is my point of view, I came here, got well, left, so that someone else could come here, get well and leave, and then that person could leave, ... I'm not selfish, so move over, let someone else get well. ... I just see it like that. The core of the community will always change, the members will *always* change, the warden will *always* change, the community is the people that are here for a long period of time or even indefinitely because they *have* to be. If they don't have to be, move over and let someone else get well, that's how I see it.

CARING WITH: SOLIDARITY

Bill's perspective is important in identifying the way in which the community is in constant flux. People come and go – and should do so if its benefits are to be more broadly experienced. The importance of caring for the community is a key way in which the Pilsdon experience offers a different perspective on care from dominant narratives of this. Google images of care and you will find images of two people of whom one is care giver, the other care receiver: a mother and baby, nurse and old person, perhaps a person with learning disabilities and a support worker. As we have seen, care at Pilson is both reciprocal and distributed. But more than that, the focus for care goes beyond the individuals who live there. It is both a community of people who come together and then move on, and a physical place that predated and will outlast the people who have made it their home. Whilst we need to understand the significance of Pilsdon in the individual lives of the people we talked to for this project, and to acknowledge that 'Pilsdon' is that shifting community of people, we also need to understand the significance of Pilsdon as an enduring project.

The notion of 'caring with' emphasises the political necessity and significance of care. This is linked to the recognition that care is necessary to both justice and wellbeing. Collective decisions about how we respond to those who may be vulnerable, ill or suffering loss, stigma and pain reflect the extent to which we are prepared to live in solidarity with others. This is not some simplistic trope of being 'all in it together', but a profound recognition of the essential interconnectedness of humanity and the more than human world. Practices in which care is valued and shared are more likely to sustain connections and increase understanding of what is necessary to live as well as possible in the world than are practices that separate and individualise troubles.

This is reflected in comments from some about the importance of knowing that Pilsdon is there even though they have not lived there for some time. Simon Smith talked of trying to resist his "craving" for Pilsdon, but for him and other wayfarers knowing they can spend time there sustains them in their capacity to live the life they have chosen. One of the themes of interviews was the mix of people you would encounter if you spent time there and the opportunity to get to know and understand lives beyond your own experience. That includes accepting that pain and vulnerability are part of the human condition and that expressions of this should also be accepted. Hilary Joyce:

> ...one girl who was there, who had developed epilepsy in her late twenties ...she needed to be around people so that when she had fits ... we used to all shuffle up on the sofa and support her while she was having a fit. That became very normal. There were all sorts of things about Pilsdon that would be considered quite abnormal in other places, like people would suddenly burst into tears and everyone would just think, 'Oh ... someone's crying'...

Hilary's description of encounters in which everyday care is a taken for granted part of life is an embodiment of the democratic caring implied by 'caring with'. Care at Pilsdon is not explicitly debated or deliberated amongst everyone, but all are engaged in it in some way. And, having had the experience of living with others in this way, many return, hold on to the possibility of return, or are simply glad that it is there in case they or anyone else needs it. For some people Pilsdon's significance in this way can be understood as explicitly political as well as personal. Pilsdon embodies a different way of living together, prioritising different values from those dominating mainstream life, and its continuing existence offers hope that collective care for others endures in spite of the dominance of individualism in western culture. James Morris suggested that powerful people could be changed for the collective good by spending time at Pilsdon:

> I think if some of the world leaders came here just for a weekend, they'd completely chill out and think, 'Wow, what a wonderful amazing life that you could actually have.' That's looking at communities as not just a way of life, but as life, as peace and tranquillity, as we could all live together, regardless of what we believe in or what the colour of our skin, or gender or whatever, on a neutral, equal level. Just do that.

CONCLUSION

Care is an ethically and politically charged practice. It changes those involved in caring relationships. It involves giving and receiving and happens in diverse and apparently mundane everyday encounters. Pilsdon offers a very different approach to care from those that dominate statutory and professional services. In the interviews this was narrated by reference to the importance of everyday interactions and relationships. Some narrated this by reference to faith:

In the day-to-day of this community, that's where the commitment is. We hold each other accountable but the commitment is really with God. When you start adding pastures and farm and animals and human beings and everything that this place holds, your relationship, your ability to do this is… it's not a direct line. It's not between you and another person, it's really a triangle. It's between you and God and that person and that person and God and you. (Michael Deegan)

Pilsdon is a physical place: an old house; gardens; soil; plants; animals and the work that is necessary to sustain them. Pilsdon is a coming together of people in a fluid mix of relationships that are complex, difficult and nurturing. Pilsdon is a way of enacting caring life together in which, when it works, people and place are engaged in a process of interweaving and creating a life sustaining web.

For some, what we have discussed here as an ethic of care is grounded in and sustained by Christian faith. This was fundamental to Percy and Gaynor's vision for Pilsdon and has been core to the wardens and members who have followed in their footsteps. For all those who embrace the opportunities offered by Pilsdon, acceptance, concern and respect for other people, for the animals and the physical world ground and sustain the doing of care and also constitute the practices of care. For those who profess a Christian faith and those who do not, being part of an enduring project that seeks to offer hospitality and care for those who are excluded, marginalised and broken enables them to contribute to the solidarity of 'caring with' others. The necessity of this to the possibility of living well together and contributing to social justice is key to the longevity of Pilsdon. The need endures, and so does the preparedness to accept responsibility. Alex Kelly:

> Well, I think it endures because people come and go, the structure changes, the buildings change, it gets refurbed but it comes back to that ethos that's at the heart of it. It does good … It's just a genuinely good thing in the world to have. From my point of view, if something is good and has a strong heart, it'll last, that ethos, which is its heart, it will last and it'll probably go on forever. I hope it does, anyway… There'll always be people who want to help and they'll always come here and they'll find this place and there are always gonna be people who need help. As long as there's that, there'll always be Pilsdon.

CHAPTER 7

———

Pilsdon: A Place in Space and Time

One of the themes that our reflections on Pilsdon as a place of care highlights is the importance of time in enabling caring relationships to form. We have also suggested that Pilsdon remains important to people after they have moved on: its significance endures in the knowledge that the place is still there, even if you are no longer in that space. In this chapter we focus more specifically on space and time.

The origins of this book are in an oral history project conducted as the community was approaching its 60th anniversary in 2018. However, the book does not offer an historical account – that did not seem the most helpful way of trying to communicate what the Pilsdon Community is, nor what it has meant for people throughout its history. But the questions of what has changed, what remains the same and what accounts for its endurance when many attempts at communal living break down after a few years, have recurred in interviews and conversations about the project. Here we offer reflections on Pilsdon as a place that has survived, struggled and flourished throughout a period of significant social, cultural and policy changes during the second half of the twentieth century and now into the third decade of the twenty first century. We reflect on key themes that we have identified throughout this account: those of community and solidarities; of living the faith; of the continuity of values and practices; of accepting vulnerability and seeking ways of enabling repair both individually and in the ways in which we live together in the world. We acknowledge the way in which the spatial reality of the buildings and the land intersect with the relational and spiritual dimensions of life within the community. We locate the responses of those who have been part of the Pilsdon Community with key changes taking place nationally and internationally in ideas and practices about community, and about responses to mental illness and addictions. Our perspective here is on the way that change and continuity co-exist and interact at Pilsdon across space and time.

The Pilsdon Community is in a constant state of being made. Through the mundane everyday interactions amongst a shifting assembly of people whose lives become entangled in this place; through the continued cultivation of the land that grows fruit and vegetables that feed the community; and through the seasonal care of animals whose lives are intertwined with those of the people, the community recreates itself and supports and nurtures those who are part of it. Through conversations about the place, past events within the community and the ideas that nourish the people who come together here, the significance of the community is explored, developed and reinforced. And through the maintenance and development of the buildings that offer shelter and a space to be together, the spatial reality of Pilsdon as a place of safety and of spiritual life sustains the initial vision of Percy and Gaynor in what is a substantially different historical context. As we embarked on conversations about this book a note of caution was expressed by one of those taking part. Would the process of discussion and writing impact the community? Would this in itself change things? To which the answer is yes, because all such conversations and the personal reflections they give rise to contribute to the making of Pilsdon. It is neither possible nor desirable to suggest that the community is established, has reached an end state, and is not rather a dynamic process of living, working and caring together. Writing this book is a part of the process of community making. The conversations that have taken place and the book that has emerged from talking and writing make their own contribution to what Pilsdon *is*.

If Pilsdon is in a constant state of being made, then the question of whether the community in 2018, when the oral history project took place, was the same as when Percy and Gaynor established it in 1958 is not the key question. The community has endured and much of what is regarded as core to its values and purpose as we write this in 2020 would be very recognisable to those who first came together over 60 years ago. At the same time, if we understand Pilsdon as a series of relations between the people who come and go, and the animals, land, plants and things that make up the community, these are in a constant state of flux. And what happens within the community intersects with changes beyond its boundaries. Though spatially distant from centres of population and in some ways isolated from the everyday realities of most people's lives, the interactions within the community, the formal requirements that have shaped specific changes, and the ideas and cultures that are debated within the walls of this 17th century manor house, are both different from and yet similar to those familiar to the original residents of the community. Pilsdon remains Pilsdon.

Doreen Massey was a social geographer who wrote eloquently about the way in which a relational understanding of the world unsettles the taken-for-granted notion that space is necessarily boundaried, that space must exist within the confines of a specific physical location: "If we really think space relationally, then it is the sum of all our connections, and in that sense utterly grounded, and those connections may go round the world." (Massey, 2005, p. 185) The hospitality that is at the core of the Pilsdon ethos requires an openness to connections that actually and potentially go round the world. So it is not separate from the changes taking place around the world. As we were writing this we (David and Marian) were unable to visit Pilsdon because of the impact of Covid 19 that caused lockdown within the space of a household. For Pilsdon, the implications were profound: there has always been a sign on the track leading to the house which says 'Welcome to the Pilsdon Community'; now, a new sign was placed in front of this stating that the community was closed to all but essential visitors. The global impact of a contagious virus demonstrates with utter clarity our interconnectedness, whilst also constraining hospitality to outsiders. In time this particular challenge will pass and one question that was being asked from early in the crisis was what impact this experience will have on ethical and political recognition of our essential interdependency. In the final chapter we reflect on what some of those who were resident in the community experienced during the lockdown and on the broader consequences of the pandemic for Pilsdon. Relationships both within and beyond the community did change during this time. If places and spaces are constantly being made through relational processes then we have to think about space and time together: "As the 'past continues in our present' so also is the distant implicated in our 'here'" (Massey, 2005, p.192). The ethical implications of this are precisely what the relational and political ethics of care which we considered in chapter 6 help us to understand and enact.

As we explore the nature of the changes that the Pilsdon community has experienced over 60 years, we hold understandings of a very different world in the third decade of the twenty-first century from that of the mid-twentieth century when Pilsdon was founded. At the same time, we recognise the enduring significance of what the community means in the lives of those who have been part of it. One practical illustration of this is that, for those not familiar with the people whose stories we were reading in interview transcripts, it was often not possible to locate their stories in time – we had to look for specific markers or references to events to locate an account in the 1980s or 2010s, for example. In chapter 8 Mary starts her reflections on Pilsdon with her sense of familiarity in hearing accounts of earlier life in the community that mirrored her everyday experience. But we do need to consider some of the key differences that mark Pilsdon's time of origin and it's 60th anniversary and we draw on interviews to illustrate key aspects of that. We start with ideas of 'community'.

COMMUNITY IN AN INDIVIDUALIZED SOCIETY

As we described in the introduction, Pilsdon is an 'intentional community'. Those who live and work there as members have taken an explicit decision to move there, for an agreed period or as an open-ended commitment that depends on their wishes or on the quality of the relationships and experiences that develop whilst they are there. Communities based in such decisions have existed for centuries across the globe: monasteries, communes, kibbutzim, housing cooperatives, ashrams, ecovillages. These vary as to whether they are religious or secular; own the land and dwellings that they occupy; hold all resources in common; attempt to practise self-sufficiency, and provide services or support to people in need. They also vary in regard to criteria for community membership and to forms of governance. Living in community is a positive choice for some for whom ordinary life or 'normality' has not been experienced as a source of inclusion, and for others who want to live according to different values from those of mainstream society. In the counter-culture of the 1960s and 70s residential communes were spaces in which to live in avowedly alternative ways and the growth of environmental movements has generated numerous examples of collective living focused on creating more sustainable lifestyles.

Visiting examples of residential communities in different countries was the source of Tobias Jones' (2007) book *Utopian Dreams*. His visit to Pilsdon as part of this project was the inspiration behind his subsequent establishment of the Windsor Hill Wood community (Jones, 2015).

But the concept of community has been invoked in many different ways in public and social policy. Eric Hobsbawm (1994) suggested the term has been used: "indiscriminately and emptily" in social and political discourse. It is applied to geographical locality; to shared interests; employment or professional identities; to shared religious or cultural commitments; to ethnicities; sexualities; identities as disabled people, and more (Prior, Stewart and Walsh 1995, pp. 153-157). A distinction is made between 'communities of choice', which people freely elect to join and are equally free to leave, and 'communities of fate', to which people are classified as belonging regardless of their personal preferences and from which they can only escape with difficulty (Hirst 1994). Community is a term that is generally imbued with a positive sense of warmth and solidarity. But many people feel excluded from a geographical community because of characteristics that might locate them in a community of identity or fate that is regarded as deviant or simply different. This includes many people who live with mental health problems (Dunn, 1999). And one of the key challenges in contemporary societies is how people who do not share characteristics, interests or identities can live well together within a shared space. The increasing population diversity resulting from migration, itself a characteristic of an increasingly interconnected world as well as resulting from the shocks of climate change, intolerance and conflict, require better ways of forging solidarities amongst different people living together in the same place (Agustin and Jorgensen, 2019).

The tension between communitarian and individualistic philosophies and politics has been a feature of both scholarly analysis and everyday ethics for much of the twentieth century. The rational, choice making individual of right-wing economists dominated neo-liberal policy making in the late twentieth century, but many, from different perspectives, are making strong arguments that neither this conception of humanity, nor the economic, political and social relations it has given rise to, is sustainable (Mason, 2015; Tronto, 2017). Those commentators on contemporary western society and culture who contrasted community-based forms of human interaction with the individualism characteristic of modern capitalist democracies (e.g. Bauman 2001; Beck and Beck-Gernsheim 2002) noted the isolating impact of individualisation. Bauman suggested that risks, problems and catastrophes which may have collective origins and be susceptible to collective responses: "seem to fall upon each one of us at random, as individual problems, of the kind that could be confronted only individually, and repaired, if at all, by individual efforts" (2001, p.149). In the context of policies relating to health, social care and welfare, and the practices through which they were delivered, a positive focus on the individual rather than the collective led to the conclusion that individual problems required individual solutions.

Within the period during which the Pilsdon Community has existed the intersection between ideas about community, individualisation and how to respond to people living with mental illness has undergone radical changes. When the Pilsdon Community was founded in 1958 long stay psychiatric hospitals were still a feature of the English countryside. In Dorset, the county where Pilsdon is located, Herrison Hospital provided long stay accommodation for patients in what was considered a self-supporting community, comprising farm, laundry, ballroom, cinema, theatre, chapel, dentist as well as wards and treatment rooms. At its height, in 1913, Herrison accommodated 957 patients. By 1979 that had reduced to 200, but it did not close until 1992, 34 years after the Pilsdon Community was founded. Today some of the old hospital buildings have been converted into smart apartments, the chapel is a health spa and the site is now the location of the village of Charlton Down. Similar changes have taken place across the country. It is no longer considered appropriate to seclude people with long term mental health problems in places separate from the rest of the population.

Evidence of abuse within these largely closed spaces and changing ideas about the best way to respond to the needs of people living with mental health problems, learning and other disabilities, led to the closure of long stay hospitals and the development of community care as the dominant policy response to needs. There were many positive aspects of this. Long stay institutions had separated out and made invisible people regarded as other and had reinforced a stereotyping of them as mad, dangerous and incapable of living ordinary lives (Prior, 1993). Emerging collective action amongst people who described themselves variously as survivors, users or consumers of services, disabled people or peer advocates supported such closures and went beyond this to campaign for broader recognition of their rights to live, be educated, work, travel, participate in cultural and leisure activities alongside everyone else (Barnes and Bowl, 2001; Sayce, 2000). But what did community care mean in practice? Assumptions that communities, defined as people living in proximity within a specific locality, would care for those discharged into their midst could not be relied upon. The historical tradition of foster care in Geel, Belgium, for those experiencing 'insanity' predates community care policy by centuries and offers an unusual example of a response based both in religious practices and a deliberate attempt at the integration of people with mental illness into 'normal' life (Roosens and Van de Walle, 2007). While long stay hospital closures led to some positive examples of neighbourhood care, too often community care meant limited support in what were effectively much smaller institutions; revolving door admissions to inappropriate psychiatric wards in general hospitals; and/or families shouldering complex responsibilities as the state stepped back in the interests of encouraging ordinary lives. In 1999 a report by MIND (a major UK mental health charity) into social exclusion argued that: "The ethos of segregation that underpinned mass institutionalisations remains. The brick walls of the old institutions have been replaced by economic and social barriers within 'the community'; they are less obvious, but just as effective" (Dunn, 1999: p.6). The report went on to cite diverse examples of discrimination, disadvantage, violence and devaluing experienced by people living with mental illness. It argued the need to create 'accepting communities.'

By definition community care policy assumed a disjuncture between residential institutions such as long stay hospitals and the community. Institutionalisation was associated with a lack of individual choice in day-to-day life and the requirement for individuals to fit a professionally dominated regime in long stay hospitals and residential homes. This came under fire from an increasing emphasis on the individual as a person capable of rational choices to whom services should be responsive. The development of markets in services was promoted to enable potential users to shop around for the services that best fit their needs and preferences. Critiques of this noted, amongst other things, that at those times when people were feeling particularly vulnerable, collecting information about different suppliers in order to weigh up the evidence and make an informed decision did not accurately describe the process that most went through to access help (Barnes and Prior 1995). But beyond this, the dominance of individualist ideology assumed that individualised care and services were both better and preferred by those living with disability, mental illness, physical health problems associated with growing older, or other problems of ordinary life. The actual and potential benefits of *collective* services were thus obscured and devalued. In her conclusion to her history of Severalls Psychiatric Hospital, Gittins noted:

> Certainly nobody I spoke to who had been a patient at Severalls expressed a desire to return to large, overcrowded wards, and some said how much they appreciated the greater privacy and comfort they now have in the new acute units. Almost all of them, however, said how incredibly

important the grounds of Severalls, the time they were able to spend there, the human contact with other patients, with certain nurses, occasionally with doctors, were to them. As one woman patient said: 'There's always a lot of love up there, or there always was. And every time I was in, there was some would give me this extra flush of love. It might be staff, it might be visitors, but there was always someone...' (Gittins, 1998, p. 221)

Some collective models of support survived the dominance of individualism. The therapeutic community movement continued to offer opportunities for healing though interaction with others. As is often the case, what constitutes a therapeutic community (TC) can be both disputed and diverse. Particular TCs have focussed on different groups including offenders, children and adolescents, people with acute psychoses and people with learning difficulties. What is common to such communities is the centrality of treatment – the therapeutic process around which the community is organised (Kennard, 2004). It is this emphasis on treatment as the principal goal that marks a key difference between TCs and the Pilsdon Community, which makes no claim to provide treatment. Treatment assumes designated professionals trained to intervene according to specific models. In spite of claims to practice democracy as well as therapy, the categorical distinction between staff and patients remains and can be the source of conflict within TCs (Spandler, 2006). As we have seen, whilst there is a distinction between members and guests, the commitment to live alongside creates a very different basis for relationships within the Pilsdon Community.

The move from institutional to community care was also influenced by the development of a more optimistic view of the trajectory of mental illness. The development of new forms of medications seemed to hold out the prospect of, if not cure, then at least control of damaging symptoms. And with the emergence of the concept of recovery the possibility of former psychiatric patients living good quality lives in community settings became further established. The concept of recovery has itself been contested, but gained prominence within both clinical and user led thinking about holistic responses to mental distress (Repper and Perkins, 2013). It has been argued that the acceptance of recovery as a basis for holistic responses to mental health difficulties has enabled better integration between services for those with psychiatric diagnoses and those seeking help for addictions. Many of those who come to Pilsdon are experiencing the consequences of both addiction and mental illness. The involvement of peer support workers in Recovery Colleges and other service contexts marks a recognition that those who live with mental distress can also contribute to others' recovery and wellbeing. The experiential knowledge of those living with and recovering from addictions has also been promoted as valuable, albeit still a site of struggle (Staddon, 2015). Relationships between mental health professionals and service users have undergone important changes which reflect broader recognition of the value of experiential knowledge as well as the fluidity of identities that make it hard, if not impossible, to define people solely by reference to a psychiatric diagnosis or its absence (Barnes, 2015).

Examples of different models of collective support have also developed within the disability and survivor movement. Even when the purpose has been that of campaigning or advocacy rather than offering support services, collective action amongst users and survivors created spaces in which people who knew what others were going through because they had had similar experiences could offer peer support (Barnes and Gell, 2012). And in some instances service users established their own spaces focused specifically on support, whether as informal drop-ins that do not require people to define themselves by reference to a diagnosis or treatment need, or, in the case of the Nottingham Advocacy Group's 'Ecoworks' project, initiatives that link the experience of mental distress both with the need to address poverty, and offer a space in which to come together, grow and cook food and engage in other environmentally sustainable creative work. The value of relationships amongst those who recognise their vulnerabilities, and the potential for living well together in a space that respects the more than human as well as the human world, has been the basis for alternative sources of care and repair whilst individualism has dominated mainstream services.

COMMUNITY AT PILSDON

Pilsdon's origins are within very different traditions from those being contested within mainstream mental health services. They lie within a Christian tradition that combines spiritual life with help to those in need. In *Pilsdon Morning* Gaynor Smith wrote of the influence of Nicholas Ferrar:

Percy's whole being assented to the way of life that existed at Little Gidding and his mind and heart were fired by the personality of Nicholas Ferrar himself. Here was a possible ideal, a life that was almost monastic but surrounded by the family and offering help to all who needed it. This was monasticism with a difference, a difference which made it a viable way of life for a married man in the twentieth century (Smith, 2008, p. 23).

'Monasticism with a difference' characterises the development of a number of different religious communities during the time that Pilsdon has been in existence. Sometimes called 'the new monasticism' this movement reflects a desire of many people to live in community in order to go deeper into a life of prayer, spirituality and service (Vincent, 2011; Wilson-Hartgrove, 2008). The movement takes its inspiration from the very first explicitly Christian community formed by the followers of Jesus, and from the early Celtic communities that adopted the rule of St Benedict. Little Gidding was a rare later example of this approach to community living. Twentieth century pioneering communities, led by charismatic Christian leaders such as George MacLeod with the Iona Community, gave further impetus to the development of the new monasticism. A key characteristic is the desire to overcome the dualism of the divine and the earthly by fully engaging with the world while practicing Christian principles; what Craig Gardiner refers to as "worldly monasticism" (Gardiner, 2018, p. 86ff).

The intentional communities that exist in the UK such as Scargill in Yorkshire, the Northumbria Community, the Community of St Anselms' in London, the Bruderhof, the l'Arche communities, Lee Abbey in Devon and the Leicester Tree of Life, as well as the Pilsdon Community, follow different rules and differ in their precise objectives. Some ask for celibacy during the time people live there as members, others do not. Some are structured to enable people to be members of the community whilst also retaining a work life outside. Some adopt what might be considered an outreach approach to services, and some offer structured programmes to guests who come solely to participate in them for short periods or to spend time in their own quiet reflection. They follow different spiritual guides: Franciscan, Ignatian, Benedictine and Celtic; and they vary in the emphasis they give to the pursuit of specifically religious goals. Nevertheless, Vincent (2011) identifies a number of common threads that run through these communities, including believing in and practicing smallness, seeking simplicity of life and being counter-cultural. The belief that living well with others should take priority over an individualised mode of life has a long and enduring history and is one of the key continuities sustaining Pilsdon throughout its history.

A distinguishing feature of community as enacted at Pilsdon is the emphasis on unconditional hospitality. It is a community that welcomes all with the invitation to live alongside. It is the only one among these new monastic communities that offers an environment in which members and guests live alongside each other for extended periods, joined for what are short, but sometimes frequent visits by wayfarers and others who are homeless and in need of emergency shelter. It seeks to offer the acceptance to people living with addictions or mental health difficulties that the MIND inquiry into the consequences of community care policy identified as lacking (Dunn, 1999).

So how do those who have experienced life at Pilsdon describe its community ethos? In her interview Gaynor reinforced the significance of the Little Gidding influence. Following its example, Percy and Gaynor saw the regular practice of prayer as the foundation on which Pilsdon should be built and sustained: "It's the prayer life, I think, really. It's been sustained by its prayer life" (Gaynor). But Little Gidding had also been established as a quite deliberate rejection of the dominant religious, political and social values of the time, as an attempt to create a way of collective living marked by simplicity and honesty. Little Gidding was, in its day, counter-cultural, and this opposition to dominant norms and practices is a core characteristic of Pilsdon, challenging the emphasis of neo-liberalism on models of social action based on the choices of individual economic actors.

> ... if you put it in Christian terms, we're working for the Kingdom, and the Kingdom is counter-cultural. I don't know quite how to put it succinctly in political terms, but yes, I think we are doing something that is holding a candle to the world to say, 'Actually, there's another way of living, there's another way of being.' We run counter to individualism. We're saying, 'It's actually better to do it together.' (Andrew Davey)

> The reason why Pilsdon is prophetic, I believe, is because it is very countercultural in so many ways ... there is no

monetary value to anything that involves the residents of Pilsdon. You are not valued monetarily by what you do or by who you are or what your circumstances are, whereas everything today seems to be how much are you worth or how much do you earn or what is it worth? … And that is what is so contrary to 20th, 21st century priorities, where the individual is all-important and all-powerful and we are a very individualistic society you might say and we have often lost what the nature of community is and how we express the common good for all involved which might be the individual good. (Peter Barnett)

The failures of some forms of alternative communal living indicate that there can be dangers in this prioritising of the community as an expression of the common good over the wants and needs of the individual. James Morris has spent time in many communities and contrasted Pilsdon with some others:

JM: I've been to communities where whatever the community's belief system is, the belief system has taken over the community. That's crazy. That's more and more institutionalisation. And it becomes quite cultic in a way, and it's not the answer, really.

Int: So do you think Pilsdon does that?

JM: No, no, I think it's very relaxed really, I think Pilsdon is quite relaxed, as a Christian community.

The value of community does not, in the Pilsdon ethos, lead either to a set of relations in which subjects are subordinate to collective doctrine, nor to an institution with strict lines of hierarchy and discipline. These can be the outcomes of a rigid communitarian doctrine, and as damaging as strict adherence to an individualised market-based approach. Rather, the aim is for people to flourish through participation in community: through the act of living together. Thus, whilst Pilsdon is an explicitly Christian community:

> ... we also say that the community is open and available to all faiths and none and we had the joy of having both Jews and Muslims, Hindu, as well as every conceivable Christian denomination, as well as people escaping, what I would call sectarian type of existence to bring back their sanity where it had been over authoritarian, to put it mildly, to the extent of abuse. And we're able to say that and to do that by, yes, in the eyes of many people having quite a liberal approach to this. I mean some residential detoxification is run by evangelical Christians who, you know, make compulsory prayers and bible study and all the rest of it for all concerned, which I'm afraid I cannot go along with. (Peter Barnett)

One aspect of this 'liberal' approach to community living is that the structures or rules that need to be in place in order for the community to function and survive are often not immediately apparent, yet are sustained over time despite inevitable changes in other elements of the community's operations.

When I first came [as prospective Warden] the thing that struck me was the ease and openness of all the people here – members, volunteers, guests … There was an ease around people. I knew that Pilsdon had been in existence for a very long time but my initial experiences were more, 'What was it today?' Approaching it as possibly being the leader of it, for me, was more about, 'What is it? What holds it together?' … I knew the history, I'd read *Pilsdon Morning* so I sort of knew where it came from and my experience didn't completely resemble that because it had modernised a bit … it took a while to recognise that the ethos was the same, the certain principles or the ways of living together actually were still there. That was something it took me a little bit longer to recognise; that it still did all the same things but just slightly differently. It changed with the times, it had moved a bit but it was the same. (Michael Deegan)

Sustaining this ethos based on what is necessary to live with people who have been thrown together is key to understanding the nature of community as enacted at Pilsdon and why and how it has continued for over 60 years. Interviewees talked, in different ways, about what was referred to as "radical hospitality": the willingness to accept people as they are, to welcome them in, to live alongside them without requiring a specific objective:

If you have got a community, then all is welcome, everybody is welcome. I've been to all sorts of different communities and the very heart of the community is to welcome people into that community. It's how we should all be living. I truly believe that. We're all flesh, blood and bone, you know, and we should all be gender fluid, and if we can wake up to realise that, then we can all make sure that everybody's ok. We're all ok. (James Morris)

An open door. Unconditional open door ... The unspecified-ness of the whole way Pilsdon works. Lee Abbey was a place to preach the Gospel and it was a place to train people to work in community ... You went because you had a reason, whereas Pilsdon, it's not specific, as I've always seen it, in any way. What we offer is an open door and as long as you're not going to burn the place down or abuse somebody, you're welcome here. You just are welcome here. You don't have to have a reason to be here. (Shirley Edwards)

Sometimes the impact of Pilsdon's open hospitality could be immediate, achieved simply through the first greeting that a new arrival receives. But the meaning of a radical hospitality extends throughout the many everyday practices that constitute community life. And it is through these that the Pilsdon ethos is transmitted and sustained:

How is it that the ethos gets passed on? How is there continuity? It's a hard one to know. I think it's in the stories that one tells, a little bit, about the past. It's in the present quality of welcome, I would say. It's how people are met and it gets passed on, that, if when you arrive, the guests particularly, because they've been welcomed, notice you and say, 'Hello.' Whoever you are. You then have already picked up that this is a place of welcome, that this is a place where it's good to welcome and it's good to be welcomed, and in a strange way that passes on a huge amount of information. ... I think there are very subtle ways in which these sorts of things get passed on. I think it's the communal things, I think it's the meal times, I think it's the celebration of living life together, it's taking care of the very mundane parts of life that are actually so important, of hospitality. (Andrew Davey)

The liberal values of acceptance of, and openness to others regardless of who they are, what they believe or what has brought them to Pilsdon does not mean, as we have seen, that the community operates without rules or standards of behaviour. Indeed, it is the way that Pilsdon embodies acceptance and respect for each other within an explicit framework of principles for living together that, for some, is at the core of Pilsdon's attraction and of its success:

There was a serialisation of Toby Jones' book *Utopian Dreams*, which was on the radio, where he described living in different communities. The phrase always stuck with me that the community that he thought worked best was the Pilsdon Community because it was, and I do remember the words, it was 'caring and compassionate but it had rules and boundaries' and this is what made the community work and this is why it was the best of the, or... well, the community that worked. So, I went on the internet and found the Pilsdon Community, flashed off an email to the warden offering my services as a volunteer for six months. (Bob Edwards)

A RELATIONAL PLACE

During the time that the Pilsdon Community has been in existence, the shift from institutional to community-based services, then the emerging dominance of neo-liberal ideologies that created markets in health and social care services, have encouraged shifts in both how relationships between those providing and those using services have been conceptualised and practised (Simmons et al, 2009). Alongside contested developments in community-based services, the growth of collective action on the part of those using mental health services, created another important influence on responses to those living with such problems (Barnes and Bowl, 2001). There have been many dimensions to such action. It has included demands to be included in decision making about individual care and treatment, but also involvement in decision making about policy and the design and delivery of mental health services. It has also included and led to important developments in the design and conduct of research on mental health issues (Sweeney et al, 2009). But it has also reached well beyond mental health services to link to other civil rights movements that have called attention to the discrimination, disadvantage and oppression experienced by those living with mental health difficulties, and it has questioned assumptions about associations between mental illness, incompetence and dangerousness. It has promoted, and in some cases provided alternative ways of enabling recovery by means of arts based, environmental and spiritual practices. Initiatives such as Ecoworks in Nottingham reflected the analysis of some of those living with mental health problems about not only the link between mental illness, disadvantage and poverty, but also the potential of sustainable engagement with the natural world as a route to recovery.

Whilst some sections of the mental health user movement were arguing to be recognised as citizens with civil rights, others saw the route to empowerment through consumer advocacy and the right to choose. At the same time, the official adoption of individualised service models meant that collective services such as day centres came to be regarded as inappropriately separating service users from mainstream society and the focus shifted to the construction of individual care packages and then to the provision of direct payments to enable people to both choose and purchase what they wanted in terms of service support. For some, the whole notion of 'care' became tarnished with a link to oppressive paternalism and rejected in favour of choice and control over individualised support services (Barnes, 2011).

The Pilsdon Community has remained largely separate from these debates and conflicts about the nature of the relationship between 'service providers' and 'service users.' But then it has never identified itself as a service provider. It has, to some extent, struggled with the idea that community decision making should include guests and volunteers, not least because the relationship between members and guests has never been that of professional/service user. Thus, guests are included in discussions, for example, about the garden: which vegetables to plant, changes to layout and responsibilities for maintaining different areas. Guests whose turn it is to cook lunch or the evening meal make the decision about what to cook. But they are not part of decision making about who should join the community nor about major expenditures or developments. Some guests have found this hard and this has contributed to the decisions of some to move on. Others, long term guests, have turned down invitations to become members because they are happy not to take on the responsibilities that come with decision making. The role of guests in supporting peers is evident from the interviews we have quoted and this is an integral part of the way the community functions.

A key theme of the account we have offered in this book is that acknowledging vulnerability is important for members as well as guests and that it is acceptance of others' humanity rather than asserting status differences that defines the way in which people seek to live together within the community. Core to the enduring nature of life at Pilsdon is the centrality of the relationships that enable both the practical maintenance of life within the community, and through which all those who come are nurtured and supported to address the troubles that brought them there. This was reflected in the words of wayfarers, guests and wardens who offer different perspectives on the nature of these relationships.

Former guest Sarah Hallett contrasted relationships at Pilsdon with those she had experienced in mental health services in the 1980s:

> But also I think what I really liked about Pilsdon, and still do, is something about the emphasis on … normalising people in a way. Because in those days the psychiatric system was very much sort of them and us, so you would have the staff, the nurses and the doctors … and they

almost would put up quite a barrier between themselves as people, real people, and themselves as mental health professionals, and they could be quite bullish really, and you were definitely told what to do, where to go. All the doors were locked at night, at times I didn't have access to my own clothes and things like that. Whereas at Pilsdon, I can't remember any of the doors ever being locked and I think the Pilsdon Community is a great leveller and … there wasn't that same boundary or even … it was more than a boundary, it was a barrier between the staff and the patients.

Wayfarer Simon Smith indicated how authority at Pilsdon is handled in a way that does not obstruct ordinary person-to-person relationships: "Michael's Michael, Mary's Mary, Kathy's Kathy…". Whilst warden Michael expressed his sense of what his relationships could encompass:

You can be hard and you can be truthful and you can do those things in love but you have to remain in relationship in order to sit in the dining room … There is affection there, there are a lot of feelings that go with it and it's a learning experience for me and I think it's a learning experience for them that it's not hard conversations and then dismissing them. It's hard conversations and we're still gonna wash up dishes together and we're still gonna work in the garden or do something, or you're still gonna come and say, 'Can I do this?' One is not necessarily gonna rub up against the other. So, that's the only way. The only way I can explain it is it's just a discipline about … you can't forget that you love them.

Relationships within the Pilsdon Community are not the same as those within mainstream mental health services and the ethical, therapeutic and political issues they embody provide a different context from that which prompted much of the growth of the user/survivor movement. But changing cultures and expectations about the nature and exercise of authority mean that the autocratic practices of Pilsdon's early years have evolved. A number of those who knew the community in its early days spoke of Percy Smith as a benign autocrat. His daughter Ruth described aspects of her experience of him: "He ruled with a rod of iron and he was a strong disciplinarian and I won't pretend I didn't resent that at times, I really did." He would allocate work tasks and tell people where to sit at meal times:

> He was quite a slave driver in some ways. Sometimes he gave people tiny, little jobs, 'cause he knew that they were either old or weak or recovering from something, so it maybe something really quite small, but they still got given a job whatever it was, even if it was just polishing that brass pot or whatever, to give them all a meaning, to help with the running of the place, in a way, to be seen to be part of it, really, I suppose? (Ruth Thurgur)

Thus, whilst guests may come to feel too constrained by the demands of community to remain at Pilsdon and this may lead to either a planned move on, or to a more conflictual ending of their time there, most of those who took part in interviews experienced the value of solidaristic relationships within the community and there was no evidence of the emergence of oppositional collective action on the part of guests. The development of peer support such as those services introduced within mainstream mental health services can be seen to have evolved organically at Pilsdon, whilst a focus on recovery as a basis for treatment both for mental illness and addictions is, at Pilsdon, better understood in terms of providing a space in which people can repair the brokenness that brings them to the community.

The process of repair, at both individual and collective level, is one that enables the creation of something new. Repairs, however carefully performed, are rarely invisible. Repairing or mending, can be a creative opportunity:

> Mending is something that human beings do all the time, re-making our lives in all kinds of ways; adapting to loss, adapting materials, appropriating cultural references, in order to give ourselves, our objects, our ideas, new meaning and a continued useful life. Everything in life is fragile. Things break, we renew, and artists are a powerful part of the current movement to remind us all that 'renew' is not simply to 'take a pill' or 'buy another one'. Imagination, courage and invention are the best tools, and ones that every human being has. (Wall, 2016)

This quote from the curator of an exhibition at an arts centre close to Pilsdon expresses a way of thinking that reflects how people who come to the community in their fragility and vulnerability are also seen as capable of renewal. And, as we argued in chapter 6, this personal renewal supports and is supported by, the development of caring solidarities amongst those who are part of the community. Renewal and repair are collective as well as individual processes. They are not the result of pursuing individual outcome objectives regardless of the way these may impact others with whom you are living. At different points in this book we have quoted individuals talking about their own or others' aggression or other damaging behaviour. Relationships within the community are not always positive and there have been occasions when people have had to leave because of the way they have behaved in relation to others, as well as people leaving because of breaking the no drink or drugs rule. Some such incidents have taken place since the history project was concluded and thus were not a subject for discussion in interviews. Some of those incidents have led to the community undergoing trauma and becoming unsettled in ways that have required considerable care to repair. The general point remains, however, that the relational nature of the place is both the source of conflict and the means through which conflict can be resolved. It is the community that must be sustained if individuals are to benefit.

SUSTAINING AN ALTERNATIVE WAY OF WORKING

The landscape of mental health services and ways of thinking about people who live with mental health difficulties have changed radically during the 60-year life of the Pilsdon Community. During this time the community has not changed in terms of its commitment to the value of living together and of community rather than individualism, nor to a belief that those with and those without a mental health diagnosis or evidence of addiction are equally valuable human beings who can live together for collective benefit. This is what Jonathan Herbert has come to write of in terms of the necessity of 'accompaniment' that enables: "a real sense of joy and freedom that can come through a mutual sense of interdependence." (Herbert, 2020, p. 65). Pilsdon has not changed in terms of seeing a safe environment as a necessary condition for recovery, and this remains the case regardless of the form of external therapy or treatment that may be available and which guests can continue to access. Rather than adopting or resisting changing professional views on therapeutic models, it has continued to focus on the fundamental need for home, food, occupation and positive relationships with others. The Pilsdon Community is not and does not seek to be a service provider and its basis in a Christian community rather than commitment to a particular model of therapeutic practice means that it has avoided many of the conflicts associated with therapeutic communities or other innovative mental health services. Michael Deegan described the approach to supporting individuals' recovery processes:

> It's listening. It's checking in, it's listening, asking how they're doing and it could be that they're new, just starting to figure out where they are. It could be somebody that's been going to recovery meetings for quite a while. Just having a check-in about how those things are going and maybe discussing a bit about what their goals are. (Michael Deegan)

Michael went on to talk about the way they seek to help people get the most out of their encounters with medical professionals, for example by suggesting questions they may find helpful to ask, or exploring diagnoses such as Aspergers that can help people understand themselves in a different and more helpful way as a preliminary to receiving more appropriate specialist support.

As we saw in chapter 5, Pilsdon's alternative way of working is also evident in the community's relationship to public services and government programmes. The determination not to become incorporated into the mainstream health and social care system has meant forgoing possible income streams. But the requirement for record keeping that would interfere with the informality of relationships, as well as be in tension with the focus on the community rather than the individual that is central to the ethos, means that the decision to remain outside such contractual relationships has not been contested within the community. This does not mean that the community is unaffected by changes within the statutory sector or by the savagery of government cuts under austerity. At the time of writing Pilsdon is the only place offering accommodation to homeless people in the area and thus is on the receiving end of requests to admit people who are unlikely to fit within this environment.

But the informality of the way in which Pilsdon has operated throughout its history *is* counter to the increasingly managerial and regulatory culture of public services. Pilsdon *has* had to change in some respects in response to this. For example, recognition as a charitable organisation required the creation of a body of trustees, and the designation as an intentional community was a consequence of minimum wages legislation and how it might be possible to side step these in a context in which members received 'pocket money' rather than a formal salary. Stuart Affleck became warden after Percy effectively chose him, but on his departure the need to recruit a new warden required the generation of a job description to underpin a recruitment process. Caroline Hillyard also suggested that it was at this point that the terminology of members and guests was adopted in order to provide a description of who Pilsdon is for. When major renovations were required in the 1990s these had to create *en suite* accommodation that marked the end, for all but wayfarers, of the night time outside trek to the toilets. And the ban on smoking except in designated areas has had a significant impact on the way in which people socialise. The smoking hut, outside the main building, is a hub for interaction that creates a separation between smokers and non-smokers.

But these adaptations to legislative and cultural shifts are adaptations rather than fundamental changes to the ethos that guides the way in which people live and work in the community. Informality has always distinguished Pilsdon from agencies providing services in the ways in which people come to the community and the way in which relationships between guests, volunteers and others change and evolve.

I think the way that we used to do, when Stuart would say to somebody, 'Come and stay, just for a short time and see if you like it,' we had no complicated application forms, nothing. It was just talks and chats and letters and just, 'Come and stay. Stay for a weekend or Monday to Friday.' Particularly important when people were claiming benefit because it's so difficult, and I think it's just as difficult today, to start reclaiming and all the rest of it and relocating your claim and applying again and all the rest of it. So it was, 'Come. You can afford to get the train or get the bus. Come and stay with us, see if you like it.' (Annie Hardie)

Whilst experiences such as the fire set by the woman that was recounted by Peter Barnett have led to exclusion criteria being made explicit, and experience more broadly has informed a sense of who is likely to both fit and to benefit from being at Pilsdon, the process of coming to the community remains less formal than in mainstream services. Homeless people can still turn up and find a place to stay on a temporary basis, and it is still possible to come for a trial week and see how it works out. People leave, but will be welcomed back for visits if they feel the need for a break or if they are facing another crisis.

There are other contemporary changes in awareness of existential crises that impact on practices at Pilsdon. In recent times, the community has been influenced by, and responsive to, the increasing global concern with environmental issues, and this is evident in, for example, changes in animal husbandry and horticultural practices. However, from its inception Pilsdon has embodied the values of simplicity in living that is counter to the consumerist and materialist ethos now identified as closely complicit in climate change and environmental degradation. It is a space that embodies understanding of the contribution of the natural environment to wellbeing, and which recognises the importance of the availability of physical space in enabling repair. It shares those aspects that were identified as positive to asylums such as Herrison or Severalls in enabling creative physical work in the natural world. And it has recognised the way that producing and preparing food in a sustainable way nurtures both physical and mental health. It has sustained and developed those practices that are now a more common feature of support services available in different localities and which are increasingly recognised as a valuable contribution to improved wellbeing (Hardman, 2020). In the context of the Christian faith of members Michael Deegan described the purpose of the gardens:

> The gardens are a means of ministry, they are not the ministry. Whether it's productive or not, I don't care. If people are learning and challenged and having fun, then the gardens are doing exactly what they're supposed to do. We're grateful for what they produce but they're never gonna be high yield, that's not why they're here.

Social changes *have* impacted practices. There is still an expectation that people will make a contribution to the community through some form of work, but the individual allocation of tasks is a thing of the past. Similarly, gendered expectations regarding who should do what kind of work have evolved at Pilsdon as they have in society generally (though have not completely disappeared – when Mary gained her chain saw licence at least one male volunteer found this hard to accept!). A major change in this respect came after the 60th anniversary when in 2019 Pilsdon's first woman warden was appointed, a development made possible as a consequence of the ordination of women as priests, but also reflecting a growing acceptance of and familiarity with women in leadership roles in all walks of life.

CONCLUSION

In chapter 3 we discussed the importance of the rhythms and routines through which community life is enacted and sustained. Those rhythms and routines sustain a strong sense of continuity in the context of a changing world. They include the apparently mundane pattern of particular meals on particular days such as Sunday roasts, or fish and chips on Fridays; the Wednesday afternoon shopping trips into Bridport. They include the daily demands of the farm and gardens, of the animals and plants, and the annual rhythms of the seasons and festivals. And they include the enduring rhythm of prayer four times a day, as Percy Smith envisaged.

For the members whose Christian faith sustains them in the difficult day-to-day as well as long term experience of living in community at Pilsdon, the continuity of what Pilsdon is, is grounded in their relationship with God; in Michael Deegan's words, "that's where the commitment is". This commitment with God, renewed through the regular act of prayer and embodied in the attempt to live life in accordance with the teachings of Jesus, in itself represents one understanding of connection across time and through space. While for those who do not share the faith (as well as those who do), the stability offered by daily and seasonal routines, anchored in repetition and familiarity of place, provides a security within which it becomes possible to face up to and reflect on the troubles that brought them to the community.

It would be wrong to suggest that Pilsdon has existed in a bubble, either practically or spiritually, unimpacted by changes in the world beyond. We have argued that the community is constantly being made and what makes it are the relationships between those who become part of the community at different times and thus bring to it ways of thinking, attitudes, behaviours of their own time, not of 1958. This process is not always trouble-free: events have sometimes resulted in the community becoming unsettled and the rhythm of its collective life disrupted. The departure of the charismatic founder led to a number of other members abruptly leaving; the tragic death of Annie Hardie's son left all feeling vulnerable and fragile; emotional relationships have occasionally formed between individuals which undermine the bonds of trust on which the community relies. These are human issues, whilst major necessary practical developments such as those consequent on the need for a compete rewiring of buildings, or the substantial renovation of accommodation, have resulted in re-organisations that have had significant and difficult impacts on everyday life for both members and guests. And in the final chapter we reflect on the impact that the global crisis of the coronavirus pandemic has had on the community.

But whatever the policy context, whatever forms of clinical or therapeutic interventions might be available, the trajectories associated with the impact of damage caused by addictions and mental illness, and the experience of caring relationships in contributing to healing and recovery, remain largely constant. Care takes place through time, it requires time to establish caring relationships and enable healing. Those who have been part of Pilsdon throughout its history have experienced changes as a result. Care is reparative – it offers a response to hurt and damage from the past, and it is purposive – it seeks a better way of living together. The experience of being part of caring relationships enables solidarity to build which is necessary for the future. This is important both at an individual level and collectively. This, rather than any specific change in policy that has had effects on accommodation or practices at Pilsdon is what is most important in understanding the community and its longevity. It is both constantly being made and, at heart, remains the same. And it remains the same because the needs it addresses have not yet been banished from the world.

It also remains the same because the traditions in which it is based and on which it draws for sustenance are enduring ones that reach deep into the collective history of humanity and humanity's relationship with the more than human world. The next chapter offers an account of Pilsdon's meaning and significance from the perspective of Mary Davies, a current member who led the history project, but who here tells her own personal story of relationship with the community that is based in her Christian faith.

CHAPTER 8

————

The Way Of Pilsdon

Up to this point Pilsdon's story has been told through the words of people interviewed for the 2018 oral history project, with reflections and analysis from two of the authors. In these final two chapters we introduce more immediately contemporary perspectives, presenting accounts from some of those living in the community during the period since the 60th anniversary that prompted that project. Here Mary Davies offers a first person account from a current member. As we noted in chapter 1, Mary's perspective is one that is different from, and not available to the other authors of this book. These are her words.

MARY'S STORY

The story of Pilsdon is now woven through my own story, and I have the privilege of being woven through it. I realised this when I went to interview Stuart Affleck for the history project, who had served as the second warden of the community from 1980 to 1994. My diary recounts my feeling that talking with Stuart, even after a few minutes, was full of familiarity. As he told me about his life and work at Pilsdon I noticed our connection; a unique connection borne from a shared life, lived decades apart. We spoke about the life, and work, and spirituality of Pilsdon, but we also spoke vulnerably about the joys and sorrows of our lives as though we were sat with a cup of tea in the Aga Room of the manor house where we had both lived at different times.

I then knew Pilsdon was an idea, not simply a place, and a way of being rather than just a charitable religious organisation; and we both carried this *way* in our bodies and our hearts. I've had similar experiences with other former members and guests who have returned to the community at anniversaries or for short holidays. Again and again I got the sense of having walked this same *way* together, having allowed the rhythm of the place to work itself into our hearts and change us. There was often a trust, an openness, which enabled a sharing of truths about ourselves that one might not have had the instinct to share with closer friends than these. Perhaps we recognise that we have been in exile together; sharing griefs, lamenting losses, and groping towards a hope of finding "home". And all the time consoled by the beauty of this place; gathering us in, enfolding us and soothing our sore and tender hearts.

However differently we have each navigated our lives, whatever our beliefs or practices, those of us who have participated in the story of Pilsdon have shared *communion*. And once we have left the physical place we remain connected because of this sharing. In the retelling of our own stories of Pilsdon we keep reinforcing and renewing the idea of this place, and it can become a consoling act during challenging times in our lives. I picked up the phone to someone recently who had lived at Pilsdon whilst Stuart was warden, who had known my predecessors here, Judy and Annie, Scott and Pookie, and for whom living in community had clearly been incredibly important. Following the death of his wife he had found himself calling this place, a place he had not visited for over 20 years, to be reassured of its continued existence; and he spoke with me as though we too had shared something vital.

This sharing a way of life decades apart, even centuries apart when we come to think of the patterns of the Little Gidding community that Pilsdon was inspired by, is incomprehensible in a world constantly changing, where societal conceptions of time and progress are linear, and where success means moving upwards. The invitation of Pilsdon, and other communities built on the wisdom of ancient monastic and contemplative practices, is a calling into a seasonal and natural rhythm, which is cyclical. It allows us to be with someone in 1978 stringing beans, in 1985 welcoming wayfarers, and in 1997 milking cows. It even mysteriously allows us to be with someone praying compline in 1658. We believe that this cyclical pattern in the landscape and our activities can hold or become the substrate through which the inner work takes place; deepening our awareness of ourselves and our patterns of behaviour by living with others.

The newsletters of the early years also present this recognisable pattern; that Pilsdon is not simply a place to find rest and renewal, it is a way of living that asks something significant of us. Only a few months after the doors of Pilsdon opened these truths of living together were being explored:

> This is not a success story and it would be cheating to write it up as such. So often life in community breaks people open, exposing them to themselves as they are, and this is one of the hardest and most painful things to take. Rather than accept oneself as one is and battle with one's own nature, the temptation is always to run away or hit out. For those who are prepared to accept themselves, Pilsdon is a place where this battling and this acceptance can take place (April 1959).

The encouragement at Pilsdon, without it being "therapeutic", is that we should all take responsibility for the work each one of us has to do, to become more at home in ourselves. The practical work grounds us, giving us a framework to have conversations, build trust, be vulnerable, and to receive and give care.

The temptation, perhaps, of coming to live at Pilsdon to "recover" from the stuff of life, is to transfer the responsibility we need to take for our own lives onto others within the community. Whilst the structures and rhythms allow us space and time to reflect, and to share our troubles and concerns with others, the work of repair is ours to do. The community can hold us as we build the courage we need to notice our patterns, and it strives to provide the forgiving and loving space we need to face up to them. The theology of Pilsdon is spacious and accepting, offering us the opportunity to "face ourselves" in a loving and self-compassionate way. The possibility we draw on, inherent in our Christian tradition, is that we can seek out and ask God to help us recover the lost parts of ourselves in this place, and imagine the possibility of becoming whole.

The Act of Dedication that we say at each anniversary comprises eight commitments; they reflect the aspiration of the community to live simply and with vulnerability, within a now 62 year old rhythm of work, prayer and hospitality. These humble statements of intent, this framework of values, are outward declarations of an ongoing work that we are invited to daily live in this place; a work that awakens us to our responsibility to ourselves, to each other, and to the world in which we live.

This *way* and the traditions underpinning it can accompany us through turbulent times and help us navigate the uncertainty and change in our contemporary lives. Something that Percy and Gaynor Smith, and their inspiration the Little Gidding Community of Nicholas Ferrar, recognised very well. They understood that the example of such a community was needed over 60 years ago, in a traumatised and fragmented society impacted by two World Wars; it is as needed today in a world that is disoriented, disconnected and disenchanted.

A HOMECOMING

In all traditions and cultures there is something hugely significant about the concept of return. It is often expressed as a form of homecoming, even as this "home" looks different to us following a journey of discovery or a period of exile. And my first encounter with Pilsdon, back in February 2016, felt more like this than an arrival at somewhere new. I recognised something immediately on walking through the archway into the farm yard. Soon afterwards I left my job and came to live in community.

Almost as soon as I changed my direction of travel towards this "home" that I had long searched to find the co-ordinates for, my brother died unexpectedly. I was disoriented once again, and overcome with a heavy grief. My first year at Pilsdon was coloured by this grief. Indeed whilst the ways of the community and the rhythms of our days held me over those desperate times, people's gentleness and quiet compassion towards me also radically shaped the way that I would find myself living with others here as the years unfolded; accompanying sorrow which I now recognised could not be taken away, only borne witness to.

I was amazed by the people that I lived alongside in those days, who daily struggled to survive their many losses within losses but who were generously able to honour my seemingly simple grief. I don't remember the details of what I did in those days or the conversations, but my body remembers being cushioned by those who barely knew me yet who understood my sorrow. It remembers the sadness which heaved out of my lungs on daily walks up the hill behind the house; and the soil and the clay and the salty sea, under nails, in the creases of hands, on my skin; the movement in its muscles, urgently demanding the load of emotion to flow through and out of my flesh and bone. Shifting hay bales and muck spreading; chopping logs with someone who moved and spoke gently like him; turning the heavy soil and hauling heavy buckets of reservoir water. Stacking, moving, and digging. Cleaning, cleansing, and calling my brother to mind, always. With each breath and each swing of the axe.

I awoke each day and sometimes there was early sunshine and hope, other days there was an unbearable weight in everything. And the gift of Pilsdon for me at that time was to be able to simply face that tangle of emotions each day; to live and breathe in it, and no more. I ate, and worked, and prayed, and laughed, and cried. Some days it felt almost euphoric to be so stripped away, to be left so present. It was simple and I was offered the space to be truthful and honest with myself about the ways loss was unravelling me. In those moments something enabled me to be, strangely, at peace with everything. A freedom, hard to explain.

As well as the weight there was a tenderness which was called out from everything in those days. It was in the softness of the early morning light as I walked down to the church, it existed discretely in my newly folded jumper laid out for me on the picnic table outside the back door where I had left it in a heap after lunch, it was there in the spaciousness of my neighbour at the dinner table as I sobbed quietly for twenty minutes, from my first mouthful to my last. It was a tenderness that somehow eased but did not bury away the harsh reality of my loss. Living through this at Pilsdon was my initiation into lamentation, and its utter necessity for my healing.

As I look out onto the garden now, I remember my first year preparing plots and sowing carrots, and I can see my body bent over, crouching, burying seeds into the soil. And I look on it now and I see all the bodies bent over, grieving. All of the activity, the conversations, the laughter, the desperation, the secrets, the shame, the jokes, the sweat, the acceptance, the forgiveness; all of it is sequestered like carbon into the soil of this place. Transforming it into a sacred piece of land.

I return often to examine my choice to come, and to remain, in community here. As I do this I am reminded of all the ways that the life and work here have changed me over the years, and quite how much I have to be thankful for. Through the difficult goodbyes, the disappointments, the unresolved conflicts, the achingly slow pace of transformation, I have learned not to look for answers or to expect neat outcomes. I have decided instead to keep searching for a language and practice that can nourish and sustain me and those around me, despite those realities, perhaps even because of them.

At Pilsdon, if we are fortunate, we find kindred who share this language and carry this way. People who are spacious, generous and hospitable, who live striving towards gratitude and abundance, who wish to give away what they have been given as a loving impulse rather than a manipulation or obligation, but who also understand that our giving away is often shadowy and complicated. We learn that just to be present to the telling of each other's stories, and not to wrestle their ending into a conclusion of our choosing, can be frightening for us but is utterly necessary. This is how we bear witness to one another's lives. We learn how to just sit and weep with others, or be silent with them, or thank them for the breakfast eggs that they made for us, or plant out seedlings alongside them, or laugh at the jokes they tell.

We abide with one another in this place, and learn to love and have compassion for ourselves as we grow in love for those we share this space with. If we allow it, Pilsdon can be a place where relationship transforms us, where imagination frees us, where beauty unravels us, where the smallest acts of kindness fill us, and where a deep mysterious knowing anchors us. This *way* is not dramatic, it is a slow and repetitive work, punctuated by small encounters and fleeting revelations each day. And we are guided in this way by the commitments we make whilst living at Pilsdon: to pray, to maintain a practice and rhythm, to live simply, to offer welcome and acceptance, to live with vulnerability, to work for the good of the other and to create safe and nurturing space. To keep returning to the beginning, and to keep trying. These commitments create a ritualised boundary, in the same way a hedgerow boundaries a piece of land, and this holds us and steadies us along the way.

COMMITTING TO THE COMMON LIFE

Rhythm

It was my turn to do lights out at the end of the day and as I walked around the yard I followed the pattern I had learned: I checked doors were closed, that the animals had enough hay, and that no cats were trapped in the corridors, I contemplated the repetitive nature of life here. How was today different from last week, when I did exactly the same thing? Wherever it is that we find ourselves, most of the content of our lives is held in rhythms and patterns. However, we are generally not given to examine the landscape of our lives each day, or to celebrate what we might have discovered. The simple rhythm of Pilsdon helps us make space to ponder the small moments of transformation, to examine the textures of our hearts, of the quality of our relationships, the hurts we experienced and the confidences shared, and the things we learned from others.

Here, at Pilsdon, I notice the incremental changes in weather and in light, in the length of the grass and the fullness of the moon. My body pays attention to the wind and the soil, to the light on the garden at different times of year, and the levels of water in the reservoir. It does not feel right to desire an unchanging, predictable stasis in which we control our temperature, grow things all year around, force things out of season. If we live here long enough we get to remember each season; how we might have felt the previous autumn, or the last time the cows jumped for joy on being released into the pasture in the spring, or who we shared our Christmas and New Year with the previous year.

The foundation of Pilsdon is built on a commitment to a framework, an order, a rhythm. A vision that Percy and Gaynor were inspired by as it was practiced by the community of Little Gidding. This form of life belongs within a tradition and history that gives it wider meaning; it is a way of living birthed from ancient ways of living in common. Pilsdon might best be understood as an inheritance from the practices of the early Christian church, and the wisdom of monasticism.

In the Rule of St Benedict, written over fifteen centuries ago, we see that a large portion is given over to "practical discussions of the ordering of life". Monks and nuns who have followed this tradition, such as Sister Joan Chittister, tell us of the opportunities that this ordered-ness creates. "The routine parts of life, the dull parts of every day" become gifts of space (Chittister, 2000). Whether we are consciously concerned with making ourselves available to "God" in this space, or we are seeking a peace and a balance in our life following times of chaos and confusion, this rhythm is essential. The monastic invitation then is that we relate to time not as a commodity, finite and to be used productively, but as a sacrament revealing the goodness and the gifts of our lives in the here and now.

In this examination of the small, ordinary ways we enter into the day and navigate our way through it, we can begin to notice changes in ourselves. Critically, this attending to our own needs and understanding of our own patterns isn't just a process of becoming freer ourselves, but that through this attention we understand how we are connected to others, and to the landscape around us; furthermore, the work we do in ourselves, or allow to be done within us, serves a purpose beyond our individual story. As the mystic Thomas Merton reminds us about the practice of the Desert Fathers, they, "withdrew into the healing silence of the wilderness (...) not in order to preach to others but to heal in themselves the wounds of the world" (Merton, 2003).

Inviting people into this rhythm, to live alongside those of us who commit ourselves to the common life, can be fraught. It takes time for people "to land" and to accept that this rhythm, and the boundaries it creates actually enable all of us in the community to thrive. There are many who resist this common way of living; in fact we all resist the parts of it that are more challenging for us. But what the monastic wisdom offers us is the insight that what we are resisting is not really "the rule" of community life but something much deeper and more significant. We are resisting the opportunity that rhythm affords us, to "go inside ourselves to clear out the debris of the heart" (Chittister, 2000) rather than to concentrate on trying to control the environment and situations around us. We are resisting the invitation into an inter-related connection with those around us. We are resisting the reality that we belong together and not as separate entities.

A significant current within the rhythmic flow of community life at Pilsdon is the attention paid to the liturgical seasons. Some of the most transformative moments that I have had are held within the context and services of Lent or Advent, Christmas or Easter. Every year, in the run up to Easter during Holy Week, our attention is turned to the final days of Jesus' life. It has always been a powerful and moving few days; so much of what Pilsdon offers us and represents can be found in the landscape of those days. We wash one another's feet, we build the tomb and decorate the garden of repose, we follow the Stations of the Cross, we wait in front of a stripped back and bare altar, and we rise early on Easter morning, light a fire and illuminate the cold church with candlelight. They are powerful days and as individuals and as a community we journey year after year through landscapes of betrayal, desolation, torture, death, longing, grief, hopelessness, to the promise of new life. These liturgical spaces can hold opportunities to find solace and renewal and a chance to tell our own stories of love and loss.

Like all rituals this practice of remembering in these ways provides stability and continuity. Rituals are moments in our year where we are reminded of the treasures of our faith: the practice of a revolutionary love, a certain kind of power that is not hierarchical or dominating, an always available forgiveness. As we follow the example of Jesus washing the feet of his disciples, for example, we re-enact his way of nurturing reciprocal relationship in a society where our politics are built around hierarchy and competition. As Beatrice Bruteau highlights "this gesture (of foot washing) carries the weight of the whole program" of Jesus. So the warden washes the feet of the wayfarer; in this they together are enacting this program: "I will no longer call you servants but friends. There is to be no distance between us...I have not kept anything back, and I have not claimed any privilege. We are friends, all equal" (Bruteau, 2005). It overturns the concept of master and servant, and requires both parties to take responsibility for enacting this disorienting new order. One of the collects in the Corrymeela book of prayer beautifully encapsulates the importance of this ritual: "We do not know what to do with this kind of love, or this kind of power. So we repeat it once a year. May we repeat it more often"; the ritual begs to be woven through all of our encounters, "every month, every day, every hour".

Critically we believe that these rituals and liturgical rhythms should not remain locked up inside the church; they are gifts which make sacred our every day. They also often mirror and illuminate aspects of our daily struggles at Pilsdon, and make profound the activities we are involved in, and the crises we face. I think particularly of

258

being with one guest on the evening of Maundy Thursday. As people were holding vigil in the house chapel back at Pilsdon, watching with Jesus as he prayed alone at the Mount of Olives, I was sat with him in the waiting room of the hospital, as he endured the grief in his own Garden of Gethsemane. The faith that we profess, the kind of love we want to be in the world, the hope that we carry, these are all manifest with meaning during these different seasons of the year. This rhythm is our breathing in, and our breathing out.

Prayer

Attending to a regular prayer office, is an essential part of the life at Pilsdon for those who have come as members. There is a church here that has been in existence since 1301, to which people have come continuously to pray; the community's worship therefore represents the tiniest fragment of the prayer life and devotion that has taken place there. For over 700 years people have worshipped in that place, and when we go down there three times a day, and to the house chapel for compline, we believe, mysteriously, that we join with them in our prayers. We recognise that they too must have endured heartache, loss, needed to lament and be angry. We recognise also that they saw the seasons come and go, and were thankful like we are when spring arrived and the hedgerows burst into life, for births and baptisms and marriages, and for plentiful harvests. They too remembered their lost loved ones in this place, and sought solace in the face of transition and change.

For me the prayer life enables an opportunity for stillness; to practice gratefulness; to give and receive forgiveness; to find our way, groping, towards love. We don't need words for this, most of the greatest gifts are given to us in the silence: a peace which passes all understanding; a compassion for ourselves and for others that can overwhelm us; a capacity for forgiveness that reaches beyond our fragile egos and defensive natures; examples from scripture and other spiritual writings, poetry and meditations that travel with us and nourish us and encourage us. We are not alone, we are not the first and only people to have felt these things, we are able to begin again, we can feel wonder, we can be truthful, we can be encouraged that the dark night of the soul is a place of transformation. That we are more than our emotions and our bodies and our thoughts.

From the point of view of maintaining a healthy community the prayer life is essential. The Benedictine Rule explains that "the corporate prayer is there to uphold a continuing awareness of the presence of God which makes praying inseparable from living, and living from praying". At Pilsdon we believe that this prayer life sustains the work out in the yard, and in the office, in the garden and the kitchen. It sustains the work of relationship; whether that be with the natural world, with others, or crucially with ourselves. "As we say our prayers in working clothes", wrote Percy in 1958, "we are conscious of a deep underlying unity between work and worship".

The significant spiritual and psychological resources available to us in our Christian tradition haven't always been made readily available to us through our experiences of religion. Sometimes they have been hidden from us, and sometimes they have been used against us inappropriately. Many who come to Pilsdon have experienced some kind of spiritual abuse which has robbed them of a loving experience of the divine. The words of scripture baffle us, and understandably we fight against the language because it has been wielded inappropriately by the powerful over the powerless for too many years. We do not make ourselves available to the mysteries in the liturgy because they make no rational sense. If, however, we can free ourselves from our associations then in the rhythm of prayer at Pilsdon we can find surprising nourishment in the words of Augustine, or recognition in the ways in which Mary loved Jesus, or a strange redemption in the mysterious power of the Eucharist, a sacrament of thanksgiving and remembrance that connects us to Christ's love for us. Our tradition is deeply flawed but contained within it is a language, practice, and wisdom that can enable us to live more courageously, and with more freedom.

Pilsdon is sometimes a difficult place to be. We bear witness to the trauma in each other's lives and feel powerless to overcome it; we travel with others who cannot find healing for their bodies or their minds. Prayer cannot fix us. Prayer is a reaching out for something that you know you will never actually grasp in your life; a struggling to unify things that cannot be unified. It is an alliance with Christ in the now who promises, eventually, to make all things new. Maintaining this practice of prayer is an important and hopeful act, and as we enter into the church I believe we enter a prophetic space where we speak out what we want the world to be; we name fragilities and weaknesses, we confront failure and falling, we meet people in scriptures who remind us of things, and who encourage us. Our imagination is nurtured. We sing through our tears. We make statements which sound impossible but are given power in this place of yearning, in the speaking out, in the voicing. And they are our words joined with other words from long ago.

I sometimes try to imagine how Pilsdon would be if you took away this element of its life. What energy would animate the work; what would strengthen the bonds of fellowship when things don't go as planned. People's experience of Pilsdon is multi-faceted and varied, the welcome needs to be wide and the acceptance unwavering, and people come and go from this place who never need to step into the church to find some kind of healing. However, the foundation of Pilsdon is utterly forged in the fire of God's love. Its structure, its reason for being, its animating force is borne out of this foundation. As Percy pondered some 20 years after its beginnings, our relationships with one another here are founded on the essential relationship "of ourselves to God" and it is on this that "I place all my hopes for myself and for this community now and in the future".

Whilst a community without this foundation would look and feel different, there are significant aspects of the prayer life that could be translated into a "non-religious" practice. A shared time and space to be together at least once a day where the gathering was not about work, or food, or even recreation; a time to bring things that were unresolvable, to share gratefulness, to be with loss and pain. It would be a space where people could come together even though they may not agree on everything; this has been essential at Pilsdon over the years. The community has been through challenging times, and times of significant disagreement and difference. It has negotiated these differences, I believe, because of the determination that seeking God's will first in all of it in the end overrides everything else.

What human beings are capable of doing in their own strength can be extraordinary, and many people succeed in supporting people through challenging times without a religious framework to hold them. In some ways my default setting is just that: keep working hard, keep learning from what has gone wrong, keep being encouraged by small breakthroughs. When my heart is broken and my energy sapped, when my own pain clouds my vision, when I am triggered by others' vulnerability; it is then that I see how little I can do on my own. The prayer time sustains us here and we withdraw into the silence like Jesus does, away from the hustle and bustle of the day. Prayer rarely brings us resolution or answers to our questions, but it holds us steady, it allows us to lament, it grants us the opportunity to name hard things and gives us a place to exclaim hopeful things, it helps us imagine beautiful things, and reminds us of the mysterious grace that forgiveness is ever available.

Simplicity

A few years ago I was talking with a wayfarer who had been coming to Pilsdon for several decades about his life on the road. He told me what he had carried with him when he first took to the road, and how it weighed him down, slowed his progress, and hindered his movement. He began gradually to look through his belongings and to pare them down to the bare essentials. A tin opener, a spoon, a sleeping bag, a few good pairs of socks and some sturdy walking boots.

These things that were important to him enabled him to survive that day, and to keep moving towards the next.

He could not be self-sufficient living like this however, he told me; relying on the provision found in the landscapes he travelled through and the hospitality of people along the way. In this way he knew he needed to understand and respect the gifts that the woodlands and the fields and the hedgerows offered to him as he made his way from one place to the next. And he also needed to become patient and socially adept, nurturing connections with people who might give him some work to do and offer him shelter for a night or two.

Some wayfarers have retained their friendships with people in convents and monasteries, in churches and family homes some 30 or 40 years after they first worked with or stayed with them. They maintain that long-standing connection with Pilsdon too. These wanderers, who move around in these ways, offer something in return to those of us who try desperately to build secure lives and invest in what we think is stability. They offer a way of being in the world that is honest about its dependence on others, even as they appear to move alone and independently; this paradox that they live is the life Jesus invites us to abandon ourselves into. In Luke's gospel we find Jesus instructing the disciples as he sends them out: "Take nothing for your journey — neither a walking stick, nor bag, nor bread, nor money; and do not even have two tunics apiece". Why does Jesus say this? What kind of a life is he inviting us to live? What secrets are hidden in this light, unencumbered way of travelling? If we have the humility to listen, the wayfarers who live like this can be teachers of these ways. The invitation to be pilgrims without extra money, protection or clothes, is an invitation into a different economy.

A commitment to living simply has always been a feature of Pilsdon's way. Just as rhythms create an external order that can enable internal freedom, simplicity can create a spaciousness that does the same, questioning the plans and expectations that we cling on to, and forcing the distractions aside. Simplicity enables us to see things for what they really are, and to have relationships with ourselves, with others and with the natural world around us that are true and real. Simplicity enables a directness in dealing with each other that is not complicated by evasion or avoidance of conflict. Simplicity invites us into a life that is more tuned in to the rhythms around us, and an impulse to nurture the natural world rather than exploit it. It makes us available for the work that matters. For me living this life is seeking Christ (that is my language, but this could mean seeking peace, seeking belonging, seeking contentment, seeking fulfilment) and I believe that he is more available to all of us here because of the simplicity of our days. As Meister Eckhart tells us, "God is not found in the soul by adding anything but by a process of subtraction".

Choosing to live a simple life is a gateway into a deeper reverence and respect for the life around us. The contemplative wisdom, again, helps us see that our relationship to material things is not simply about non-possession, it is about fundamentally considering "nothing as private property". Esther de Waal highlights for us that this: "is a delicately crafted theology, in which the attitude towards our talents and possessions and towards people all inter-relate". In this the ancient monastic practices of simplicity show us "the possibility of the totality and wholeness inherent in all of life" (de Waal, 1990). It is a radical standpoint which offers us insight into a different kind of economy; one which is based on interconnectedness rather than consumption. Whilst we do not take vows at Pilsdon, we try to live a life where we share as much as possible, and we keep reminding ourselves that everything we have been given is a gift which we too must give away.

The practice of giving away what we have is a radical one, but we have glimpses of how we too might feel freer, lighter, more connected to that which is around and about us moment by moment if we do. We must not over-romanticise this "giving away", however; and neither should we imagine that simplifying complicated lives is easy. Some people come to Pilsdon with nothing; homes, jobs, relationships stripped away from them as certain patterns of behaviour jeopardise a settled life. Other people might have taken advantage of them, exploiting their vulnerability. Some will have spent their whole lives on the edge, living with such scarcity that the idea of "having nothing" is not something to aspire to, it is deeply traumatic. Some of us may come to Pilsdon *thinking* we are prepared to give what we have away, but soon realise that whilst we might have simplified our external world by coming to live in a community like this, we can continue to live in complicated ways. Holding on to ideas about ourselves, hoarding expectations about our life, over-attached to certain ideas and ways of thinking. We gather these things around us to preserve our system of reality, guarding our world view to the exclusion of all others. But these things too we are asked to give away.

Our lives are stripped back to basics at Pilsdon, and the work we do is not about expanding what we have but maintaining what we need to sustain us. We enjoy the simple pleasures: the first tomato of the season being divided into six, sprinkled with salt and put to our mouths with eager anticipation; the sight of a row of carrot seedlings emerging; witnessing an impossibly small seed transform into delicate green shoots; being brought a jumper from a clothing donation that someone knew that you would have picked out yourself. We are known in these simple exchanges and we see others in these small revelations.

We are committed to honouring the natural world we live amidst, believing that we are bound in a network of relationship with the plant, insect and animal life around us. Living a life of simplicity, hospitality and prayer allows us to make space for these relationships, and to recognise how necessary they are for our thriving. Our garden and farming practices are also shaped by this commitment to treading lightly on the earth and we manage our grazing land and vegetable gardens in a way that nurtures biodiversity and habitat retention. We hold a hope that visitors and guests will be impacted by this way of living and working, and that they might take away with them a commitment of their own to respect the environment which sustains us all.

Welcome

I write this as we are living through the third lockdown of the Covid 19 pandemic and we are about to mark the one year anniversary since we closed the community to wayfarers, visitors and new guests. A year since we rang all those people who were planning on coming to volunteer, to get some respite or to start a new chapter living with us in community; having to break the news to them that they would not be able to be with us for the time being. Signs were put up letting people know that we were "not open", and the church was closed – and remains so up until now – to anyone outside of the community. The final chapter of this book considers the practical, emotional and spiritual impacts of lockdown. It has had radical impacts on the welcome that the sign at the entrance to the community declares, and that many whose stories are recounted in this book recognised in their experience of coming to the community.

Over those first few months we found ourselves having to make heart-breaking decisions when a few wayfarers did show up, often hungry and tired, desperate for a bed and a hot meal. Each situation required a different response and over that time we tried to be hospitable in all the ways we felt we could be: offering showers, tea, sandwiches, clean clothes, space in our church meadow to pitch a tent. But these were difficult times as we witnessed our wayfaring friends carry on walking once they knew they wouldn't be able to stay. Pilsdon, which had been for people a place to lay their bag down for a few days, could no longer accommodate them. We have sat uneasily with, and lamented, the loss of being able to fulfil our vision as a place of welcome over this time. The flow of people arriving at our door began to slow, and eventually almost completely stopped. Now hardly anyone phones to see if they can send someone to stay with us, and no-one has "turned up" unannounced for months, a situation inconceivable for anyone who has lived here over the years.

There are no keys in any of the doors to the manor house and, in "normal" times, this has meant that any time of night or day people may arrive and, if they know the place, make themselves a cup of tea and find a bed to sleep in. To live in such a place with open doors invites us to ponder the openness of our own hearts too; we notice where the arrival of others, unannounced, throws us out, brings chaos, challenges our sense of control, alters our plans. And we might wonder what these unexpected arrivals teach us about our holding back, our fear, our own sense of scarcity.

I have had some difficult conversations with guests who have found it especially hard to welcome certain wayfarers. And let us not over-romanticise, some can be difficult, eccentric, and disruptive. With one I talked about the poem written by Rumi, *The Guest House*, where new arrivals are welcomed "even if they're a crowd of sorrows, who violently sweep your house empty of its furniture", since, after all, they "may be clearing you out for some new delight". Welcoming new arrivals into our midst can be uncomfortable, but it is necessary for our own growth and change. We all struggle with the welcome for various reasons, be it anxiety, impatience, tiredness, having been disturbed and disrupted by challenging behaviours or stories over too many years, our personal boundaries of time and space tested to their limits. And what some of us find easier to welcome, others find triggering or challenging; the people who annoy and irritate us can pass by others unnoticed.

I suppose what we all look for, and is hard to live without, is that the welcome is returned with a sense of gratitude.

This outcome, what we hope to get back, cannot be the reason that we offer this hospitality. However, gratitude is a powerful practice, and when we see it enacted through people who have next to nothing it is a truly transformative attitude to be around. A few years ago a wayfarer arrived for Christmas having been living in his car for months; he had never been to Pilsdon before and he was visibly amazed at what he encountered. On Christmas Eve a few of us had tiptoed around the community after lights out, placing a stocking on the doors of everyone sleeping there that night. When I wandered down to the church early on Christmas morning I found him there, in the silence and the dark. He shared with me what the welcome had meant to him, and what a surprising gift it was. He carried no sense of entitlement to this hospitality, which was freely offered; it was freely enjoyed, and freely returned through his grateful heart. He saw that he had discovered a hidden treasure, and it made me see the treasure of Pilsdon even more brightly.

The welcome is also about shifting something within us to create room to hear the different opinions, ideas and experiences of life that people bring with them. The prayer above the Common Room fire place summarises this for me: "Make the roof of Pilsdon wide enough for all opinions, oil the door of our house so it opens easily to friend and stranger, and set such a table in our house that all may speak kindly and freely around it". The welcome must remain wide, and we must not look to what will be taken away from us in the process, but how the challenge of the other will change us for the better, and enrich the common life that we live.

However, the negotiation between the welcome of wayfarers and visitors, and the wellbeing of those who live here permanently is not straightforward. Our lockdown experience has enabled those who call this place home to relax in ways that they may have found difficult before when people were coming and going. Negotiating between the safety of the permanent residents and the safety and welcome we can offer strangers is not straightforward. We all have to work hard to resist excluding others who we know will bring a challenge to our rhythms, and who are unpredictable. We must endeavour to follow the teachings of Jesus and welcome the stranger whenever we can. As we do we make room for the unexpected, and the gift, and the enriching of others. We also welcome the difficult parts of ourselves. During Advent last year we reflected on the mechanisms of exclusion that we participate in; these can be in obvious ways through the groups that we belong to and the systems we are a part of, but they can also be more subtle including "our tendency to condemn, exclude, and make wrong those parts of ourselves we deem defective or unsatisfactory" (Bachelard, 2020). Our welcome becomes an attempt to subvert this mechanism of blame, exclusion and condemnation.

And whilst we have become acutely attuned to the reality that not everyone can come and be with us at the moment, during the pandemic, it is worth remembering that in fact we can't, and don't, welcome everyone even in the freest of times. To be welcomed in one has to have a basic respect for the house rules which are there to keep the place safe. If people arrive inebriated or aggressive, or threatening to the community then they will be asked to leave. What remains important, however, is that a person's approach to the door of Pilsdon is met with an attitude of openness. Just because a person may not be able to stay it should not be experienced as a rejection, or a humiliation. Wherever possible a cup of tea or space for some conversation and exchange is important.

A key aspect of the welcome is the ongoing and unfolding nature of it; where we have been welcomed, we then extend that welcome to others. And this can happen very quickly. I have seen people arrive and after only a short while, busy themselves making tea and showing others around who have arrived perhaps just a week or two later. People can and do practice hospitality in this place, even if they think they have no *material* thing to offer to others, since it is about being generous with ourselves. We see hospitality in action here as a sharing not only of what we have, but who we are. For most of us our impulse to welcome remains strong and more than a couple of people who have come to service our boilers or fix our fire alarm system have no doubt been overwhelmed with our tea-making and need to show hospitality during the various lockdowns. We realise that the impulse to welcome utterly feeds us too.

Vulnerability

The invitation to be honest about ourselves is one of the gifts of living in community at Pilsdon; this has been woven into the fabric of the place from the beginning. In reading old newsletters it is a recurring, and challenging, theme: "Occasionally people arrive who have not told the truth about themselves", Percy wrote in 1959, "and then Pilsdon seems a very hard, unrelenting and even unloving place".

This call to be honest will come as somewhat of a shock to those who consider that time spent in a Christian community should be an experience where we are buffered against the harsh experiences of life. That we might find respite from the unhealthy choices we have made, or a place to escape from the reality of our situation. On the contrary, Pilsdon is a place where we are asked to be truthful with one another; and over its nearly 63-year history the community is well versed in the exposing of raw nerves.

This can be a confrontational experience for some, arguments and disputes may disrupt us and force us to look at our behaviour and how it impacts on others; at other times new recognition and awareness comes through compassionate conversation and tenderly asked questions. Right from the beginning this truth-telling work has seemed vital at Pilsdon; a way to build healthier relationships with each other, with ourselves, and with God. "We meet at a deeper level and share the inside of each other's lives – what we are when our defences are down and we dare to be vulnerable" (Newsletter, 1959). For some, however, this work is unbearable, and life in community ultimately unliveable.

Vulnerability is talked about a lot these days, and we are being encouraged everywhere to be more vulnerable with each other: to share, to admit those things we have got wrong, to ask for help. The actual practice of "being vulnerable" is much trickier; what can we share, and with whom is it safe to? We often do not come to Pilsdon feeling able to share immediately, but over time we can find the courage to become more vulnerable as we work and live together, and we might be able to casually and gently speak of our experiences with those with whom we have built trust. When we see the example of others who turn up, at rock bottom, we are also challenged and reminded of the precariousness of our own life. In these moments the honesty and openness of new arrivals can have a profound effect on us. At some point during our life in community our own addictions and attachments will be revealed to us – maybe gently, maybe harshly – and it is up to each of us to decide whether or not to face them.

The beautiful thing about living in this community with others, who have decided in their own way to face themselves too, is that we have a shared map and we navigate the terrain together; this happens in surprising ways and sometimes we are supported by surprising people. I have seen someone who had been on the receiving end of another's angry verbal abuse become the very person counselling and guiding them back into community, with their empathy and forgiveness. The acceptance and empathy of others is critical as we begin to tell our stories; sharing the space with others who do this work with us dissipates our shame and makes us feel safer. As the poet Adrienne Rich writes, "No person, trying to take responsibility for her or his identity, should have to be so alone. There must be those among whom we can sit down and weep, and still be counted as warriors" (Rich, 1995). We do not go about "saving" each other, rather we do our best to befriend and accompany; and in so doing contribute to a grace-filled circular economy of forgiveness, rather than a linear and competitive one.

The dynamic between vulnerability and trust is subtle and always changing in community; new people arrive and we need to open ourselves up to their coming. The things in which we have placed our security are shifted, and the positions in the community that we have established are questioned. The terrain is always moving. We need to have the courage to keep letting others know how they have hurt us or to listen openly to how we have hurt them. If we do not do this regularly then resentments can build and misunderstandings can grow. If we stop communicating then trust is eroded and we become less likely to share our concerns and fears.

In order for Pilsdon to be a safe and nurturing space, where being vulnerable can be practiced, the warden and membership must also pay attention to their own needs; recognising what Percy Smith described in one sermon as the "equality of our brokenness" in this place. It might be easy to focus attention on those who have come to live in community as a result of crisis, but the work of honesty is especially important for those who lead. And it is this work that brings us closer together as a community, breaking down a sense of hierarchy and offering a different model of leadership that is vulnerable, reciprocal, and Christ-like. Our reactions to behaviour will have an impact on the health of the community if we do not pay attention to our fear, pain, shame and hurt.

Creating and sustaining safe and nurturing space is, however, easier said than done. That which enables one person to feel listened to, may feel stifling to another. One approach might enable someone to open up and make another shut down. How do we hold open that space for others to express their own hopes and fears when it can make us feel unsafe and overwhelmed? There are no easy answers to this, only a need for those involved to faithfully turn up and have the hard conversations, despite the differences of opinion and approach. Again, drawing on the wisdom of the founder of Pilsdon, we must accept the inevitability of difference and sometimes even division in community. And we cannot overcome it by "laying down forms on which to agree and making rules and regulations to which all must subscribe".

Some of the most challenging conversations I have had at Pilsdon have been with other members who have not felt heard by me, or do not agree with my way of doing things; challenges that drill down into my insecurities and blind spots. Staying with others in that difference of opinion or approach, staying with others in the painful misunderstandings and broken trust, this demands a lot of us. It requires energy and emotion to navigate carefully and compassionately, it requires courage to stick around and hear what others think of you, it requires discernment to know how to sift what needs to be addressed and to guard your peace through it all. But there are incredible fruits from going that hard way with people.

It is a challenge to talk about the ways in which we travel through these landscapes of difference with people because here, at Pilsdon, the unfolding of relationships happens so incrementally. You realise suddenly that a year has gone by and much has been said, and done, much has been exploded and forgiven, much has been explained and understood, much has been left untouched, much has been learned, more has been forgiven, trust has been built, and knocked, and built again, work has been undertaken, but this "sticking with", this commitment to relationship is worth it. It just is.

Having compassion for oneself as these conversations take place is as important as having compassion for the other. This is some of the toughest learning I have encountered. It is here that the resources of my faith have bolstered me. And it is at this point that I have returned to the foundation of community life here for members, the desire to do the will of God through it; in Percy Smith's words:

> This trust in the revealing of God's will is the tap root of life in a Christian Community, the tap root which gives it strength and stability, and the fibres which nourish the community and encourage it to grow are the loyalties and sympathies of those, who have the same love and are of united soul, even when not necessarily of one mind. [...] the Holy Spirit of God is equal to the task of creating what we most certainly cannot create ourselves – a Christian Community.

It is hard to bear when people leave the community in a desperate state, sometimes it can seem they leave in a worse state than when they arrived. Naturally we want people to find the peace and resilience that they need to flourish, but the journey towards this, for all of us, involves our admitting we cannot do things on our own. It can be hard telling people they need to leave when they have broken one of the very few rules, but in their breaking of them they have already demonstrated their aloneness, their separateness from the community. In a sense they have already broken away from the common life through their actions. This is not about blame, or a judgement that they could have done things differently if they had only tried. This is about a common human struggle, our inability to ask for help. It is about believing that we can sort everything in our own strength, lying to cover over how terrified we are, imagining somehow we can regain control. At these times it can feel as though people are leaving in a terribly vulnerable state, with a wound that is open and bleeding. But often at this stage they have already put on their familiar armour, and have roughly patched their familiar wound; in a sense they had already stopped "being vulnerable", unable to be honest with themselves or others about what it was they desperately needed.

Someone who I have lived with for over five years told me a few weeks ago that he had just come to a challenging realisation that without this place he would not still be alive. He said that in his moments of lost-ness, which come and go, the community was the thing that kept him steady and safe. To speak such truth, to have the courage to say that you need the help of others to get you through, to hold you, to face up to life with, this is the treasure we can find here. To endure life together and through that enduring see a beautiful awareness emerge of each other's fragility, and be granted the privilege of being entrusted with that fragility. If we all come with a willingness to go that "hard way", as Adrienne Rich has put it, then it is a very beautiful thing (Rich, 1995). The only thing. And it is Pilsdon's role in the world to create a healthy enough space, a prayer practice that holds our capacity to do this, and a natural environment that mirrors it, where people are enabled to go the hard way, at least to the extent that is possible for them to.

Community

I had a dream before I arrived at Pilsdon that I was in a room and around me there were a group of people all dressed in similar colours, and they were standing together drinking tea and talking about simple things. This is the picture of community life for me. Every time we go into the common room or smokers hut and talk about jigsaw puzzles or our favourite biscuits, planting trees or taking cuttings, we are making connection and deepening relationship; we are making meaning together in this place, in these small ways.

I have tried here to talk meaningfully about this simple thing; this simple, hidden, small community. Knowing that many of those people that I have shared this place with over the years, with whom I have talked about anything from great novels to wood turning, from owning parrots to being homeless, would find different ways and different words to illustrate their experience of this place. They might not even recognise my version of community life. But then describing Pilsdon in words has never been an easy task. As Percy and Gaynor wrote at the end of their first year here in 1959, Pilsdon "has to be lived in and shared in order to be understood". Stuart too, when reflecting on the making of a TV programme about the community made in 1986, recognised that whilst the filming was important for many people, "for some it fell short of showing Pilsdon as it seems to them. No camera, no pen, no brush can capture the atmosphere that is Pilsdon".

Whilst my description of Pilsdon is a personal one, I hope it honours the people who have fundamentally shaped my experience of it. Those people who have made Pilsdon their home, who have built potting sheds, dug vegetable beds, cleared the yard, laid the fire, set up for dinner, faithfully turned up to pray, and repaired windows and doors over many, many, years. They are the fibres of this place much more so than the members who come and go. My commitment to community is also a commitment to each of these precious lives; they have taught me much and it is their faithful and quiet allegiance to Pilsdon over the years that have brought such continuity and stability, even as they look to the rhythms and rituals of Pilsdon for theirs.

At the anniversary the final commitment we make is to community, "accepting one another within the love of God". But what does this mean? What is this "love of God"? For me, it is an encircling where we are all held equal, where we are all connected, where we all belong. It dwells, as Thomas Merton (2003) tells us, in the mysterious indestructible reality at the core of each one of us; "this innermost hidden center of ourselves remains invincibly whole and undiminished (no matter how badly we may have trashed ourselves in patterns of self-destructive behavior) because it is that in us that belongs entirely to God". Being *this* love for each other is a big ask, in fact it is an impossible one, but we are committed in this place not to the being but to the *becoming*, to the *trying*. For the completion, for the wholeness to be known in our hearts, we must continue to wait for Christ.

What is it that I commit to each and every day when I wake up and say "yes" to this little place? I commit to holding this precious fragment of God's Kingdom up to the light. This fragment is small, but like any fragment or trace of bone or of blood, its DNA contains a map to the whole. We cannot know what this fullness, this wholeness of life is, or looks like, but I think we get further towards it at Pilsdon.

Over 40 years ago Percy spoke of this community being a very small part of the church as a whole, and wondered, as we do today, "whether far too much energy and enormous concern is not spent on the structure and institution and organisation, which Jesus Himself so conspicuously neglected". Our task, like Jesus, is not to be concerned with this, but to stake everything on living a life to reveal God, and "to become a community that would act as leaven and salt and light amidst darkness and corruption and death". This community is a small place with connections to a much bigger world. It holds within it an intentional urge towards social justice and towards a good way of living together with the more than human world. The *way* of Pilsdon is an idea, a hope, an example within which we can share our lives and develop the connections necessary to repair brokenness and challenge exclusions.

Pilsdon is about arrivals and welcomes, but it is also about leaving too. When running around the lanes in the early morning I often think about life "beyond Pilsdon". I am reminded to absorb the landscapes around me, and be grateful for the spaciousness of my life here. I am reminded to listen attentively to those here who have so much to share and teach me. I am reminded to love what is in front of me as fully and as attentively as I can, knowing that there will come a time when I don't see the daffodils arrive in front of the church or the apple trees come into blossom in the orchard, and when I won't sit down for Christmas dinner with these precious friends I have made, or sing in the New Year with them either.

Talking with Stuart, Gaynor, Ruth and all the others who had made their home at Pilsdon over many years, was very important for me. To see the imprint that living this life has left on their hearts is poignant and heartening. What is it that any of us take with us when we leave this place; whether we have lived here 3 months or 30 years? We take a way of being, and of sharing, of noticing and accepting; we take a hope, and a promise that ultimately we belong to each other. I hope one day, when I have moved on, that someone who is living at Pilsdon will cross my path, and will ask me about my time there, and how it has shaped me and changed me. And I hope that I too will have the generosity to delight in the fact that someone is living that precious life still, holding the rhythm and abiding in the goodness of that place; keeping its spirit alive. My experience of Pilsdon is just a fragment of the whole, but along with everyone else's it belongs here too.

CHAPTER 9

Epilogue: Community in a Time of Pandemic

The stories of Pilsdon and Pilsdon's story continue to develop as the community is sustained by new people coming to be part of it, as the world beyond changes (for good or ill), and as people who are finding it hard to find a place for themselves within the world opt to live for a while in a different place and with different people. In the previous chapter Mary started to reflect on what 2020/21 meant to those who were living there at the time of the coronavirus pandemic. Her chapter emphasises both the continuity and change at the heart of the community. This period was a time in which David and Marian's relationship with Pilsdon also underwent a significant shift. Whilst we started this book assuming that the oral history interviews carried out in 2018 would constitute the source material, the events of 2020/21 indicated a need to go beyond that. A new warden, Sue Langdon, had been appointed in 2019 and she was faced with the need to respond to an environment that had changed in sudden, unexpected and unwelcome ways. If we needed evidence that the story of Pilsdon could not be concluded by reflecting on the accounts offered in 2018, we couldn't have been confronted with a more powerful demonstration than the consequences of the pandemic for the life of the community.

In this final chapter of the book we recount more of what the impact of the pandemic was on the Pilsdon Community, and we reflect more broadly on what we might take from the community's continuing life through changing times.

THE LOCKDOWN EXPERIENCE

On 17th March 2020, as the coronavirus pandemic surged throughout Britain and the government advised people to avoid all non-essential contact, the Pilsdon Community closed its doors to all visitors. A sign appeared in front of the welcome sign on the front cover of this book: the community was closed to all but essential visitors. This decision was taken by the warden following a meeting of the whole community (members and guests) and was communicated to the trustees. One week later, the government issued the order for a legally enforceable national lockdown, with the instruction that everyone should 'stay at home' except for certain specified essential activities. People from different households were prohibited from meeting. From that moment, the Pilsdon Community became defined as a single household, comprising at that time 17 adults and two children. Later, Sue reflected back on the extremity of what they were faced with in the early days of the pandemic, an understanding substantially enhanced by her nursing experience and public health knowledge:

Having closed the community a week earlier than the first national lockdown, I knew it would be two weeks before we would find out if any of us had contracted Covid 19. Several things occurred to me simultaneously. I realised anyone who became ill would probably be shipped off to hospital, triaged and only those with the best chance of life would be given treatment and others would simply be isolated and probably die alone. It was important that our everyone should be cared for and allowed to die here among us if the need arose. So we created a five bedded infirmary and managed to obtain nursing equipment sufficient to give basic care. I prayed that I would be given the strength to care for them and to instruct others who could relieve me if I succumbed to the virus myself. We were fortunate that after two weeks it was clear no-one had become sick and that we could go forward with strict protocols in place to prevent us becoming infected in the days and months ahead.

The rapid escalation of the virus and reports in the news were extremely frightening and given the vulnerability of some our guests I needed to make this conscious and to find safe ways of letting that be expressed safely. Those of us with responsibility of leading the community needed to address our own fears too while we endeavoured to support everyone else. In the midst of exacting business we invested time sharing with each other and processing our individual concerns. Using guided meditation enabled us to express our own fears. Mary, Franti and I moved psychologically and spiritually into a more intimate and dynamic way of being together and this enhanced our capacity to 'hold' the community safely.

Also a more collaborative approach involving the whole community was essential to our well-being. Ideas and suggestions were shared, discussed and evaluated with various individuals who had the capacity to participate. Mutuality and shared vulnerability held us all as one body as we found the way ahead.

Spiritually, living in the present moment in a hope 'not of rescue' but a 'knowing' everything would unfold exactly as it was meant to. This depended entirely on living out of a heart centred space alongside clarity of thought. We became more contemplative in our times of prayer, (less wordy and structured), with an attitude of deep listening. Synchronicities led us through our days and all we needed was given.

We can enlarge on the consequences of the pandemic from conversations with Sue and others who were living in the community during this period.

The decision to close the community even before government instructions made this necessary was prompted by one of the members having a health condition that required them to be shielded, and three other people being aged over 70 and classed as highly vulnerable to the disease. Several other guests had significant health conditions, such as diabetes, making them more vulnerable to serious illness should they become infected with coronavirus. There were particular anxieties about the risk of infection if wayfarers arrived unexpectedly with an unknown recent history of contacts with others. This was a time, perhaps like no other, when the background experience of members was called upon to manage a situation that presented new and diverse challenges. The substantial nursing and public health management experience of the warden enabled her to quickly identify the major sources of risk and to develop a plan for mitigating them. Various practical measures were introduced in the community during March, including enhanced personal and collective hygiene routines; preparation of rooms should isolation become necessary for anyone; building up food stocks, and construction of a covered area where deliveries could be left without need for personal contact. Regular events like the weekly shopping trip into Bridport ceased, the church was closed to the public and all planned visits from people outside the community were cancelled. Early experiences with hospital visits for some guests led to both an awareness of the pressure being faced by health services and the importance of taking precautionary measures: changing clothes and showering, even after accessing outside health services. Because the community did not 'fit' criteria for agencies to receive personal protective equipment, home-made protection was utilised.

While such steps meant significant change to some familiar Pilsdon routines and certainly made a difference to the everyday life of the community, there was arguably a much more profound impact on the philosophy and values that have always governed how the community operates.

Mary wrote of her perception of this at a time when the community was still closed to new guests and wayfarers:

> The welcoming of friend and stranger utterly shapes the place of Pilsdon, and the unexpected gifts and challenges hidden in the lives of those who arrive are essential for our common life and our individual transformation.
>
> We know, however, that the living out of Pilsdon's "closure" is not straightforward. Somehow as we work to preserve the life of the current community and its continued functioning in a stripped down version of itself, we know also that what we are doing is preserving the welcome for the future too, the hospitality that we long to offer again soon. We recognise also that during this time we have been able to practice welcome and hospitality in other ways: noticing and accepting difficult or hidden parts of ourselves perhaps, and learning to be more available to those who we might have lived with for a long time but had not had the opportunity to get to know so deeply until now.
>
> We have continued to be a place that people reach out to when they are struggling, and many have continued to call in order to be reassured of Pilsdon's existence during this time of change and uncertainty. The welcome we try to give to others' stories and experiences of lockdown over the phone, or as a touchstone to which those struggling with their mental health during this time has remained vital.

Pilsdon's fundamental principles of openness, hospitality and acceptance had to be recalibrated and – temporarily, it was hoped – held in abeyance. As Mary indicated, this had immediate implications for Pilsdon's relationship to wayfarers, which is at the core of the community's tradition of 'radical hospitality': "There was a general opinion that we shouldn't welcome them. And it came from the people who had themselves been wayfarers. That was my sadness, I was really sad" (Sue Langdon).

This opinion expressed by guests was one indicator of the high level of anxiety being felt within the community in the early days of the pandemic. Sue realised this had to be acknowledged: "I knew if I didn't let them let that out it would just go underground". The overriding priority became one of ensuring the survival of the existing community, both physically and psychologically.

The consequences of lockdown were starkly apparent when a wayfarer, well known to the community and who experiences serious mental illness, turned up unannounced on a dark wet night. He entered the main house, causing considerable upset among the guests who were present and requiring Sue to be called from the church where she was about to commence evening prayers. She led him to one of the outside rooms used by wayfarers and offered to get him a meal, while explaining that he would not be able to stay; fortunately, he understood the situation and left. The normal reaction of people in the community would have been to welcome him in and make him comfortable; instead, fears generated by the pandemic produced the opposite response. Recognising and responding to such fears became a key concern for warden and members in addition to their own anxieties: "We were carrying the unconscious as we always do here, unconscious material, and of course we had our own fear to deal with." (Sue Langdon)

As time went on, whilst people adapted to new, more restricted routines, particular events necessitated responses. The community has always sought to enable those who have had to leave (because they have been drinking, been aggressive or using non-prescription drugs) to return if they demonstrate that the reasons for their departure no longer apply. One man who had been a popular guest but who had started to drink during his time at Pilsdon asked to come back. Following much discussion and reflection within the community this was agreed. However, after considerable collective effort on the part of members and guests to prepare quarantine quarters and processes for enabling meals to be delivered safely to him, he arrived demonstrating that he was, in fact, still drinking and was not allowed in. Sue reflected:

> This community, because they'd liked him, had turned themselves inside out to get that cabin ready for him... The effort we put in, everybody gathered up furniture, clothing, bedding, we thought of everything...

The importance of dealing with personal anxieties and fears amid the general uncertainties of the pandemic was a key issue for the warden and the other members, both regarding their own ability to cope and to sustain the community as an unthreatening place of safety. Sue had to address her own deeply felt fears that she might never see her children and grandchildren again: "a visceral fear in my gut ... emotions that have no name but flood through every cell of your body". She worked with the other current members through guided meditation in order to get in touch with fear rather than avoid it. Her view was that: "You won't die of fear, [but] if we don't deal with our fear it will leak out. We're going to have to deal with everyone else's conscious fear." Ensuring that the fear didn't 'leak out' by trying to behave normally was a deliberate strategy: "I was very conscious, going about the community – just be ordinary".

One effect of the community being in lockdown was an intensification of the issues around 'living with others' explored in earlier chapters. With the community effectively cut off from external influences, relationships between those present became an even more important factor than usual in maintaining a stable and positive social environment. It is inevitable among a large group of people that particular friendships and alliances will form, but members thought it important to avoid the development of exclusive relationships during a time when the community needed to function strongly as a collective and Sue had to intervene on one or two occasions to ensure this did not happen. Reflecting on the lockdown experience, she also felt that for at least one person it acted as a 'crucible', enabling them both to reach a personal crisis and come through it: "Someone sitting in a pot on a flame, that's the transformational process ... we've been the crucible for him." Here, Sue is referring to an episode in which one guest reached a crisis point after a long period of struggle, culminating in extreme verbal abuse of another guest including unfounded accusations of serious misconduct. Once the crisis point was passed, and the accuser recognised that he had behaved in a completely unacceptable way, he felt he had no option but to leave. However, the matter was resolved when the guest on the receiving end of the abuse explicitly forgave him and said he should stay. This act of forgiveness was something the second guest said he could never have contemplated when he first came to Pilsdon, but he had come to recognise as a necessary part of living together; for Sue Langdon: "That for me is the absolute essence of this place, that at some stage we meet our own neediness in our own vulnerability and we need each other". Learning how to forgive is fundamental to the acceptance of others that we have described as a basis for living with others at Pilsdon.

An incident occurred during the first lockdown which demonstrated the community's capacity to come together in supportive response to individual vulnerability and provided a vital and positive outlet for collective emotions. Mary has written movingly about her early experiences at Pilsdon when her beloved brother died. In the summer of 2020 her greatly loved young dog, Laddie, was killed by a vehicle in a nearby lane. Sue Langdon recalled:

> The fact that he was killed allowed this community to grieve. They had something to grieve and they had an opportunity to show Mary how much she was loved... We had been so protected from other people's trauma and because people hadn't had anywhere to put their grief for what was going on in the world, Laddie became the keeper and the holder of it.

The community's response to Mary's loss echoed other occasions in the past when traumatic events centred on particular individuals became a trigger for expressions of solidarity. In the wider context of the global trauma of the pandemic, from which Pilsdon was largely isolated, it also became a means of giving emotional recognition to the significance of external troubles and of expression of the healing that living in community can offer.

We saw in earlier chapters that every warden at Pilsdon has had to confront questions of authority and accountability for decisions in the context of community living. Sue's preferred approach as warden to the exercise of leadership and responsibility is through what she refers to as "flattening the hierarchy". This means that, where possible and appropriate, guests contribute to aspects of decision making and are asked to take responsibility for leading certain activities. Sue adopted this approach more explicitly as the pressures of lockdown on her and the other members increased, although this had to be done carefully and informally. In her early response of setting up an infirmary she sought particular help from one guest who she saw as both able to learn basic nursing techniques and physically strong enough to move anyone who was ill and unable to walk. In other contexts she turned to others:

> Where I can, I do. This is a community… [but] to extend that fully to the guest community would be giving some people more responsibility than they could manage and it would be unfair to do that. But some of them, for example … I didn't make it formal, but I would go and talk to Eddie and say, look, I'm making an infirmary here, I would welcome your ideas … I did it with Eddie, I did it with Matt … he was very helpful.

We have discussed earlier questions about the extent to which guests are and want to be involved in decision making. It is likely to continue to be the case that the approach to this will be fluid, informal and responsive to both situation and person. The very particular context of the pandemic highlighted the relational priorities that need to shape decision making processes. In what might appear a trivial indicator of the change in relationships between guests and members Sue spoke about one consequence of members and volunteers taking over the regular weekly shop that guests had enjoyed before the pandemic:

> We would go out once a fortnight and do a massive shop for all the butter mintoes, chocolate eclairs, get money…I got to know people better, I got to know what their treats were, it was a kind of intimate thing to be doing.

Having later experienced doing this ourselves, we (Marian and David) recognise the force of this. Being entrusted with people's bank cards to get cash for them felt quite moving. Being new to this process Marian also experienced the shame of mistaking chocolate eclairs for cakes! These intimacies are one example of how living in community opens people up in ways that can be unfamiliar and that create different kinds of attentiveness to one's self and others.

The pandemic created more of the kind of practical management challenges that we discussed in chapter 5. Financial calculations were necessary to determine the impact on the community's capacity to stay afloat with more limited numbers of guests than had become usual.

In the early days there was some consideration of the possibility of needing to ration food. A crisis of water supply when the community's reservoir collapsed had to be dealt with. Ongoing issues such as the need to replace some member accommodation continued to require attention, and a decision about renting out a separate cottage to generate income became more urgent.

The lockdown also required continuing to manage external relations in this unwelcome context. These generated new possibilities as well as unlooked for challenges. Some people who had been used to Pilsdon's open, welcoming culture had to be persuaded that they could not simply drop in to the house or church. On the other hand, the community became part of a broader network of exchange with the local food bank and another residential community: some of Pilsdon's garden produce went to feed others whose access to fresh food had become problematic and the community was the recipient of vast quantities of dried pasta! And communication with others via newsletters, by telephone and email demonstrated the enduring importance of the community as a source of hope and imagination for people recognising there can be other ways to live:

> Lots of people have been re-evaluating their lives, lots of very wonderful phone calls where we have been given an opportunity to share our vision and reconnect to the original vision Percy and Gaynor had, and people wanting to do the same. One family wanted to come from Canada, five kids...lots of people wanting to come and join us and be members...(Sue Langdon)

Whilst there has been little longer-term impact in terms of applications for membership, these contacts are illustrative of the processes of reconsideration of priorities and aspirations that the pandemic prompted in the world beyond the community. The imperative to live life differently that was a consequence of new constraints on how people could work, meet with others and move from place to place, led many to hope that future 'normality' might look rather different from life prior to 2020. Whilst these constraints impacted on life in the Pilsdon Community, the way in which life is lived in this place did not undergo fundamental change. The enduring nature of caring for animals, growing food and supporting others in difficult times, demonstrated what the pandemic exposed as fundamental to what is most important to living well with others in all places at all times. The importance of maintaining connections with others beyond the physical space of the community reflects the position of Pilsdon as part of a web that links people and values across space and time. The intensification of relationships within the community during the pandemic is only part of the story. It was not only those who already knew about Pilsdon who looked forward to a time when they could physically be there again, it was also those for whom the existential shock of pandemic led to a search for alternative ways of life who recognised in the community a source of possibility. The particular significance of this for those sharing in the Christian faith was described by Sue when she recounted the experience of celebrating the Easter liturgy in Pilsdon's church:

It's only the religious communities that lived as one household that could have done that on Easter morning. There is both the responsibility that you are taking with you every other person who couldn't be there...you are bringing new life, resurrection for all of us. In this dark place that the world is in, here we are coming to say there will be new life. Whether you believe the religious elements or not, for all of us...It's to do with humanity and the way humanity faces suffering, the way humanity surrenders...how does it come together to support. It's all there in the liturgy if you know how to read it.

The lockdown at Pilsdon was eased a little during the summer of 2020 as the national 'stay at home' restrictions were lifted, although the community remained closed to new guests and wayfarers. Volunteers were able to return subject to certain conditions: residential volunteers had to receive a negative test certificate for coronavirus before they could move into the community, and day volunteers could only do outside work, had to maintain social distancing from members and guests and could not join them for meals or breaks. Marian and David recommenced working at Pilsdon as day volunteers in September 2020 and then, having received negative test results, joined the community as residential volunteers for four weeks in October (and spent two more periods there as residential volunteers in the first half of 2021). This spell of living in the community gave us the opportunity to talk informally to people about their experience of the lockdown and also to record a small number of interviews.

The role of volunteers was particularly important at this time. Two of the members, a married couple with young children, departed at the end of August to pursue a new life elsewhere, leaving just the warden and two other members, Mary and Frantisek. One residential volunteer arrived for a six month stay, another came for a month in September and a third had arrived in early July, becoming a full residential volunteer after a period of two weeks quarantine. When we went there in October, none of the three remaining members had had any significant time off since March and were feeling extremely tired and stressed. The presence of the group of residential volunteers made it possible for each of the members in turn to take a two weeks' break.

Craig, a young man raised in the Bruderhof Community, had been living in a small Bruderhof house in London at the start of the pandemic. He came to Pilsdon as a residential volunteer in early July, partly from a desire to move on from his Bruderhof background and partly because he had heard that Pilsdon needed additional help. He was interested in eventually working in social care, and the opportunity offered both a stable place to live during the lockdown and the chance to broaden his work experience. He reported that he had felt very safe throughout the lockdown at Pilsdon, with very little contact with people from outside but at the same time, "I've absolutely been able to keep up communications with friends and family. But I have a friend who was planning to visit me here and we've had to put that off unless he can get tested". However, in October 2020, when national restrictions had eased, Craig was himself planning a week's stay at one of the Bruderhof communities where he had family and friends. As someone whose whole life had been spent living in a defined community, his overall sense of Pilsdon was of a place with a strong dimension of communal living but in which people had significant time to themselves, which he saw as a positive aspect. He summed up his feelings about living at Pilsdon during the pandemic by saying: "I love being with this diverse range of people. I relish meeting different kinds of people and getting to know them. I much prefer that to being largely on my own in London"; and he felt that his understanding and awareness of people whose experiences and ideas were very different had expanded considerably at Pilsdon and was something he would carry with him in the future.

For some guests lockdown was a time of considerable anxiety, both because of the awareness of risk of infection and the need to avoid it, and because of lack of personal contact with friends and families (and worries about what might be happening to them). One guest developed a high level of mental stress resulting in an inability to cope with communal life and left during the summer; another, as described above, passed through a personal crisis but was able to stay. Despite general anxieties, however, guests who have spent this period within the community recognised a number of positive aspects of being closed off from wider society in an environment in which the rhythms and routines of daily and seasonal life were sustained. Thus one of the longer established guests, Eddie, who plays a major role in maintaining and repairing the community's physical infrastructure, responded to the question about how he had viewed the lockdown period with one word: "Peaceful!" Like some of the other longer-term guests, Eddie had enjoyed the respite from the disruption that the presence of wayfarers can sometimes bring; while it was good to see them, they also created extra pressure and he appreciated the sense that the community was "less crowded" than it sometimes was. One of Eddie's regular jobs is preparing Friday night's fish and chips, and as he said, with slight exaggeration: "Cooking fish and chips for fifteen is a bit different from doing it for forty-eight!"

While other guests expressed similar feelings, there was also an ambivalence regarding the absence of wayfarers and other visitors. Simon, who has lived at Pilsdon for twelve years, recognised that not being able to offer hospitality was a difficult issue for the community but also felt that: "It's been quite nice just being us for a while". However, he normally liked having wayfarers around for short stays and by October was "ready to have them back". Another guest, Jack, is on his second stay at Pilsdon and found it: "strange not seeing wayfarers. I feel sorry for them, they've got nowhere to go". Jack had not been at Pilsdon when lockdown started following a crisis in his time in the community. He was someone who had experienced the positive impact of relationships formed within the community for ongoing support: in the time away from the community he had reflected on the importance of the place and the people there and had been offered hospitality by a regular residential volunteer with whom he lived for three months. He was allowed back into the community and spent his initial two weeks in quarantine carrying out stream clearing work. He reflected on the welcome he received on his return and the absence of any sense that people were judging him. He was able to develop his interest in art, as well as contributing to the community through his work. This "gets you away from the madness", he said.

Perhaps this experience has enabled some to become more aware of the significance of Pilsdon's hospitality. Jack also saw the benefits to those able to be in the community that arose from lockdown, such as guests spending more time with each other because they were unable to see family and friends, and opening up more to each other because they understand the kinds of mental health problems they each have. He suggested this might be more difficult for members who have to keep their emotions more private and for whom it is time away from the community that can enable them to deal with their stresses. The reciprocal help that guests can offer to members might just be a smile and making them a cup of tea or coffee.

Like Simon, Jack's reflections on time in the community during the pandemic highlighted its significance as a place of safety. This sense of safety, of being in an environment that gave them much greater protection from the risks of coronavirus infection than was being experienced by the great majority of people in the UK, was widely shared among those resident at Pilsdon during lockdown. For Jack it enabled a greater focus on developing a skill he hoped would enable him to earn a living when he eventually was able to leave, and it provided an environment in which his mental health problems were not a source of stigma. For Simon, who sees himself as being a longer-term resident in the community, the routine and work has offered a sense of supported continuity and, whilst it has been more difficult to see his young nieces and nephews, he has been able to maintain family contact and has not been unduly worried about them.

For two of the guests resident during this period, being in lockdown at Pilsdon was different because they had arrived in early March only a short time before it began and therefore had very limited experience of what 'normal' life in the community might be like. Joni is a young woman who applied to Pilsdon with a history of mental health difficulties and problems with alcohol and drugs. She knew about Pilsdon from a family member who had had some work involvement with the community. She came knowing that it was a Christian community, that it involved farm work and that the guests were mainly older men. Her expectations have largely been met, although she had been looking forward to meeting wayfarers and other new people – she referred to the "new energy" you get from being with different people and how she appreciates meeting new people. She was also rather surprised that more time was not spent with others in view of the number of people living in the community. For her, hearing different perspectives and views is a way of enabling you to think about things in new ways. In coming to the community she was looking both for an opportunity for peace and contemplation, and for the stimulation and inspiration that others can offer. Nevertheless, she appreciated having space and time to herself and felt there was "more kindness" at Pilsdon than she had been used to. She shared Jack's experience of the value of being with others who understand the kind of experiences you are going through: "we've all been through things, there's an understanding whether people tell their story or not". She also enjoyed the routines of work and, having previously struggled with a full-time job, appreciated both the variety of work at Pilsdon and the day-to-day differences in the time commitment required for work. A particular highlight for her, having had some experience of theatre work and singing, was the opportunity to form and lead a small choir involving members, guests and volunteers. This met weekly for practice, was starting to give some performances within the community and had resulted in very positive feedback to her that had contributed to her sense of being valued. Joni stated that, regarding the pandemic: "There's nowhere else I would have preferred to be … it's a lot luckier than being stuck in a house seeing few people". She felt she had had: "space to grow I wouldn't have had elsewhere".

Alex had arrived around the same time as Joni. In his late thirties, Alex has a long history of mental health problems. He was made redundant in 2013 after an extended period of illness and then lived with his parents for six years in what he described as: "a chaotic, dysfunctional family". He felt he needed a different way of life and began to explore the idea of living in a community. He discovered information about Pilsdon, partly from an on-line article by Tobias Jones, and was attracted to it as it seemed to be a caring and supportive place. Alex spent a couple of years learning more about communities, and specifically about Pilsdon, and became more and more enthusiastic about the possibility of living there. His optimism about what it might do for him demonstrated the importance of alternative possibilities: "Pilsdon helped me a lot before I even set foot in the place because it gave me hope. It provided a long-term goal of where I wanted to get to". He applied to the community in December 2019, completed a trial week the following

February and joined fully in early March just before the lockdown commenced. Alex's trial week experience left him feeling "euphoric"; he recognised that he: "had an almost Utopian view of Pilsdon". Perhaps inevitably, his view had become more nuanced after six months in the community and he struggled with some aspects of community life. However, his overall reflections on being at Pilsdon during the pandemic crisis are very positive:

> I felt incredibly fortunate to be here at that time. I'd go as far as to say Pilsdon has been a life saver for me. My mental health is like being on a tight-rope but it's been stable ever since coming here, there are people around to speak with, it's easy to take for granted but I'm much less lonely than I was. So that continues to be a good consistent positive.

Alex also appreciated the outdoor life at Pilsdon: "I've been in the best mental health and also fitness since I was eighteen. The exercise has been really good, being out in nature, being with the animals." Like others, he does miss the opportunity for chatting with wayfarers and other visitors who he feels bring "a freshness and enthusiasm", and cited that absence as a negative of the lockdown experience within the community.

DEEPENING OUR OWN RELATIONSHIPS

The pandemic was both a constraint and an opportunity for us (David and Marian) in terms of our relationship with Pilsdon. It provided both the opportunity and the impetus for this to become closer. At first we, like others not already living in the community, were unable to visit. Later, when things eased over the summer of 2020, we were invited to spend time there as residential volunteers. As in other successful volunteering contexts, this met both some of our needs and some of those of the community. We offered some additional person power to relieve the demands on members, and we brought new conversation and presence in the unfamiliar experience of closure within the community. For us it meant companionship at a time when we were unable to visit friends and family who were spread across the UK and elsewhere. We missed people. We, like others, also missed many of those activities that made up our everyday lives. We struggled with the sense of anxiety evoked by an unanticipated existential threat that spoke of the evolving crisis in humanity's relationship with the more than human world. We puzzled over recognition of our own circumstances, living in a house with a garden we could cultivate, beautiful countryside where we could walk, space to be both together and apart, in contrast to the situations of those trapped within small living spaces in which adults and children were having to live, work, play and learn without access to the natural world. This pandemic did not feel to us like the visions of Armageddon we knew from dystopian fiction and film, but it reinforced awareness of inequalities and vulnerabilities. As well as companionship, spending time living at Pilsdon gave us a sense of both purpose and possibilities.

The balance of our insider/outside identity shifted. We became a part of the Pilsdon story as well as developing our own stories of the community. In Zoom and telephone conversations with friends and family we had something to talk about. This has impacted the way in which we have written some parts of this book. Our experiences as residents have not led us to any fundamental revisions in our thinking about Pilsdon and how it works, but what they have done is to enable us to deepen our understanding by sharing in everyday lives within the community and to know in our own, different way, of their significance. We have experienced the rhythms and routines of meal times and of breaking off physical labour to go and have coffee and conversations that range over the mundane, the nostalgic and the philosophical. We have taken our turns at floor cleaning, milking cows and working in the dairy. And we have been part of teams of people shifting muck, taking down Christmas decorations, re-decorating accommodation and spring cleaning, during which some have spoken to us of frustrations about medication and the impact of mental illness, as well as hopes and aspirations for their future lives. We have seen what is required to ensure the survival of the place when the unexpected happens: dealing both with the consequences of pandemic and localised impacts of a reservoir breakdown. We have experienced at first hand the beauty of the stars in a night sky unaffected by light pollution, the peace of looking out of our windows onto the enclosed farmyard, and the lifting of spirits seeing new shoots emerge in the spring. We have listened with sadness to accounts of people we knew in the community whose mental health deteriorated and who had to leave, or who took their own decisions to leave and did not survive. And we have been glad to meet up again with people who had moved on, but returned for a period of respite. We recognised that Pilsdon had got under our skin.

In the inevitable editing and re-writing that is part of the process of writing a book, we saw that we needed to emphasise some things that we had recounted in others' stories, to use some different words, or to offer a more detailed reflection on some issues. Being residents has had an impact on us as it has had on those whose stories we have told throughout this book. The community has become an important part of our lives. It has probably not transformed the way in which we think about its importance, nor has it changed our position with regards to our own lack of religious belief. But it has deepened our understanding through direct personal experience of what Mary has described as the 'Pilsdon way.'

FINAL REFLECTIONS

The account that Mary has given in the previous chapter is not one that we could offer. A key aim in this book has been to understand Pilsdon from different perspectives of people who have been part of the community over many years. It is those different perspectives and different experiences that make up both the place and the idea that is Pilsdon. But Mary's account also illustrates the enduring significance of those things that the community shares with other ways in which people have sought to live life in common in very different times and places. Living well with people who are very different, living well with the physical environment, with animals and plants, and weaving all into a web of care capable of nurturing the present and the future, are vital to all of us whether or not we share in any religious faith. There is value in looking to different traditions and different starting points to learn better how to do this. Those traditions include the monastic traditions of the Christian faith; the knowledge of indigenous peoples whose ways of life have not separated humans from the land and what grows on and under it, from other animals or from spirits that inhabit the lakes and hills in which they live. They include humanist values and principles that draw on ancient stoic and epicurean philosophies; and the insights from an ethic of care that starts from the necessary relationality of what it is to be human and asks us to acknowledge our interdependence with both the human and the non-human world. The significance of all these ways of thinking about how we can live well together have been increased by the pandemic and the wider environmental crisis that we all face. Both the causes and consequences of Covid 19 have revealed only too clearly how out of sync we have become from those things that nurture us and which are necessary to our, and their, survival.

Understanding how Pilsdon works means we need to understand the importance of faith to those who established and who continue to sustain it. But we also hope to learn things that can be helpful beyond Pilsdon. We want to take Pilsdon with us as we interact with others beyond this particular space. And we also want to think about what we can contribute to Pilsdon from other ways of thinking and struggling around care and justice. The three authors of this book have different starting points for this. We use different language. Our relationship with Pilsdon is different. But we share a commitment to the importance of respectful and reflective dialogue and in this book we have tried to offer ways of understanding the significance of Pilsdon that can speak to audiences who do not share the Christian faith as well as those who do.

As we draw this book to a close we can suggest that the experience of the pandemic has heightened awareness and understanding of the importance of places like Pilsdon. That importance encompasses the specific value of acceptance and the opportunity to live with others offered to people whose lives have been damaged by the troubles they have experienced, and who have found little help elsewhere. It also encompasses the broader experience of living with others who are different from us as an antidote to both the fragmentation of individualism and the tribalism of monocultures. It embodies the relational ontology of what it is to be human and creates enduring solidarities. Pilsdon encourages understanding through living our interdependence with the more than human world, and it offers exemplars of sustainable ways of living that respect rather than exploit the natural environment. In all these ways it has created an environment in which it is possible to acknowledge vulnerabilities, to be safe, to learn to care and be cared for, and to grow. Those things have remained consistent throughout its now more than 60-year history. As the community prepares, hopefully, to open its doors to wayfarers on their journeys, and to new guests who have heard about its accepting hospitality, this place in the Dorset countryside continues to offer an example that extends beyond its physical location and into the future.

References

Abrams, L. (2016) *Oral History Theory*, Routledge.

Agustin,O G and Jorgensen, M B (2019) *Solidarity and the 'refugee' crisis in Europe,* Palgrave.

Bachelard, S (2020) *The Subversion of 'Sin'*, Benedictus.com

Barnes, M and Bowl, R (2001) *Taking Over the Asylum: empowerment and mental health,* Palgrave.

Barnes, M. (2007) 'Participation, Citizenship and a Feminist Ethic of Care', in S Balloch and M Hill (eds) *Communities, Citizenship and Care: Research and Practice in a Changing Policy Context,* Policy Press.

Barnes, M (2012) *Care in Everyday Life; an ethic of care in practice,* Policy Press.

Barnes, M (2015) 'Beyond the Dyad: exploring the multidimensionality of care' in M Barnes, T Brannelly, L Ward, N Ward (eds) *Ethics of Care: critical advances in international perspective*, Policy Press.

Barnes, M and Gell, C (2012) 'The Nottingham Advocacy Group: a short history' in M Barnes and P Cotterell (eds) *Critical Perspectives on User Involvement,* Policy Press.

Barnes, M and Prior, D (1995) 'Spoilt for Choice? How consumerism can disempower public service users.' *Public Money and Management.,* 15, 3, pp. 53-58.

310

Barnett, P and Barnett, M (2011) 'The Long History', in J Vincent (ed) *Christian Communities,* Ashram Press.

Bauman, Z (2001) *The Individualized Society,* Polity Press.

Beck, U and Beck-Gernsheim, E (2002) *Individualization,* SAGE.

Brannelly, T (2015) 'Mental health service use and the ethics of care: in pursuit of justice' in M Barnes, T Brannelly, L Ward, N Ward (eds) *Ethics of Care: critical advances in international perspective*, Policy Press.

Bruteau, B (2005) *The Holy Thursday Revolution,* Orbis Books.

Chittister, J (2000) *Illuminated Life: Monastic Wisdom for Seekers of Light*, Orbis Books.

Dunn, S (1999) *Creating Accepting Communities. Report of the MIND Inquiry into social exclusion and metal health problems,* MIND.

Emond, R. (2003) 'Putting the Care into Residential Care: The Role of Young People', *Journal of Social Work* 3(3): 321-337.

Gardiner, C (2018) *Melodies of a New Monasticism: Bonhoeffer's Vision, Iona's Witness,* Cascade Books.

Gilligan, C. (1982) *In a Different Voice: psychological theory and women's development*, Harvard University Press.

Gittins, D (1998) *Madness in its Place. Narratives of Severalls Hospital, 1913-1997,* Routledge.

Hardman, I (2020) *The Natural Health Services. What the great outdoors can do for your mind,* Atlantic Books.

Held, V. (2006) *The Ethics of Care: Personal, Political and Global*, Oxford University Press.

Herbert, J (2020) *Accompaniment, Community and Nature: Overcoming Isolation, Marginalisation and Alienation Through Meaningful Connection,* Jessica Kingsley.

Hirst, P (1994) *Associative Democracy,* Polity Press.

Hobsbawm, E (1994) *The Age of Extremes: The Short 20th Century, 1914-1991,* Michael Joseph.

Jones, T (2007) *Utopian Dreams: In Search of a Good Life,* Faber and Faber.

Jones, T (2015) *A Place of Refuge: An Experiment in Communal Living. The Story of Windsor Hill Wood,* Quercus.

Kennard, D (2004) 'The Therapeutic Community as an Adaptable Treatment Modality across different settings', *Psychiatric Quarterly*, 75, 3, 295-307.

Kittay, E F (1999) *Love's Labor. Essays on Women, Equality and Dependency,* Routledge.

Mason, Paul (2015) *PostCapitalism: A Guide to our Future*, Allen Lane.

Massey, D (2005) *for space,* Sage.

Merton, T (2003) *New Seeds of Contemplation*, Shambhala Publications.

Norman, R (2012) *On Humanism,* Routledge.

Prior, L (1993) *The Social Organization of Mental Illness,* Sage.

Prior, D, Stewart, J and Walsh, K (1995) *Citizenship: Rights, Community and Participation,* Pitman Publishing.

Puig della Bellcasa, M (2017) *Matters of Care. Speculative Ethics in More than Human Worlds,* University of Minnesota Press.

Repper, J and Perkins ,R (2003) *Social Inclusion and Recovery: A model for mental health*, Balliere Tisdall

Rich, A (1995) *On Lies, Secrets and Silence*, W W Norton & Co.

Roosens, E and Van de Walle, L (2007) *Geel Revisited. After centuries of mental rehabilitation,* Garant.

Sayce, L (2000) *From Psychiatric Patient to Citizen,* Macmillan.

Simmons, R, Powell, M, and Greener, I (eds) (2009) *The Consumer in Public Services: Choice, values and difference,* Policy Press.

Smith, G (2008) *Pilsdon Morning,* The Pilsdon Community.

Spandler, H (2006) *Asylum to Action. Paddington Day Hospital, therapeutic communities and beyond,* Jessica Kingsley.

Staddon, P (ed) (2015) *Women and Alcohol: Social Perspectives,* Policy Press.

Sweeney, A, Beresford, P, Faulkner, A, Nettle, M and Rose, D (eds) (2009) *This is Survivor Research,* PCCS Books.

Tronto, J. (1993). *Moral Boundaries. A Political Argument for an Ethic of Care,* Routledge.

Tronto, J (2013) *Caring Democracy: Markets, Equality and Justice,* New York University Press.

Tronto, J (2017) 'There is an alternative: *homines curans* and the limits of neoliberalism', *International Journal of Care and Caring*, Volume 1, Number 1, March 2017, pp. 27-43.

UK Government, *Setting Up and Running a Charity,* www.gov.uk

Vincent, J (2011) 'The Communities Option', in J Vincent (ed) *Christian Communities,* Ashram Press.

Waal, E de, (1990) 'Introduction and Commentary', in A Parry OSB, *The Rule of Benedict*, Gracewing Publishing.

Wales Council for Voluntary Action (2012) *Faith and hope don't run charities*, WCVA.

Wall, J (2016) *Mending Revealed: Exhibition Catalogue*, Bridport Arts Centre.

Wilson-Hartgrove, J (2008) *New Monasticism: What It Has to Say to Today's Church*, Brazos Press.

This book is printed on paper from sustainable sources managed under the Forest Stewardship Council (FSC) scheme.

It has been printed in the UK to reduce transportation miles and their impact upon the environment.

For every new title that Matador publishes, we plant a tree to offset CO_2, partnering with the More Trees scheme.

For more about how Matador offsets its environmental impact, see www.troubador.co.uk/about/